Trilegal

Praise for the book

'This book is not just about the growth of a law firm; it is a chronicle of how institutions take shape in a traditional profession that is beginning to modernise. In telling Trilegal's story, it vividly captures the larger journey of Indian law from small chambers of legacy to practices of governance and scale. This engaging account of Trilegal shows how professionalism, trust and collective decision-making can create an inspiring template for law practice in India.'

– Hon'ble Mr Justice (Retired) Sanjay Kishan Kaul
Former Judge of the Supreme Court of India

'This book is a fascinating account of how a new generation of lawyers built an institution in step with India's own transformation. Trilegal's story is one of the democratisation of legal firms, in harmony with how India has changed after the liberalisation of 1991 and the flowering of Indian talent.'

– Nandan Nilekani
Co-founder and Chairman, Infosys, and Founding Chairman, UIDAI (Aadhaar)

'The evolutionary trajectory of Trilegal is in many ways the story of India's law firm market – from family firms and charismatic founders to collective leadership and globally competitive practices. This incisive book captures that transition with unusual candour and insight. What sets this evocative account apart is that it speaks not only of victories but also of doubts, reforms and reinvention. It is rare to find such honesty in a profession that often guards its secrets closely.'

– Abhishek Singhvi
Fourth-Term Sitting MP; Former Additional Solicitor General of India; Member, Congress Working Committee

Trilegal

The Making of a Modern Indian Law Firm

Akshay Jaitly

JUGGERNAUT BOOKS
C-I-128, First Floor, Sangam Vihar, Near Holi Chowk,
New Delhi 110080, India

First published by Juggernaut Books 2025

Copyright © Akshay Jaitly 2025

10 9 8 7 6 5 4 3

P-ISBN: 9789353452117
E-ISBN: 9789353457372

The views and opinions expressed in this book are the author's own. The facts contained herein were reported to be true as on the date of publication by the author to the publishers of the book, and the publishers are not in any way liable for their accuracy or veracity.

All rights reserved. No part of this publication may be reproduced, transmitted or stored in a retrieval system in any form or by any means without the written permission of the publisher.

Typeset in Adobe Caslon Pro by R. Ajith Kumar, Noida

Printed at Saurabh Printers Pvt.Ltd

To my partners – past, present and future

Contents

Introduction   xi

Part 1: Origins and Context

1. What Do Law Firms Actually Do?   3
2. Law Firms in India: A Brief History   11
3. The Founders before We Became Founders   20

Part 2: The Founding Story

4. Cricket Scores and Châteauneuf-du-Pape   35
5. Gathering Everyone In   43
6. The 'Why' and the Founding Values   53
7. Trilegal Is Born   63

Part 3: The Early Years

8. One Firm: Testing the Waters   71
9. Law Firm Structure: Equity and Compensation Choices   76
10. Money Matters and Decision-Making   85
11. Delhi: Early Deals and Clients   93
12. Mumbai: Early Deals and Clients   98
13. Bangalore: Early Deals and Clients   103
14. Lessons in Collaboration: Building the Telecoms Practice   108

15. 'How Do You Get Your Work?'	115
16. Our Early Offices (and How They Shaped Us)	121
17. Opening Up the Partnership	127

Part 4: Growing Up

18. Taking Stock	135
19. Allen & Overy: Making Best Friends	139
20. Pantone 484	149
21. Crisis in 2008 (No, Not That One)	156
22. New Partners and Tweaking Compensation	164
23. The Neemrana Sessions and Other Ways to Learn	169

Part 5: Building an Institution

24. Calling Time on the A&O Relationship	177
25. We Get Served Some Brutal Facts	183
26. Refresh! Going All Equity	190
27. The Amarchand Mangaldas Split and Lateral Movement	195
28. The Long Kiss Goodbye	202
29. Recognition and Renewal	208
30. The Guts of the Trilegal Lockstep: Our Levels-Based System	215
31. Crisis and Transition	223

Part 6: Moving to Market Leadership

32. A Short Note on Numbers	231
33. The Power of Compounding	237
34. Leadership, Scale, Risk and Growth	242
35. Becoming a Lateral Magnet	249
36. Specialisation: Building Practices from Within	255
37. Specialisation: Strategic Practice Development	264
38. Support Functions: Getting Out of the Way	273

39. The Lawyer-Led Innovation of our Technology Backbone	280
40. Impact, and Lessons for Institution Building	288
41. 25 Years of Change and What Next?	297
A Note on the Regulation of Law Firms	308
Notes	312
Acknowledgements	318

Introduction

Many people have established law firms. Millions more have started businesses. Why is Trilegal's story worth telling?

When we set up in early 2000, there were fewer than ten lawyers in the firm, six of them the founders. Today, the firm has about 1,200 lawyers, including 145 partners, making it possibly the largest full-service, top-tier firm in India. How did this happen?

Law firms in India have traditionally been family-run, or founded and controlled by one or two key individuals. Trilegal followed a different path: six founders, widely dispersed ownership and collective decision-making. This model set us apart from other top-tier Indian firms and invited curiosity about how we operated. Over time, that curiosity widened into questions not only about how we stayed together, but also about how we scaled, governed ourselves, navigated alliances, dealt with crises and responded to a changing market.

Just a few years after we started, people were already asking how the six founders had stayed together for as long as we had. Shortly after Reliance Industries split, I remember being asked: 'Even brothers fail to stay together in business – what's your secret?' Twenty-five years on, barring one amicable departure, the founders remain at the firm. This is one of the questions the book will address, but not the only one.

I had never taken much interest in the theory of why founders stick together but it seemed useful to see what leading management thinkers had to say, and how their ideas related to our own experience. Simon Sinek's idea of the 'why' highlights the role of a shared purpose beyond profit.[1] Jim Collins talks about 'getting the right people on the bus' and in the right seats.² Peter Drucker stresses the importance of open, honest and frequent communication.³ And Collins and Jerry Porras underline mutual respect and trust as foundations for long-term collaboration.⁴

These principles sound obvious, even trite, but I found them deeply relatable, and each remains part of the Trilegal story. Our 'why' evolved from wanting to create a positive workplace to having the ambition to compete at the top end of the legal market. The founders brought different but complementary skills, experiences and personalities. We disagreed often, and sometimes deeply, but communicated constantly. Even if we rarely said it out loud, each of us saw merit in others' abilities and believed they acted in what they thought were the firm's best interests.

But theory only takes you so far. There is always an element of mystery – perhaps even alchemy – in why some ventures succeed. And then there is luck – the randomness of the universe. Malcolm Gladwell's account of Bill Gates in *Outliers* shows how timing, context and opportunity shape even the most famous success stories.⁵ Gates acknowledges luck, as do Warren Buffett,⁶ Phil Knight,⁷ Reid Hoffman⁸ and, most explicitly, Jeff Bezos.⁹

We acknowledge luck as well. In our case, three early strokes of luck stand out: first, that six young lawyers with shared personal and professional values came together at the right moment; second, that this happened a few years after India's transformative 1991 reforms – before legacy firms could capitalise on a liberalising market and scale up; and third, that the founders maintained the chemistry needed to stay committed to each other and the original vision.

Luck, however, is not a strategy. It explains moments, not careers. What is replicable are the lessons we learnt: how to translate values into governance and incentives, how to make partnership structures work, how to sustain culture through and in spite of growth, how to navigate alliances and how to adapt to a market that has changed almost beyond recognition since 2000.

This book is about those lessons. It is about building a small and unknown professional services firm into an institution. It is about the decisions, mistakes, experiments and adjustments that shaped us, and the people – both inside and outside the firm – who influenced us. Additionally, since Trilegal's story unfolded alongside the evolution of the modern Indian legal market, this book also offers a lens on that wider transformation.

Part 1

Origins and Context

1
What Do Law Firms Actually Do?

Unless you happen to be a law student, a client or someone otherwise orbiting the somewhat insular world of corporate legal practice, you might struggle to answer a simple question: *What on earth does a corporate law firm actually do?*

If this is you, you are not alone. Here is a typical conversation many corporate lawyers have found themselves having with members of the general population.

> **Random Person**: And what do you do?
> **Corporate Lawyer**: I'm a lawyer.
> **Random Person** [*trying to display their knowledge of the legal profession*]: Ah, high court or Supreme Court? Civil or criminal? [*If the interlocutor is a policeman, they may well ask 'Tis Hazari or Patiala House?' – referring to the best known criminal courts in Delhi – to establish complicity as a fellow insider in the legal system.*]
> **Corporate Lawyer**: Oh please get me out of here.

Most, but Not All, Lawyers Go to Court

If this conversation were to continue and the corporate lawyer were to say that he or she didn't go to court at all and was something called a 'corporate lawyer', the most predictable response would be a blank one. The more worldly wise might nod knowingly and quip, '*Accha aap liasoning ka kaam karte hain* [Aha, you are in the 'liaisoning' business]?', a barely polite euphemism indicating that they know some lawyers who perform the sometimes questionable task of 'dealing' with government authorities on behalf of their clients – mildly unethical middlemen at best, out and out purveyors of illegal rents at worst. The idea that there exists a category of lawyers who neither go to court nor facilitate dodgy quid pro quos has not quite penetrated the imagination of the general public.

As the judiciary is one of the three pillars of the modern nation-state, the court system and the legal practitioners who appear in court are central to the popular image of lawyers. After all, it is these aspects of the legal system that are most concerned with the rule of law and delivery of justice. And the facts reinforce the stereotype – over 95 per cent of India's qualified lawyers are litigators, most of them solo practitioners. Only a vanishingly small percentage work in law firms focused on corporate practice. Whether in a large metropolis or in the smallest mofussil town, when people think 'lawyer' they think 'courtroom'.

It is an image rich with symbols – an advocate in flowing black robes, addressing a judge seated on a high platform in even more elaborate robes, polished teak – and the stakes are always very high, the tone is dramatic and everyone holds their breath as the protagonist advocate brilliantly argues a point upon which the entire case irresistibly pivots in favour of their client. The legal scholar Marc Galanter also observes that the public images of lawyers are largely shaped by adversarial courtroom roles, and the quieter but equally vital work of counselling and transaction structuring are sidelined.[10]

Real Lawyers vs Bollywood Lawyers

Dramatised impressions of the legal profession come mostly from popular culture, films in the old days and OTT series today. These mediums convey a grossly inaccurate view of what happens in a courtroom. Day-to-day proceedings in most courtrooms across the country are drab, boring and often soul-destroyingly tedious. Hearings are adjourned again and again, and lawyers waste countless hours – even days – waiting for their matter to be called. Judgments can take years, even decades. The common (and generally correct) perception is that justice in India moves at a glacial pace.

'Real' courtroom life in India does not lend itself to being depicted in Bollywood (or any of the other 'woods'), though independent cinema can sometimes capture the pathos of the common man's search for justice through the courts.[11] Despite improvements, including through specialised courts and tribunals, overall pendency in Indian courts remains. Massive, with over 50 million cases languishing in the system.[12] The cliché immortalised by Sunny Deol in *Damini* (1993) – '*tareekh pe tareekh* [date after date]' – captures the reality as well as anything else.

On the other hand, law firms have figured far less in popular culture. Shows like *Ally McBeal* and *Suits* are set in law firms, but these too largely stay within the world of litigation and adversarial battles. In India, law firms hardly appear in popular culture. A recent exception is *Illegal*, the Amazon Prime series whose fictional Delhi law firm happens to have a managing partner called Janardhan Jaitley (no relation), whose son – Akshay Jaitley, if you can believe it – also works there. You could call it coincidence or something to do with the fact that one of the actors in the series, Satyadeep Mishra, used to work at Trilegal and is a dear friend. The storyline revolves around a death row appeal and a sexual harassment lawsuit – compelling subjects but still well within the courtroom drama genre.

The Legal World beyond Courtrooms

Far from crowded courtrooms lies the hidden arena of corporate law – a world that exists out of public sight, in quiet offices, plush boardrooms and long email chains. When businesses need to navigate regulatory landscapes, structure complex deals and anticipate risks in a new business, they contact a different breed of lawyers – the corporate lawyer. These lawyers operate within the formal economy, advising companies, financial institutions, investors and entrepreneurs. Broadly, their work falls into two categories: disputes and transactions.

The contentious or disputes side is easier to picture. Corporate litigators represent clients in business disputes. This could take place in various forums: from the Supreme Court of India and high courts down to district courts, and increasingly in specialised regulatory bodies and arbitral tribunals. But for most larger firms, the transactional side dominates. Based on the Trilegal example, I'd estimate the ratio is roughly 75:25.

Transactional lawyers structure, negotiate and execute business transactions: mergers and acquisitions, financings, joint ventures, public offerings and commercial agreements. The transactional side is less intuitive. When my children were small, I struggled for years to explain what I did for a living; 'No, I don't go to court' was never a satisfying answer.

Transactional Lawyers Are Risk Managers

Corporate lawyers are, in essence, risk managers. When a company wants to acquire another business, corporate lawyers anticipate what could go wrong and build protections into the deal structure. If the target company has hidden environmental liabilities or pending litigation, corporate lawyers structure warranties and indemnities so that their client does not bear those costs.

The work could involve conducting due diligence to identify legal risks, drafting and reviewing contracts, and advising on regulatory compliance. As risk can be expressed in monetary terms, one reason why transactional lawyers are paid high fees is because they help their clients protect or make large amounts of money.

This work has become more important as India's economy has formalised and integrated with global markets. When Tata acquired Jaguar Land Rover or when global private equity funds invest in Indian start-ups, these transactions require lawyers who understand both Indian regulations and international deal-making. Legal complexity grows significantly when deals cross borders, involve multiple regulatory approvals or require sophisticated financing structures.

Some of what corporate lawyers do overlaps with other business professionals like chartered accountants and management consultants. The difference lies in their tools: while accountants work with balance sheets and consultants analyse market data, lawyers operate within the vast and intricate framework of the law.

Another useful way to explain the difference between disputes lawyers and transactional lawyers is to use an analogy from medicine. Peter Attia, the longevity expert, distinguishes between Medicine 2.0 (which tries to fix medical conditions after they arise) and Medicine 3.0, which prevents conditions from arising in the first place through nutrition, exercise and lifestyle interventions.[13] Disputes lawyers practise the legal equivalent of Medicine 2.0 – a problem arises for a client and they find a solution for it. Transactional lawyers are like preventive care doctors, exponents of the legal version of Medicine 3.0. They know where problems tend to arise and they take measures to prevent them using contracts and the law.

Specialised Expertise for Complex Business

Modern corporate practice is too complex for generalists. Larger firms will have specialist groups: corporate, banking, tax, real estate, competition law, capital markets, labour and employment, technology, and energy and infrastructure.

For example, a fintech company going public needs capital markets lawyers who understand how the technology is affected by securities regulations. A pharmaceutical company entering India needs specialists who can navigate drug approval processes. A real-estate fund building a nation-wide portfolio needs lawyers who understand land acquisition laws state by state.

What a Typical Deal Might Look Like

Consider, for example, the bare bones of what might happen when a multinational company wants to acquire an Indian family business:
- **Structuring the Deal**: Should they buy shares or assets? How to minimise tax impact while satisfying foreign investment

regulations and share valuation guidelines? Should the promotors be asked to stay on for some years? Lawyers design an optimal structure balancing legal compliance with tax efficiency and business needs.
- **Due Diligence**: Lawyers spend weeks, even months, reviewing everything from employment contracts to environmental clearances, looking for problems that could cost millions later. They review corporate records, regulatory filings, vendor contracts, employee agreements, leases and more – searching for risks, particularly non-obvious ones.[14]
- **Documentation**: Transaction agreements might run into tens or hundreds of pages, with dozens of annexes. Lawyers draft share purchase agreements, shareholders' agreements and ancillary contracts.
- **Negotiation**: Who pays if the company faces a retrospective tax claim? What happens if key employees quit? Lawyers negotiate key clauses like warranties, indemnities and non-compete obligations. All of this could take several months.
- **Closing**: On closing day, lawyers coordinate multiple document signings, regulatory approvals and fund transfers, perhaps across different time zones. Once conditions precedent are fulfilled, they manage the formal signing and financial settlement – when the money actually changes hands – ensuring the deal 'closes' cleanly.

A Real-World Example

A great illustration of the process outlined above is Trilegal's long-standing work for Heineken in India. From the time the company first sought to deepen its presence in the country, the legal challenges were layered: how to structure its entry, comply with foreign investment regulations and manage relationships with Kingfisher (which involved Sridhar Gorthi – one of the founders – once being offered a 'lift' back from Dubai on Vijay Mallya's private jet). Over the years, we advised on licencing arrangements, foreign exchange regulation compliance, shareholder agreements and the governance frameworks necessary to build a durable presence in the tightly regulated alcohol industry.

In 2021, Heineken acquired an additional 14.99 per cent stake in United Breweries from the Debt Recovery Tribunal, taking its total shareholding to more than 61 per cent and giving it majority control.[15] The work required transactional execution, navigation of regulatory approvals and, later, defence in high-profile competition proceedings.

This is how corporate lawyers operate outside the courtroom spotlight: structuring cross-border investments, aligning them with local regulation and staying engaged through both the relatively smooth phases of deal-making and the potentially adversarial stages of regulatory scrutiny.

The Value of the Work

Done well, this work creates substantial economic value. When lawyers structure a deal efficiently, they can save clients millions in taxes. When they spot a hidden liability, they prevent catastrophic losses. When they draft clear contracts, they enable large investments and prevent disputes.

The work is intellectually demanding, legally complex and commercially critical. However, it does not lend itself to the cinematic drama of courtroom showdowns; no blockbuster films are being made about a perfectly worded limitation of liability clause.

As India's economy has matured and diversified, corporate law firms have become indispensable to the business ecosystem. The top firms in India advise the largest Indian and global companies on billion-dollar deals, regulatory challenges and corporate strategy.

Law firms in India are not new – they have existed for almost two centuries – but their scale, specialisation and visibility have expanded significantly only in recent decades. Understanding their history helps explain how corporate law firms have evolved so dramatically in recent times – from colonial-era partnerships serving British trading companies to today's sophisticated institutions advising on multi-billion-dollar deals.

There is little dedicated scholarship on the history of law firms in India (there should be), and an exhaustive exploration is beyond the scope of this book. But a brief and gap-filled overview will help contextualise the evolution of Indian law firms up to the early twenty-first century.

2
Law Firms in India: A Brief History

The Indian law firm landscape in 2025 bears little resemblance to what it looked like even a quarter of a century ago. At the turn of the millennium, the largest law firm in India was Amarchand & Mangaldas & Suresh A Shroff & Co. (hereafter Amarchand Mangaldas), which probably had around 200 lawyers. There were perhaps three or four firms with a hundred lawyers on their books. Most large firms were based in Delhi or Bombay (now Mumbai) and only a handful had offices outside of those cities. Even Bangalore (now Bengaluru) was a bit of a legal services backwater back then.

In the past 25 years, India's nominal GDP (gross domestic product) has grown almost nine times, from US $468.4 billion in 2000 to $4,190.0 billion in 2025, with GDP per capita rising from $442.75 in 2000 to approximately $2,400 in 2024.[16] Law firms in India have had to grow to service the explosion in commercial activity that has fuelled this growth.

How Big Is the Indian Law Firm Market Today?

It is hard to tell. Given that few firms release data publicly, it is unclear how many lawyers in India work in law firms. Here is a highly speculative and definitely inaccurate estimate.

In 2023, the Ministry of Law & Justice revealed, as a reply to a Rajya Sabha question, that there were 2,013,081 advocates enrolled with State Bar Councils.[17] This seems like a significant underestimate but let's go with it. Asian Legal Business's 2024 ranking lists the

25 largest Indian firms by size. Their published numbers add up to approximately 9,400 lawyers.[18] Extending this survey to the 26–50 bracket (each 50–200 lawyers) gives us a cumulative 14,000–15,000 lawyers. Another study suggests that 12,000 lawyers are working in India's top 100 firms.[19] An informal December 2024 report found 7,421 law firms across India.[20] Subtracting the 50 largest ones leaves roughly 7,370 smaller firms. These might employ 1–20 lawyers apiece. Taking an average of 10 lawyers per small firm yields approximately 75,000 lawyers.

Adding the two tiers together (15,000 + 75,000) puts the law-firm workforce in the 90,000–100,000 window. So, India has just over 2 million registered advocates, but less than 5 per cent work in a law firm of any kind; the rest practise as independent litigators, in-house counsel or government law officers.

Accuracy of numbers aside, this is remarkable growth. Other aspects of the law firm ecosystem have also seen enormous change. Salaries have gone up by many multiples, hundreds of law schools have mushroomed all over the country – with approximately 70,000 law graduates joining the profession annually[21] – and joining a top-tier law firm is almost as desirable today as joining a top corporate.

How did this dramatic transformation of the law firm market take place?

A Hereditary Profession?

India's caste system has existed for thousands of years. For much of this time, caste dictated the contours of an individual's social and economic existence. It determined whom one could marry or eat with, where one could pray and which profession one could pursue (the most relevant restriction for this account). While traditional societies worldwide have witnessed sons following in their fathers' occupational footsteps, the rigidity of hereditary succession has been particularly pronounced in India, entrenched in the caste system's deeply ingrained stratification of labour, and its notions of purity and pollution.

Despite significant legal and societal shifts, vestiges of the caste system persist, particularly in social spaces. However, the rights to equality embodied in the Constitution of India and the need for skilled workers in a modernising economy have eroded explicit caste-based restrictions on a person's choice of occupation.

Yet, the enduring practice of the child (still most often a son) stepping into the shoes of the parent remains a palpable feature of contemporary Indian economic life. Family legacy and hereditary control continue to define the contours of twenty-first-century corporate India, with family-run, promoter-driven enterprises still contributing to a significant share of listed companies.[22]

The legal profession is no exception. The practice of law in India was historically a semi-hereditary profession with many well-known families of advocates dominating the upper echelons of the profession. This pattern extends to law firms as well. Many of India's most established firms remain predominantly family-controlled, including prominent examples like Anand & Anand, Cyril Amarchand Mangaldas (CAM), Fox & Mandal, Khaitan & Co, Shardul Amarchand Mangaldas (SAM) and Singhania & Co.

The Colonial Foundation

Unsurprisingly, the history of law firms in India is closely connected to the establishment of the British colonial legal system. During the eighteenth and nineteenth centuries, as the East India Company expanded its rule over the Indian subcontinent, there was a concerted effort to introduce a legal framework modelled on English common law. This led to the formation of the first courts in the presidency towns of Calcutta (now Kolkata), Bombay and Madras (now Chennai). This was initially done through the establishment of 'Mayor's Courts' pursuant to the Charter of 1726. These were then replaced by the Supreme Court of Judicature in Calcutta in 1774, established under the Regulating Act of 1773 and subsequent Royal Charter in 1774.[23] In addition to its judicial functions, the Supreme Court had the power to enrol advocates.

While legal practice in those early years was mainly the dominion of English barristers who would interpret and apply English law within the colonial context, the Bengal Regulation Act of 1793 allowed qualified Indians to enrol in the Sadr Diwani Adalat, the highest civil court under the British administration. This was followed by the Legal Practitioners Acts of 1846 and 1879, which enabled Indians to act as pleaders and *vakil*s – legal professionals with rights to appear in certain courts.[24]

The First Law Firms (1830–1920)

Formally organised law practices remained embryonic during this period. Legal practice was predominantly individualistic, though occasional informal partnerships among Britain-trained lawyers popped up to address the demand for legal services brought about by the expansion of the colonial administration and commerce, particularly in the presidency towns.

These informal partnerships provided the groundwork for the emergence of more structured legal practices. The first law firms in India appear to have been Crawford Bayley & Co. (established in 1830) and Little & Co. (founded in 1856), both in Bombay. Initially, as partnerships among British lawyers, these firms served mainly British companies and expatriates, specialising in areas such as commercial transactions and shipping law.

Crawford Bayley & Co. grew to become India's oldest continuously operating law firm. It maintains its historic presence in Mumbai's Fort district, where it has operated for nearly two centuries.[25] Little & Co. represented the East India Company, the Secretary of State for India and the Government of Bombay Presidency. They also acted as solicitors to the Great Indian Peninsula Railway and assisted in the incorporation of the Tata Iron and Steel Company.[26]

The first law firms founded by Indians were established in Bombay in the last quarter of the nineteenth century, predominantly (but not exclusively) by members of the Parsi community. Tyabji Dayabhai was founded in 1872 by the pioneering Badruddin Tyabji – the first

Indian barrister to practise in the High Court of Bombay and a founding member of the Indian National Congress – in partnership with Dayabhai Edulji. Wadia Ghandy followed in 1883, Kanga & Co. in 1890, and Mulla & Mulla came soon after in 1895. An exception to the dominance of Bombay-based firms was Fox & Mandal, founded in 1896 in Calcutta as an unusual partnership (for its time) between an Indian, Gokul Chandra Mandal, and an Englishman, J.K. Fox. All these firms are still in existence.

Three of India's most consequential law firms today trace their genealogy to the period around World War I. The first, Khaitan & Co, was established in 1911 by Debi Prasad Khaitan. In addition to being a top legal practitioner, Khaitan was an active participant in India's independence movement and a contributor to the drafting of the Indian Constitution.[27]

Two firms – SAM and CAM, both of which formally came into existence in 2015 – are descended from Amarchand Mangaldas, founded in 1917 by Amarchand Shroff and Mangaldas Mehta. In 1980, Amarchand Shroff's son Suresh A. Shroff and his wife Bharati took over the firm. In 1994, following the death of Suresh Shroff, his sons Shardul and Cyril took over the Delhi and Bombay offices, respectively. The legacy firm split in 2015, which was a major event in the history of Indian law firms that we will explore later.

Post Independence: Nationalisation and the Licence Raj

The unification of India's fragmented legal profession through the Advocates Act of 1961 was a key development during this period. The colonial system had created a complex hierarchy with barristers, vakils, pleaders and *mukhtar*s. This legislation abolished all distinctions and created a single class of 'advocates' who could practice in any court across India, ending over 200 years of hierarchical divisions.

The socialist, planning-based economy of this period was dominated by the public sector, seen by Prime Minister Jawaharlal Nehru as the guardian of the 'commanding heights of the economy'.

Many previously private companies – including Air India (and eight other airlines), oil and gas companies, heavy engineering firms, and all banks and insurance companies – were nationalised. Most significant private investment came from a handful of large, family-owned business groups, many of whom later formed the Bombay Club.[28]

Nationalisation was a bonanza for law firms. Bank nationalisation occurred in two phases – 1969 (14 major banks) and 1980 (six more) – bringing over 90 per cent of banking business under government control. Insurance sector nationalisation was equally complex, with the Life Insurance Corporation of India Act (1956) amalgamating 243 insurance companies. Each nationalisation required asset–liability transfers and led to valuation disputes and compensation proceedings.

The Industries (Development and Regulation) Act of 1951 required licences for virtually all significant economic activities. The Licence Raj system created demand for specialised expertise in navigating regulation and dealing with the government. India's distaste for participating in the global economy threw up legal work in foreign exchange regulation under the Foreign Exchange Regulation Act (1973) and import–export licencing.

Corporate Work in Socialist India

In this period, firms handled corporate transactions despite the regulated environment. For example, Khaitan & Co managed India's first corporate demerger for the sugar companies Balrampur Chini Mills and Tulsipur Sugar Company Ltd in the 1950s. This was complex since the Companies Act only contemplated mergers. The firm also handled the 1948 Bennett Coleman & Co. deal between R.K. Dalmia and the Sahu Jains, and the Indian Express split in 1990 following Ramnath Goenka's death.

Otherwise, the period was litigation-dominated. Corporate and commercial transactional work remained minimal due to state ownership, limited private activity and restricted foreign investment. The drafting and negotiating skills that corporate lawyers are known for today were relatively unimportant, with many corporate destinies determined by regulatory restrictions or political influence.

Law firms often operated under the chambers system inherited from British practice – lawyers working together under the same brand sharing costs but not revenues – with most lawyers working as sole practitioners. Practice-building relied heavily on family and community connections. The major industrial houses developed strategic relationships with specific law firms. The Birla–Khaitan & Co relationship exemplifies this – the firm grew alongside the Birla Group.[29]

Liberalisation Changed Everything

Economic liberalisation in 1991 transformed the destiny of Indian law firms. The policies initiated by Prime Minister P.V. Narasimha Rao and Finance Minister Dr Manmohan Singh opened the economy to foreign investment, reduced trade barriers and deregulated key industries. Significant parts of the economy opened to private and foreign capital, dramatically increasing the range, size and complexity of business transactions, along with the need for competent transactional lawyers to execute them.

The Indian legal market in 1991 had very few of these lawyers. This was not a question of ability. India had produced many excellent legal minds, but low demand for transactional lawyers meant that most of the country's top lawyers were displaying their brilliance in the courtroom, and the best and brightest graduates of Indian law faculties (there were no dedicated law schools then) were not rushing to join law firms. In any event, Indian law firms had been shaped by decades of practice in a closed, tightly controlled market. Thanks to a lack of opportunity, they had little experience of the complex, large-scale, cross-border transactions that came with the influx of foreign capital and increased private participation.

Initially, foreign clients, considering an unfamiliar overseas market like India, preferred to work with legal advisors they knew and trusted. They hired familiar international legal counsel, especially those experienced in complex, cross-border, high-value work in other parts of the world. The largest markets for legal services were (and continue to be) the US and the UK, so most international lawyers working on India-related cross-border transactions in the 1990s had American or British accents. However, these cross-border transactions were taking place in India, which meant that Indian law would apply to them. This mandated the involvement of Indian qualified lawyers. As a result, in the first decade post liberalisation, the legal team for an international client doing a cross-border deal in India almost always included both international and Indian law firms. Often, even simple documents like residential lease agreements for foreign executives were reviewed and approved by international firms.

By the time Trilegal was set up in 2000, legal staffing for transactions in India tended to be like this:

- **Purely domestic deals**, where both clients were Indian companies, were handled exclusively by Indian law firms.
- **Outright referrals**, where an international client contacted an international law firm, which then referred the transaction to an Indian firm. If the international firm was confident about the Indian firm's capabilities, their involvement would end there. This was relatively rare at the time.
- **Collaborative arrangements** involved an international law firm working with Indian firms in varying proportions. The international firm remained involved to ensure that delivery met client expectations. Their involvement was deeper if the deal was unprecedented in India, involved a new sector, was of high value or strategic importance or part of a larger, multi-jurisdictional transaction requiring global coordination.

New Firms and New Models

By the early 2000s, the effects of liberalisation had taken hold. The combination of India's GDP growth and international exposure was transforming the entire legal landscape. The second factor, international exposure, was more important for law firms than the growth of the economy per se. This allowed Indian law firms to participate meaningfully in complex cross-border transactions, first as support to international law firms and later as independent advisors in their own right.

This period saw the rise of several new firms, beyond those that had existed before liberalisation. Some continued to be run as family enterprises but also began to include another type of firm – those established and substantially controlled by one or two key individuals. Examples include AZB (formed originally as a merger of two founder-dominated firms – Ajay Bahl & Co. and Chambers of Zia and Bahram [earlier Chambers of Zia Mody] – and which for much of its existence has been steered by its founders Ajay Bahl, Zia Mody and Bahram Vakil), Dua Associates (run by C.R. 'Ranji' Dua) and Luthra & Luthra (run by the late Rajiv Luthra). These founder-controlled firms, together with the family-dominated firms, are referred to in this book as 'the traditional firms'.

There was another category – firms that appeared to operate on a more broad-based partnership model. Examples include DSK Legal, Economic Laws Practice, IndusLaw, J. Sagar Associates (JSA), S&R Associates and Trilegal. Among these, JSA is a rare example of one that transitioned from its roots as a founder-led firm to one that follows a collective leadership and decision-making model. Of all the firms mentioned, there are six that are considered to be in India's top tier: AZB, CAM, JSA, Khaitan & Co, SAM and Trilegal.

Among these six, one stands out for its unique founding philosophy: a partnership established without familial ties among its founders, or domination of one or two individuals. It was deliberately structured, from the beginning, to depart from the traditional law firm model. We believe that this difference is the reason behind that firm's rise to the top tier.

It is now time to dig into the story of that firm. Let's start by meeting the founders.

3

The Founders before We Became Founders

The Trilegal founders[30] have a few key features in common. We are all solidly Gen-X, we come from similar social backgrounds and, significantly, none of us had any lawyers in our families.

While our personalities are pretty different, we shared certain formative experiences that would later become central to Trilegal's DNA – the ability to embrace the moment when being thrown in at the deep end and expected to swim, having the sharp sense that high quality work with great attention to detail would set us apart, and the confidence (foolhardiness?) to take on challenges beyond our experience level.

Anand Prasad

Anand was born in 1968 into an army family. This meant that he travelled all over the country in his childhood, living in big cities like Bombay and Poona (now Pune) and smaller towns such as Jammu, Deolali, Chandrapur and Jabalpur.

As Anand puts it, he grew up thinking that there were essentially three possible career paths for him: to be an engineer, a doctor or a loser(!). As he got to high school, since his father was an army engineer, and a number of his friends were heading in that direction, he picked engineering as well. After taking an entrance exam and missing out on engineering school by a few marks, he did what he says was a 'natural progression' – a BSc in mathematics.

Up to this point, Anand's education had largely been in Jabalpur. By the time he completed his BSc in 1987, his father had been posted to Pune. Again, as everyone he knew there was doing an MBA, he decided to follow suit. He planned to take the entrance exam for the Symbiosis Business School (now the Symbiosis Institute of Business Management) but fate intervened by giving him a bout of chicken pox, and he missed the exam.

Now, the building that housed the MBA programme at Symbiosis also hosted a computer programming institute. With a year to kill, Anand enrolled in the institute. Instruction was only for three hours a day, and a bored Anand decided to wander into some law classes, which were held in the same building. Anand makes the unverifiable claim that he had great talent as a programmer. In any event, computer software's loss was the legal profession's gain because, by the end of the year, he had developed an interest in the law and abandoned the ideas of both business studies and computer programming, and decided that he wanted to become a lawyer instead.

While Anand was completing his law degree with a first class, his father was posted to Delhi. The principal of Symbiosis suggested that he join his parents in Delhi post his graduation, and offered to introduce him to an advocate on record (AOR)[31] there. Working for free, which at the time was the norm in early days of law practice, did not cut it with Anand. His dad's boss then introduced him to a senior advocate and member of the Bharatiya Janata Party's (BJP) National Executive, Dr N.M. Ghatate.

After joining Dr Ghatate's chamber for the princely salary of ₹750 a month, Anand focused on constitutional and criminal law, and bumped shoulders with state chief ministers and union cabinet ministers. This was very exciting and Anand was making political connections, but hobnobbing with powerful people wasn't much good for putting food on the table or fuel in his motorcycle.

Then, on the court circuit, Anand met Ujjwal Rana, a partner at Gagrat & Co., a commercial litigation firm. The money offered was better and Anand jumped. After three years there, in 1996, Anand was on course to take the AOR exam, having completed five years of practice in the Supreme Court of India.

By now, post liberalisation, a number of commercial law firms focusing on transactional work had sprung up in Delhi, and they were paying even associates more than young partners in the litigation firms were receiving. So, while there was an offer of partnership at Gagrats, Anand looked instead towards the emerging world of transactional law.

He joined Dua Associates – a young, rapidly growing firm set up by Ranji Dua, formerly of Dadachandji & Co., which itself was one of Delhi's first commercial law firms. Anand recalls that the instincts that he had developed as a litigator were all wrong for the practice of transactional law, and he had to re-skill, swallowing his ego and learning from colleagues with fewer years in practice than him.

This willingness to adapt, learn new skills and dive into unfamiliar territory would eventually serve our common enterprise well when Trilegal took shape.

Karan Singh

Karan was born in 1971 and grew up in Calcutta, in a household where English was the lingua franca and sport was a way of life. He attended a Jesuit school, where he was never particularly studious but did well enough to stay out of trouble.

His father worked for the Calcutta Port, often spending three or four days a week aboard ships. When back on land, he was (and remains till today) a keen sportsman, playing golf, badminton and squash. In his youth, he had played cricket for Jammu & Kashmir and badminton for the Services.

Karan's childhood revolved around the typically genteel lifestyle of the Calcutta club scene. Days were spent cycling to the club, playing sports and forging friendships. His upbringing was typical of the English-speaking middle and upper-middle class in Calcutta – culturally Indian, yet linguistically and socially Westernised.

Karan recalls that at home he never spoke any vernacular languages. His parents spoke in Punjabi and occasionally in Hindi to each other, but never with him or his brother. At school too, Hindi was peripheral, learnt with a tutor and spoken only with a handful of Marwari classmates. Even today, asking Karan to speak in Hindi guarantees a few laughs. He does a killer Bengali accent though.

In high school, Karan opted for the science stream, but his less-than-excellent academic performance limited his choices for higher education. However, he was convinced of one thing by the time he finished school – that he had to leave home and leave Calcutta. The last two years had been stifling and he was desperate for a new beginning.

Law was not a deliberate choice for him; it happened almost by accident. A school senior and friend, then in the first batch of the National Law School of India University (NLSIU or NLS), encouraged him to apply. The process was informal and flukey; the application was filled out at the last minute and Calcutta happened to have a test centre.

He got in. The opportunity to study in Bangalore, regardless of the subject, offered him that escape he was looking for. In hindsight, law school was the perfect fit for him. The first year wasn't demanding, and allowed him to settle into a new city and environment. From the third year, he began to carve out a niche for himself – doing well in law moots, representing NLS and becoming one of the top mooters of his cohort. Competing with students from prominent legal families, and holding his own, gave him a new sense of confidence. He started believing that he could be a good lawyer.

He describes those five years as having shaped the course of his life not just professionally, but personally as well – forging friendships that have endured over decades.

Securing a campus placement with Arthur Andersen was a big win for him. His parents, while supportive of him going to law school, had (not unreasonably) harboured a stereotypical view of an Indian legal career: a life in court, with long struggles and delayed and uncertain financial rewards. Joining Arthur Andersen, and earning a salary that allowed him to live independently in Bombay, came as a surprise to them. From the day he graduated, at 23, Karan has never taken another *paisa* from his parents – a quiet but significant point of pride.

A moment with his father stays with him. At 25, during a casual conversation, his father remarked – not with mockery but with sincerity – that Karan would one day inherit the family house because buying property in India was beyond reach. 'People don't buy homes here,' he said. 'They live in their parents' homes.' When Karan bought his first house at the age of 30, with a loan shared between his wife and him, it was as much a statement to himself as to the world that it was possible to break free from the middle-income trap and chart a different course.

His early years at Andersen were foundational. There, he felt he learned the true meaning of client-centricity, something that served him well when he moved to Lex Inde (established by Akshay Chudasama and Rohan Shah) two years later. This laid the foundation for being able to impress clients and build trust quickly. At Andersen, Karan had observed something that was rare in India at the time: young professionals, in their early 30s, building businesses without patronage or old-world networks. This bolstered his belief that success could come from merit and enterprise alone. This proved important later, along with his ability to break away from the status quo to do something ambitious and different.

Sridhar Gorthi

Sridhar, like Anand, also came from an army background. Born in 1972, he is the youngest of the founders. Like many army kids, he grew up all over India, including Jammu & Kashmir, Punjab and Delhi. It was the quintessential Indian army childhood – moving every three years, making new – often tight-knit – friends and socialising in army clubs.

And like Karan, Sridhar says that he was not academically inclined. His interests lay in theatre, music, sports and hiking.

But like many kids at the time, he was pushed into one of the science streams in school – 'PCMB' (physics, chemistry, maths and biology) – but with zero interest in any of these subjects. In the twelfth standard, in 1989–90, fate intervened and Sridhar encountered a career guidance counsellor at the Army Public School in Delhi, who Sridhar remembers well and is still in touch with. Mrs Tandon introduced him to the idea of law as a career, conducted an aptitude test and even handed him the NLSIU application form. He filled it out without thinking.

Now, while Sridhar's father was in the army, he was actually a military lawyer in the Judge Advocate General's department (so Sridhar did come from a legal background, but his father practised military law, nothing resembling commercial legal practice). This had not influenced Sridhar's decision to become a lawyer, as he never really saw his father as a lawyer – to Sridhar, he was an army officer first and foremost.

Before Mrs Tandon changed the direction of Sridhar's path to higher education, he too was considering joining the army while his parents wanted him to be a doctor. Law school was the middle ground – it seemed to make everyone least unhappy. Because he had been preparing seriously for the entrance exam to the National Defence Academy, he was over-prepared for the relatively easier law school entrance exam and ended up sixth on the merit list, joining NLSIU in the third year of its existence.

From his first month at NLS, Sridhar, like his new classmate Karan, knew he was in the right place. He was not academically outstanding, but corporate and financial law subjects interested him. He recalls that his generation, which went to law school from 1990–95, was probably the last to go through college without the Internet. Everything was handwritten or typewritten. Research meant poring over physical case law books, a dying skill that online resources have made redundant.

He continued with old interests: theatre, debates, music and sports. Mooting – and evenings with beer and Bob Dylan in the pubs of Bangalore – contributed to building a friendship with Karan. In their third year, they partnered and won the NLS selection moot and represented the school in a moot in Kerala. They won that, sweeping all the awards, including first place, best speaker and second-best speaker. Sridhar's father had preserved the clipping of a news article on the moot that had appeared in a Malayalam newspaper, which Sridhar discovered while going through his father's papers after he had passed away.

Sridhar and Karan became part of the first cohort from NLS to be fully recruited through campus placements. They joined Arthur Andersen when the 'Big Six' accounting firms (after 1998, it became the Big Five; Big Four today) were making their first forays into legal practice. In hindsight, the timing was fortuitous, with Sridhar and Karan graduating at a moment of transformation in the Indian legal landscape.

Sridhar also recalls the influence Andersen had on his professional ethos and not just because it was his first job. Andersen prided itself on being ahead of the curve – more expensive, more meticulous and uncompromising in work quality. Bosses like Bobby Parikh and Ashok Wadhwa who went on to become household names in the professional services world held them to high standards and remain close connections even today. Producing documents to the highest international standards became second nature. Exposure to global clients proved invaluable, offering a glimpse of what excellence looked like on the world stage.

Yet, with remarkable foresight, Sridhar was keenly aware of the limitations of an accounting firm structure. Indian regulations prevented these firms from practising law in the fullest sense. Litigation was off-limits, as was the ability to issue formal legal opinions – privileges that only lawyers and law firms enjoyed. Initial hopes that these restrictions would be lifted faded, and despite attractive pay and the company of brilliant colleagues, Sridhar wanted a different kind of professional life with not just success, but a reputation built squarely within the legal fraternity. Only full engagement with the practice of law could offer that.

This soon led him to leave Arthur Andersen to join Akshay Chudasama and Rohan Shah's Lex Inde. In stark contrast, this was a small, fledgling practice with an unusual niche focus on Japanese and Italian clients. The work was broad, varied and exciting – work for Sumitomo Corporation one day and Bulgari the next, advising on litigation, regulatory registrations, foreign exchange regulations, stamp duty matters and corporate law. He says it was an 'incubator-like' experience, forcing young lawyers to stretch themselves across disciplines and responsibilities.

With Chudasama frequently travelling abroad to secure new clients, Sridhar stepped into a management role much earlier than he had anticipated, taking care of day-to-day operations of the firm. Billing, hiring, business development and work allocation became part of his routine – invaluable early exposure to the realities of running a law practice.

Prem Ayyappa

Prem spent his school years from kindergarten to the tenth standard at Vidhya Vardhaka Sangha in Bangalore after his family moved there from Bombay. In the eleventh standard, he switched to St. Joseph's College of Arts and Sciences (now St. Joseph's College and part of the same group of educational institutions that Rahul Dravid went to) for his last two school years. Prem says that he got into St. Joseph's more for hockey-related reasons than academic ones, which is a credible claim not because he isn't clever but because he was in fact an exceptional hockey player.

Although initially enrolled for undergraduate studies at St. Joseph's, he ended up giving a shot at the entrance exam for the newly established NLS, encouraged by his mother, who happened to see an advertisement in the newspaper for this unknown, one-year-old law school. Prem says that he just about secured admission, ranking fifty-ninth out of 60 merit applicants, and also claims that he passed his final exams to complete law school by a whisker.

After law school, Prem started his career with Khaitan & Co, initially in Calcutta, and was then moved to their Bangalore office. His early work focused on disputes, real estate and compliance, with little exposure to transactions. He later moved to work with Markos Vellapally, attracted by what seemed like better financial opportunities – a couple of thousand rupees more a month mattered a lot in those days – and the fact that some of his friends had already left Khaitan. At Markos Vellapally, he did a mix of corporate and litigation work, finding the experience both more interesting and rewarding.

But he was not settled and, as we will see later, was ready to do something different.

Rahul Matthan

Rahul was born in Madras in 1971, but his childhood spanned several Indian cities owing to his father's changing job responsibilities. He spent short stints in Delhi and Bombay, where he attended Bombay Scottish. He finally went to St James' School in Calcutta, where he completed his schooling. His father worked at Bombay Suburban Electric Supply (BSES; now Reliance Energy) in Bombay, before taking up a position with General Electric in Calcutta. His family later moved to Madras and finally to Bangalore, but Rahul stayed behind in Calcutta with his aunt to complete his eleventh- and twelfth-standard education at St James. This proved key to him becoming a lawyer.

At school, Rahul, like Sridhar, was a science *wallah* and has retained a deep interest in science throughout his life. Initially, he had thought that he would go to university in the US; he had appeared for the SAT and planned to pursue a liberal arts education with a science orientation. But when those plans fell through, law, somewhat serendipitously (like for the rest of us), became his backup plan. He too had no legal legacy in the family, other than an uncle who was an engineer with a law degree and had a thriving arbitration practice in Bombay, and became a specialist in civil engineering arbitration. It was only through a senior at school – Nikhil Nayyar from the first batch of NLS – that he heard about this new law school in Bangalore and decided to apply.

Getting into law school turned out to be a transformative accident. At the time, NLS was operating out of a series of tin sheds on the outskirts of Bangalore. Since there was a shortage of hostel rooms, the administration encouraged local students to commute from home. This meant that Rahul (who was living with his now Bangalore-based parents) became a member of about 15 of the 60 students in his cohort (including Prem) who shared a different rhythm of life compared to their hostel-residing peers. Commuting from home in Bangalore and occasionally hanging out after hours with this bunch of lads was a dynamic that created a unique camaraderie among them, which endures till today.

In addition to his friendship with Prem, Rahul also became good friends with Sridhar. They had various interests in common, theatre in particular, with Rahul directing a play in which Sridhar had a starring role. In his fifth and final year, Rahul took military law as one of his subjects and in a neat little coincidence, Sridhar's father, as a senior military lawyer, was one of his examiners.

Rahul's batch at NLS was the first to have gone through a campus recruitment process, borrowing from a practice that was already common at the various IIMs. Looking back, this signalled a key shift, with campus hiring being an important pathway to placing students graduating from law school today. He joined Dua Associates – one of the biggest names in the Indian law firm world at the time and one of the few larger firms with an office in Bangalore.

Rahul staying in Bangalore later became a key element in the formation of Trilegal.

Akshay Jaitly

I was born in 1967, making me the oldest of the Trilegal founders. My father, who was in the Jammu & Kashmir cadre of the Indian Administrative Service, was posted as deputy commissioner in Poonch, a small border town. Thanks to the absence of local family support and rudimentary medical facilities, my parents decided that I should be born in Bombay, where my grandparents lived. I spent the first 10 years of my life in Srinagar, Jammu and Leh.

We moved to Delhi in 1977, where I went to Modern School. I did just well enough to get into St. Stephen's College in 1985. There, over three stimulating and fun years, I studied history, played football, did a lot of theatre and made many friends.

With no definite career plans, I took one of the two options available to history honours graduates from Delhi University – going abroad for higher studies. The other choice of course was to take the civil services examination, which I had no interest in. Off to the US I went, for a master's in international affairs at Columbia University. After two years of great learning and horizon broadening there and an internship at the World Bank in Washington DC, I returned to India to work as an energy policy analyst at the Tata Energy Research Institute (now The Energy and Resources Institute). These were exciting times; the Earth Summit – the conference in Rio de Janeiro that led to the United National Framework Convention on Climate Change – took place in 1992 and I got excellent exposure to both energy policy and climate change issues, something that would later influence my choice of specialisation as a lawyer.

In the back of my mind, I had always thought of law as a career option and enrolled in evening LLB classes at Delhi University Law Faculty's Mandir Marg outpost. This was a big change from Columbia, where you were encouraged to have and got extra credit for having an opinion. At Mandir Marg, I was chastised for answering a question in greater detail than the lecturer would have liked. 'You think you know more than me?' were his words as he threw me out of class. I never went back.

I then ran into the first of the series of coincidences that led me to be part of Trilegal's founding team. Deepak Thakran, a cousin's friend, arrived with application forms for Oxford University, asking for my help as I 'had been abroad to study'. Before helping him, I photocopied the forms, deciding pretty much on the spot to apply to study law at Oxford. In 1993, I went to England, graduating two years later.

I was idling in London at my friend Vikram Sahu's flat, preparing to come back to India and prostrate myself before a senior counsel to become a litigator, like most other law graduates of my generation. My mother was visiting. 'Why don't you do a few months with a lawyer here first?' she said.

Despite being tempted to ignore this well-meaning but naive motherly suggestion, I remembered a rowing brochure from University. The law firm Ashurst Morris Crisp (now Ashurst) had advertised in it, with pictures, on facing pages, of Jonny Searle MBE in a suit (with the caption 'Trainee Solicitor') and in a boat (with the caption 'Olympic Rower', referring to his gold medal in the coxed pairs event in Barcelona in 1992). Underneath, the firm had claimed that it had a Delhi office, which was interesting.

With nothing to lose, I called their switchboard. 'Can I speak to someone with something to do with India please?' I said. My call rang through to a secretary who, fobbing me off, gave me the fax number of a Geoffrey Picton-Turbervill. *That's that,* I thought, *she's got rid of me, where on earth will I find a fax machine?* (Readers under 30 can Google 'fax machine'.)

An hour of lounging later, the phone rang: 'This is Philip Hurst of Ashursts, I believe you rang me.' Twilight zone moment. In 1995, caller ID was almost unknown, so I had no idea how he had my number. I gathered my wits – we spoke – he was interested – I was called for an interview – I got the job. I joined Ashurst Morris Crisp in June 1995, with the same Geoffrey Picton-Turbervill as my first boss. I was placed in the energy and infrastructure practice and a significant chunk of my work involved India.

The learning curve was steep. Large London law firms still had fairly rudimentary training systems, and old-school partners emphasised learning by doing. Some tasks were easy and occasionally boring, like filling out forms for a change of directors. Others were more challenging, such as drafting memorandums of understanding or preparing advice for clients. It was common to be handed work outside your skill set, with the expectation that you would 'just get on with it'.

Working with Geoffrey also taught me something invaluable that I shared with my co-founders and later became part of Trilegal's values:

fierce attention to detail. Geoffrey was known for his precision – every comma, every defined term, every cross-reference had to be perfect. This exacting standard initially seemed like overkill to me, but I came to understand its importance. Details matter deeply in law, not just for accuracy but as a reflection of care and thoroughness. In a profession that isn't allowed to advertise, a key component of demonstrating your wares is the quality of the documents you produce.

The Seeds of Trilegal

Looking back at our individual journeys, shared traits emerge that later became essential aspects of the Trilegal working style. Though we developed these characteristics in different environments, they found their way into our firm's identity.

The first trait was the willingness to take on tasks beyond our comfort zones. Whether it was Anand transitioning from litigation to transactional work, Sridhar managing an office early in his career or my being thrown into a practice area I knew nothing about, we all embraced the challenge of figuring it out as we went along.

Second was placing a high premium on attention to detail. From Karan and Sridhar's training at Andersen to my experiences with Geoffrey at Ashurst, we learnt early that excellence lies in the minutiae. This later became a hallmark of Trilegal's work product.

Third was a certain independence of spirit. Each of us had made unconventional choices – Rahul leaving Dua Associates to set out on his own, or Karan and Sridhar choosing the then-unusual route of working in the legal department of an accounting firm.

These varied experiences later formed the basis of a shared belief that the traditional structures of Indian law firms desperately needed reinvention and gave us early hints about what a modern Indian law firm could aspire to be.

Part 2

The Founding Story

4
Cricket Scores and Châteauneuf-du-Pape

The Deal That Started It All

It was a matter in which I was out of my depth that triggered a series of events that ultimately led to the formation of Trilegal.

It was late 1995. James Nimmo, a senior and rather flamboyant corporate partner, showed up in my room with a stack of files. James was very much an old-school boss, who believed that the mere fact of your employment in the firm entitled him to assume that you were capable of doing anything that he chose to entrust you with. Tossing the documents onto my desk he said, 'Andrew Millet was working on this deal. He has been sent to a client on secondment for some months. It is an acquisition of shares of a company in India. You're Indian. You do it. There's a meeting with the client on Monday [this was a Thursday], make a list of all outstanding issues.'

James didn't wait for me to reply and marched out of the room. If he had, he would have heard me squeak 'but I've never worked on a share acquisition before' or 'I'm only four months into the profession and don't really know my backside from my face'. But he was gone and I was left to get on with it, which wasn't unusual for that day and age. James himself had little interest in the deal, given its relatively small size and apparent lack of complexity. MAI plc (later Garban plc), a UK foreign exchange broking business, was acquiring 50 per cent of Merwanjee Securities, an Indian foreign exchange broker, then controlled by the late Udayan Bose – one of the pioneers of modern Indian investment banking and chairman of Lazard India. Coincidentally, Mr Bose's daughter Piusha worked with Trilegal from 2005 to 2009 and is currently a senior lawyer at Freshfields in London.

The deal was complex enough for a newbie like me and the learning curve was steep. I had never even seen a shareholders' agreement before and there were terms and concepts in it that I had never heard of. For instance, what on earth was a 'right of first refusal'?[32] This seemed to me to be a collection of words that did not naturally belong together or, at the very least, were in the wrong order. And what in God's name was a 'Texas shoot-out clause' doing in a legal document?[33] My approach to getting stuck on something was to bombard slightly more experienced associates with questions. I got stuck a lot, so there were many questions, with many friendly and patient colleagues making time to answer them. It is a source of happiness that some of these noble souls who helped me back in 1995–96 are still friends.

I gradually got to grips with the file, and the matter progressed slowly, over a period of days and then weeks. The client, Phil Moyse[34] of MAI plc, was very gentle with me. I suspect that he had realised that I was a wet-behind-the-ears rookie, but appreciated my attention and willingness to work hard and muddle my way through the matter.

At some point, Indian legal advice was required for the transaction. Dua Associates, which at the time had offices in Delhi and Bangalore, had given some initial advice on the deal and I was told to get back in touch with them to take the matter further. Mobile phones were still relatively rare; I certainly didn't have one at the time. I was given a landline number and told to contact a certain Rahul Matthan, who would be the 'Indian counsel' on the deal. If this were to have happened in the Internet age, particularly after the invention of Google (and even more so LinkedIn), I would have looked him up and discovered at least some basic facts about him – rough age, educational background and the like. As it was, I was flying blind. All I knew was that there was a lawyer in Bangalore who was familiar with the file, who most likely knew a lot more than me about the structure of such transactions and certainly the law – a safe presumption, as by that time I had only been a lawyer for about eight months.

As it happened, this Rahul Matthan had graduated from law school only a year earlier, in 1994. He had precisely one more year of legal experience than I did. The circumstances of Rahul's involvement in the deal were similar to mine – relative lack of interest in the deal from our bosses. Rahul had been put in charge of the file from the Dua Associates side, which meant that the two lawyers meant to take this deal across the line had just over two years' experience between them. Not quite 'the blind leading the blind', but almost, given the complicated regulatory issues that the deal would encounter, as we shall see. Now, Rahul too had no idea who I was or how experienced I was. He just knew that there was this lawyer in a foreign law firm that he had to impress.

As a result of this mutual ignorance of each other's scant legal capabilities, we spent a few weeks pussyfooting around each other, being somewhat formal, and taking care not to reveal our relative inexperience and ignorance. This dam of polite deference broke during the 1996 Cricket World Cup. Fanatic, nerdy Indian engineers in the US hadn't yet invented Cricinfo and the ball-by-ball cricket updates it now provides. And what could be more important to a 20-something NRI in London than his team's fate in a key group game (India vs Australia, if I remember correctly)? I called Rahul on the pretext of asking him something about the deal but after a while I couldn't contain myself. 'What's the score?' I blurted out. That was it. The conversation initially focused on our mutual interest in cricket, and we soon became comfortable enough to reveal to each other that we were both lowly associates who had been handed the MAI deal thanks to our bosses' disinterest.

The transaction progressed slowly, but little by little we got it closer to the line. In December that year, Rahul came to London on a work trip with Deepak Adlakha – one of the young Dua Associates partners – and we hosted them for dinner at a Thai restaurant, where we also invited our common client Phil Moyse from MAI. This was our first meeting in person. Rahul reminds me that within a few minutes of meeting on the street, the leather soles of the fancy-dress shoes he was not used to wearing slipped on the wet cobblestones outside my office and he had landed flat on his backside!

In early January 1997, the deal was finally signed. I had to host the formidable but gruffly friendly Mr Bose in Ashurst's London office. I recall his surprise at seeing this young lad and no one else in the meeting room. The agreement contained several conditions precedent to be satisfied for the transaction to close, including obtaining approval for MAI's investment from the Foreign Investment Promotion Board (FIPB) of the Ministry of Finance of the Government of India (GoI) – the gatekeeper of foreign investment into India at the time.

Meanwhile, my bosses in London decided that I should be sent to Delhi on secondment to Dua Associates. Ashurst had a close relationship with the firm at the time and with Mr Ranji Dua himself, and I was being despatched to learn first-hand how business was done in India.

The FIPB Saga

I arrived back home in Delhi in January 1997. These were still the heady days of new types of economic activity post liberalisation. The Dua Associates office in Delhi was awash with all sorts of cross-border transactions, foreign clients and lots of hungry young lawyers eager to work on these shiny new internationally flavoured deals. Every morning, lawyers would crowd around the fax machine, waiting for new instructions from clients.

The contrasts with Ashurst were stark and interesting. While the content of the work was unsurprisingly similar, the atmosphere in the office was remarkably different. Things were more relaxed, people hung out with each other more and, in general, the vibe was more informal in a nice desi way. I enjoyed the atmosphere and found it easy to make friends. The work was interesting and varied. In London, as part of the energy and infrastructure group, I had worked mainly on oil and gas transactions, and some projects in the electric power sector, other than the odd piece of India-related acquisitions work such as the MAI–Merwanjee Securities deal.

In Delhi, my canvas was much broader. Dua Associates, like most Indian firms at the time, wasn't large enough to be organised into formal practice areas – there was just a broad separation between transactional and disputes work, and even there some lawyers did a bit of advisory and a bit of contentious work. This was a period rich with learning. In the year that I was there, I worked on matters as varied as setting up power projects; investments into hospital, food and IT businesses; build-to-fit lease agreements; the privatisation of the Orissa (now Odisha) State Electricity Board, and the then-new SEBI (Securities and Exchange Board of India) Takeover Code. My primary bosses, Deepak Adlakha (whom I knew from when he had visited London with Rahul in 1996) and Munish Sharma, were generous with their time, shared their knowledge freely and became friends (which they remain till today).

Going back to the MAI–Merwanjee Securities deal, as Rahul was in Bangalore and the FIPB was in Delhi, it was decided that I – with my previous knowledge of the deal – would be responsible for filing the approval. This involved the tedious and stressful task of putting together the long-winded FIPB application (with its numerous appendices), making 11 copies and ensuring that each page was attested, before lugging it across to the FIPB in Udyog Bhavan to file it. I recall celebrating the filing with a hot sweet chai and a cigarette in a nearby dhaba.

A funny thing happened after we filed – nothing, for months.

Concerned by the time the approval was taking, we paid the FIPB a visit through the good offices of a retired bureaucrat that Dua Associates worked with. What followed was a 10-month saga that was instructive about the mindset and functioning of the Indian state at the time.

I remember being led into the chambers of the officer in question, who bolted to attention when we entered. Rules of bureaucratic hierarchy meant that the gentleman I was with, though retired, remained forever our host's 'senior'. Tea and snacks were consumed and small talk was made. Finally, we came to the point. In principle, the FIPB would be happy to give the approval, the Officer explained, but the GoI was unfamiliar with the concept of foreign exchange broking and unclear about whether it was an activity into which foreign investment was – or should be – permitted.

At the time, the FIPB had a Ten Commandments-like list of activities that non-banking financial companies with foreign investment could perform, and foreign exchange broking was not one of them. So, for the FIPB approval to be given, the first step was for foreign exchange broking to be included on this holy list.

This wasn't going to be simple, despite the willingness of the Officer to help. We were asked to prepare a presentation explaining why foreign exchange broking should be included. This was done and was followed by another couple of months' silence. Another meeting with the FIPB revealed that the government still wasn't quite clear about what foreign exchange broking actually was. Worse, they assumed it to mean foreign exchange 'trading'. The difference is significant. When an entity is engaged in trading, it buys and sells foreign exchange itself and is, therefore, a market participant. A foreign exchange broker merely puts willing buyers and sellers of foreign exchange – generally banks and other financial institutions – together, who then conclude the transaction in their own names as principals.

Given the prevailing economic orthodoxy of the time, with its statist bias and suspicion of foreign capital, the FIPB's fear of allowing foreign direct investment (FDI) in foreign exchange was understandable, just as their failure to appreciate the difference between 'broking' and 'trading' was shocking. After a few more months of sending clarificatory explanations, the FIPB added foreign exchange broking to the list. Finally, our FIPB application was back in play. This was in October 1997.

The Importance of Châteauneuf-du-Pape

Looking back at my year at Dua Associates, two developments proved crucial for Trilegal's future. The first was meeting Anand

Prasad. The second was finally closing the MAI–Merwanjee Securities deal.

Anand had joined Dua Associates in 1996. While he had five years of experience as a lawyer, he was still learning the ropes of transactional law practice. We didn't work together much, but the Delhi office wasn't very large and our paths crossed frequently. Though Anand and Rahul knew each other as fellow associates at Dua, they weren't particularly close, working as they did in different cities.

By late 1997, Dua Associates had decided to establish a Mumbai office, partly to challenge Amarchand Mangaldas on their home turf. Anand was sent to Mumbai to help Satish Kishanchandani, then a partner at Dua Associates, open the new office. None of us could have imagined how these connections would later come together.

It was probably in November 1997 that the MAI FDI approval finally came through, and we were ready to complete the transaction. A closing meeting took place in mid-December in Mumbai. Given the key role he had played in the earlier stages of the deal, and probably also to make sure that I wasn't making any fatal mistakes, Rahul was asked to come up from Bangalore to be part of the closing. Phil Moyse of MAI flew in from London.

The closing took place without much incident. To celebrate, Phil kindly invited Rahul and me for a fancy dinner in the Oberoi Hotel, where we were also staying. After a great meal, which involved the two young Indian lawyers being introduced to a couple of bottles of a rather delicious Châteauneuf-du-Pape[35], Phil retired to bed leaving Rahul and me with the remainder of the wine and the growing relaxation that it was bringing about.

As we got more loose-lipped, Rahul asked me what my plans for the future were. I explained that I didn't see myself as an immigrant to the UK and planned to come back to India relatively soon. But, during my year in India, my exposure to traditional Indian law firms had made one thing clear – I was not going to be able to work for any of them. The contrast between the freedom I had experienced at Ashurst and the tightly controlled top-down environments I had witnessed in India had convinced me that I would have to do something on my own.

'I'm planning to leave Dua and do something on my own as well,' said Rahul. 'Shall we try and do it together?'

In the spirit of drunken camaraderie, I said yes.

And just like that, with the help of a couple of bottles of fine French wine, the idea of Trilegal was born. It seems appropriate that a decision that would shape our professional futures – and eventually make a contribution to the changing face of Indian law firms – was made not in a conference room after careful deliberation, but over a chat in a hotel, fuelled by bravado and Châteauneuf-du-Pape. Perhaps that's how the best partnerships begin – with a little liquid intervention and a leap of faith. And wasn't it Louis Pasteur who said, 'A bottle of wine contains more philosophy than all the books in the world'?

There's a nice little aside to this story. While we were enjoying our closing dinner with our client in the restaurant downstairs, Rahul had invited some of his NLS pals to his room upstairs to hang out and watch cricket (a one-day tournament in Sharjah). Among these friends were Sridhar Gorthi (soon to become a founder of Trilegal) and Srinivas Parthasarathy (who joined us as a partner in 2009 and remained with the firm for almost a decade). But, of course, none of us knew that.

5
Gathering Everyone In

I was slated to rejoin Ashurst in early 1998 at the end of my secondment, and it was decided that this would be in their Tokyo office. Many Japanese companies were beginning to take India seriously as a business destination, and it was felt that having an Indian qualified lawyer on the ground in Tokyo would be useful. I was actually offered a choice between Tokyo and Singapore. My decision to choose Japan was based as much on my personal curiosity – Japanese culture promised greater richness and variety – as on the fact that my grandfather had been India's first ambassador to Japan and I had grown up on stories of my mother's childhood there.

Rahul and I agreed that we would stay in touch and keep talking about the idea of our own firm. We expected that it would take about three years (the expected duration of my Tokyo stint) for things to play out. We left it there and went our own ways – with him going to Bangalore and me, a few months later, to Tokyo.

I loved my time in Tokyo, which happened to be my wife and my first married home. But most relevant to the Trilegal story are the contacts I made there. This included Japanese companies, particularly the *sogo shosha*s (the trading houses) – including Mitsui, Sumitomo, Mitsubishi and Marubeni – Japanese law firms and the Tokyo offices of various international law firms. Mitsui & Co., a Japanese trading house I worked with extensively in Tokyo, exemplifies the deep loyalty of Japanese clients – they remain an important firm client nearly three decades later.

I worked on a range of different matters in Tokyo which fell into two broad categories. First, while I was by no means a specialist yet, working on power projects in both London and Delhi, and now in Tokyo, meant that I was beginning to be considered a 'projects lawyer' developing experience on energy and infrastructure projects in India and the Asia Pacific region.

Growing business ties between India and Japan meant that I was given a range of other India-related work. This ranged from joint ventures for auto parts, to investments in steel manufacturing companies, to advice on issues of Indian corporate law. Recall that I had never actually studied Indian law. Thanks to India's past as a colony of the UK, my UK law degree was recognised in India. This had enabled me to enrol as an Indian advocate. However, despite my year in India with Dua Associates, I was fairly ignorant of many areas of Indian law. Google still didn't exist.

My two sharpest tools in dealing with Indian law issues in my work were therefore the venerable tome *Guide to the Companies Act* by A. Ramaiah and frequent calls to Rahul and Anand to ask them about things that I did not know, in an updated version of the strategy developed during my early days at Ashurst. I called them so often that their mobile phone numbers remain two of the few that I still remember.

As far as my employers were concerned, I was to return to the London office after my time in Tokyo and carry on from there. However, fate intervened in a number of different ways.

Plans Change

A few months after I arrived in Tokyo, India conducted a series of nuclear tests. Pokhran II took place on 11 and 13 May 1998. Owing to the memory of the devastation and misery caused by the atomic bombs dropped on Hiroshima and Nagasaki during World War II, this was a particularly sensitive issue for Japan. The Japanese government immediately imposed sanctions on India. Ongoing transactions and projects between Japan and India (and

Indian companies) continued, but the Japanese government wasn't encouraging its major corporations to look at new business initiatives in India.

More significantly, the East Asian economic crisis started affecting Japan by the end of 1998. While Japan was relatively less affected and bounced back faster, much of the work in Ashurst's Tokyo office was international, and particularly in Southeast Asia. By the spring of 1999, my bosses decided to downsize the office, anticipating a significant reduction in work. I was asked to go back to London and moved there by August 1999.

But things had been developing in the background and this change in plans accelerated the timeline for what Rahul and I had discussed that December 1997 night in Mumbai.

We had remained in regular contact throughout my time in Japan, not just because of my questions on Indian law but also to keep the discussion going about our plans to work together. Our wine-aided pact made in Mumbai was inching forward through these long-distance conversations. As we talked, it became clearer and clearer that we were both unhappy with the traditional law-firm structure in India.

Rahul

By early 1998, Rahul's frustrations at Dua Associates were mounting. As early as year two of his legal practice, It had been signalled to him that partnership was in the offing in the not-too-distant future. It was also suggested that Dua Associates was planning to set up offices overseas, first in London and then in Tokyo, and that Rahul would be sent there. Time passed and these promises were not showing signs of materialising. Rahul decided that his days at Dua Associates were numbered.

Rahul left Dua Associates on 31 March 1998, and on 1 April the doors of Matthan Law Offices opened to the public. For the first six months, he was the sole practitioner of that law firm, until his classmate from NLS, Prem, joined him (more on this later). The firm grew in bits and pieces for the next year or so, and Rahul (I think over-modestly) believes that his fledgling firm would have gone down an utterly unremarkable path if Trilegal had not happened.

Anand

By the summer of 1999, another element of the picture that would lead to Trilegal being founded was emerging. Anand's move to Mumbai had not worked out. He had disagreements with the partners in Dua's Mumbai office and wasn't enjoying the city either – it felt too crowded and commuting was terrible. He was used to Delhi, where his motorcycle got him to work in 20 minutes and his flat wasn't the size of a matchbox. In Mumbai, it took him more than an hour in cramped local trains.

Looking for an opportunity to move back to Delhi, Anand jumped at an offer of partnership from Diljit Titus of Titus & Co. in early 1999. Coincidentally, Diljeet Titus was a batchmate of mine from St. Stephen's College. It was a great commercial proposition – Titus would pay Anand 30 per cent of everything he billed out. During the 10 months that Anand was there, he pocketed over ₹30 lakh, a fortune for a relatively young lawyer.

Despite the money, Anand didn't enjoy the work environment. It wasn't about how he was treated; while it was clear that Titus was the big boss, Anand was shown a degree of respect. However, he felt that the firm was structured unfairly, with some people being favoured over others for less than meritocratic reasons. He found the atmosphere in the office to be casual and unprofessional, at times even chaotic, and he saw that many colleagues were unhappy with how they were treated. This wasn't the sort of place that Anand wanted to make a long-term commitment to. By early 1999, he had decided to break away and go it alone – a sentiment that resonated with what Rahul and I had been discussing.

Anand got back in touch with me in early 1999 to see what my plans were. During the first half of that year, our conversations evolved into a three-way dialogue among Anand, Rahul and me. It led remarkably quickly to an informal understanding and a metaphorical handshake on Anand being part of the emerging plan to set up a new law firm together.

This was our next leap of faith.

What united the three of us at this point was a shared disenchantment with the traditional Indian law firm model: Rahul's experience with unfulfilled promises, Anand's frustration with arbitrary and unprofessional structures, and my own observations during my secondment at Dua. Each of us wanted something more meritocratic, transparent and professionally run.

The Mumbai Connection

Around the same time, during the course of 1999, Rahul mentioned that two of his friends from Mumbai – Karan Singh and Sridhar Gorthi, both from NLS – were potentially interested in being part of the venture. The web of connections that would lead to the constitution of Trilegal's founding group was expanding, driven by similar experiences and shared values.

Rahul's recollection is that he was in Mumbai for work and visited the Lex Inde office to see Sridhar. They weren't in the same year at NLS, but Rahul knew Sridhar well thanks to common interests like plays and debates. He used the opportunity to sound Sridhar out about the potential new law firm. Rahul was particularly keen on Sridhar, and possibly Srinivas Parthasarathy ('Partha' to his friends – whom Rahul also knew thanks to shared co-curricular interests), joining us. Karan was not part of that group at NLS, and Rahul didn't initially have him in mind for the venture.

Rahul says that during those discussions in Mumbai, Sridhar suggested that Karan would be a better fit for the new firm and Rahul accepted Sridhar's judgement without question. This reflected the trust between them, and was another example of the risk-taking instinct that we have in common. Plus, Partha had already joined a dot-com.

So the connections worked like this: Rahul and I started the conversation about the firm, I brought Anand into the picture, Rahul got Sridhar involved and Sridhar brought Karan along for the ride. Soon after this chat in Mumbai, around July or August of 1999, Sridhar and Rahul came to Delhi to meet Anand and me (I was in transit between Tokyo and London) to discuss the idea of having Sridhar and Karan establish the Mumbai office of the new law firm.

But why did Sridhar and Karan want to leave Lex Inde? Like Rahul and Anand, they were also experiencing the limitations of existing firm environments, albeit in different ways. They agree that after about two-and-a-half to three years at Lex Inde, they began contemplating doing something independently. There were, however, shades of difference in their reasons for leaving.

Sridhar felt that Lex Inde wasn't scaling. The firm's growth was slower than he had hoped for, leading to a gradual disenchantment. This echoed the frustrations that Rahul had experienced at Dua – the sense of hitting a ceiling in a firm where the path to growth was unclear. While Sridhar's reasons for leaving related more to his perception of Lex Inde's stagnation, Karan's decision was shaped by his growing awareness of what he sought in a professional environment.

About a year before they left, a client he had worked for during his Andersen days called Lex Inde, asking for Karan. He wasn't around, and Akshay Chudasama answered the call and passed on the message. Karan handled the client's acquisition and billed for the matter. When it came to determining the origination credit, which typically entitled a lawyer to a percentage of billings, there were different perspectives on how the arrangement should apply in this particular case. After discussion, they reached an amicable resolution but the experience prompted Karan to reflect on his career priorities and what kind of professional framework would best suit his aspirations. It reinforced his desire to work within a structure where expectations and recognition systems were clearly articulated from the outset. This aligned with a broader theme among the founding partners – the importance of building transparent processes where everyone understood how contributions would be acknowledged and rewarded.

While deciding that staying at Lex Inde was not an option, Karan wasn't quite sure about what he would do next. He briefly considered doing a master's degree abroad or relocating to Singapore, but deep down he felt that it was a choice between building something new or leaving the profession altogether. When the opportunity to be part of the founding team of Trilegal came, Karan grabbed it. Though he knew Rahul only in passing and had never met Anand or me, he jumped. Here was yet another leap of faith in the Trilegal founding story.

The pieces were falling into place, driven by circumstance and the desire to do things differently – felt by all for our own separate reasons. We didn't see it quite like that at the time, but we were setting out to reinvent what an Indian law firm could be.

Making It Real

Between me being shipped back to London, Rahul deciding that he was going to take off from Dua, Anand becoming ready to leave Titus, and Sridhar and Karan planning to branch out on their own, the plan to set up a firm together was brought forward. We decided that it made sense to launch in the beginning of the financial year (FY) 2000–01.

I could have gone back to Delhi from Tokyo instead of moving to London in August 1999. But I knew that an important source of potential work would be my friends and contacts in the offices of large international law firms in London. I had been out of touch with that market for three years, and spending several months in London to rekindle those contacts seemed like a good idea. It was. During the six months I spent back in London with Ashurst, I reconnected with many old friends and colleagues, including those who had moved to other firms (always a good thing when you want to expand your contact base!). Many of them ended up being a source of work in the years to come. There was a personal reason too. My wife Isabelle – who is French and whom I had met in Oxford in 1994 – had lived away from France for over seven years by that time. She was very happy to move to India with me but wanted to spend some time in Paris first. We decided that while I spent six months in London, she would be in Paris with family and friends, and that we would visit each other as much as possible.

During this period, there was a key issue to work out: Where would the new law firm be based?

Even before Anand became part of the plan, Rahul and I had considered the question of where the new firm should be located. Rahul was tied to Bangalore from a social and familial perspective, and had the beginnings of a practice rooted in Bangalore's emergence as a technology hub. In fact, in early 2000, Rahul published the first book on technology law in India: *The Law Relating to the Computers and the Internet*, but more on that later.

I, on the other hand, had family and contacts in Delhi – which was the more natural professional fit for a lawyer working in sectors in which the central government and regulators were key actors. Despite that, we felt that being in the same office might benefit our new law firm so we toyed seriously with the idea of me living in Bangalore once I returned to India.

This did not happen. My wife made it clear that she wanted to be in Delhi, which had a more substantial French population. She also felt that finding work would be easier there. She was proved right on both counts. Also, if Anand came on board, a Delhi office would make sense. Finally, with Karan and Sridhar becoming part of the plan, the idea of launching a firm with offices in three of India's main commercial cities began to feel like a very attractive proposition. This also resonated with the fact that Anand, Rahul and I had seen the advantages that Dua Associates was enjoying by having three offices. This three-city approach would prove to be critical for the future of the firm.

In early November 1999, it was time to quit Ashurst. I went to see my boss, Geoffrey Picton-Turbervill. Geoffrey had sought out the peace and quiet of a small meeting room to work on some documents. I remember knocking on the door, fearful of his response to me telling him that I wanted to quit. I explained that my intention had always been to go back to India, and that I was going to take a leap and launch a new firm with a bunch of other young lawyers.

I needn't have been scared. Geoffrey, who is possibly the best boss I have had, took the news with customary grace and calm. He was full of praise. 'I have the greatest respect for people who do entrepreneurial things. All the very best and I hope we get the chance to work together in the future,' he said. He wasn't just saying that; Ashurst became a top referrer of work to Trilegal in our initial years, and I remain in touch with Geoffrey – who went on to become one of the best-known energy lawyers in Europe and the Middle East.

Simultaneously, Anand decided that he had to leave Titus. Together with Upamanyu Hazarika, a litigator friend, he took up a small office in a basement in Nizamuddin East in anticipation of the formation of Trilegal. Upamanyu Hazarika, now senior advocate, was briefly part of the firm before he left in our first year to be a sole practitioner, which was always his plan. For the purposes of this book, I refer only to the six partners who remained in the firm for a longer period as founders.

Almost in parallel, Sridhar and Karan left Lex Inde in November 1999 and set up Singh & Gorthi. With advances from a supportive client and a loan from Karan's wife, they rented what was to become Trilegal's first Mumbai office in Dalamal Mansion for ₹50,000 a month – yet another leap of faith, this time on behalf of an early client.

Sridhar had initially proposed setting up the Mumbai office with funding from Rahul, Anand and myself but when he conveyed this to Karan, he resisted, insisting, 'No, we'll raise the money ourselves and do this together.' While this might have been Karan's childhood experiences and fierce desire for financial independence at play, this approach has stood us in good stead. Being equal contributors and sharing responsibility was to become a key element of the firm we had not yet set up.

In December 1999, during a short work trip to Mumbai, I made a quick detour to Bangalore to meet Rahul, and in the process met Prem Ayyappa for the first time. Fate had come knocking for Prem some months earlier in the form of his NLS classmate Rahul, who had approached him saying, 'Look, I'm leaving Dua Associates, want to join me?' After some hesitation, Rahul's persistence and finally an ultimatum convinced him, and he joined Rahul under the banner of

Matthan Law Offices, which had already been set up some months ago.[36] Prem came to pick me up at the Bangalore airport. Rahul was directing a play, *A Midsummer Night's Dream*, and we got to know each other, chatting in the parking lot during Rahul's performance.

The launch date for the new firm was emerging as 1 April 2000 and I returned to India in January 2000. We decided that it was finally time for all of us to get together in one room – at this point, Anand and I hadn't even met Karan. The room in question turned out to be in Sridhar's sparsely furnished rented flat on Carter Road in Bandra. The first meeting of the firm that would soon be called Trilegal was about to begin and the lack of chairs meant that some of us were sprawled on the floor.

The moment of truth had come.

What would this new firm of ours look like?

6

The 'Why' and the Founding Values

Trilegal's foundational motivation is captured in Jayanth K. Krishnan and Patrick W. Thomas's essay 'Being Your Own Boss: The Career Trajectories and Motivations of India's Newest Corporate Lawyers'.[37] As they point out, we weren't alone in wanting greater control over our destinies – many firms established since the 1990s shared similar motivations. (A key difference: most were founded by one or two individuals, but there were six of us.)

'Being your own boss' is a good starting point, but not much more than that – motivations for running your own shop vary. For many, the main (and totally legitimate) reason is money. In 2000, even top Indian law firms paid poorly, and rewards were disproportionally retained at the top. The desire to pocket a larger share of the value they created has motivated many Indian law-firm founders. The Trilegal founders are no different. Creating a vehicle to make a good living as corporate lawyers was important. But for us, something deeper was at play.

Social psychology literature, as Krishnan and Thomas note, confirms that workplace satisfaction stems from far more than financial rewards. What we experienced in 2000 – and what has become more pronounced today – is that knowledge workers, especially professionals, seek alignment with their organisation's values and culture.

Here, returning to Simon Sinek's idea of the 'why', or the deeper reasons behind establishing an enterprise, is useful. For us, that 'why' emerged from our collective frustrations with previous workplaces and, more subtly, the opportunity we saw in liberalising India's emerging legal landscape.

The India We Found Ourselves In

To understand why we made the choices we did, it is important to look back at India's business environment in the 1990s. The economy was dominated by Indian, family-owned industrial houses. Given the disproportionate importance of government and government-owned businesses, maintaining close relationships with the government was crucial for official patronage. Further, painfully slow court proceedings meant contract enforcement was often unsatisfactory. Consequently, the details and quality of contracts – a large part of law firm work – were considered relatively unimportant.

Law firms selected lawyers partly on expertise, but family connections and the ability to navigate government and political landscapes were at least as important. Most deal-making happened behind a few closed doors, where discretion and personal connections were key. The legal market for transactional work was driven by connections and access, not expertise and professionalism.

The Trilegal founders had neither personal connections with established business houses, nor legal background or patronage. This meant we needed a different approach – an innovative plan coupled with self-belief to overcome our inherent limitations and succeed. Our personal experience of traditional firms' lack of incentive structures for lawyers who didn't share the founders' surnames led us to believe we needed to articulate foundational values, not just to set us apart from traditional firms also to have a critical ingredient for success.

What We Did Not Want

Our individual professional experiences in the Indian law firms we had worked in were similar to the experiences of our friends and acquaintances in other prominent firms. This shared dissatisfaction was a key element in bringing us founders together: we were quite clear about the sort of law firm we did not want to work in.

As discussed, Rahul had encountered unfulfilled promises of partnership and international postings. Anand was unhappy with a less than professional work culture which financial rewards did not compensate for. I had seen the contrast between the clear career progression afforded to associates at Ashurst, and the uncertain futures that young lawyers at traditional Indian firms were faced with. Sridhar had grown frustrated with the lack of growth potential. Lastly, Karan wanted a clear and unambiguous compensation system.

The perception of inequity that many Indian corporate lawyers felt was not limited to the distribution of material rewards. Traditional firms were top-heavy and hierarchical, sometimes with almost caste-like distinctions. For instance, it was not uncommon for certain toilets to be earmarked for the senior-most partners, and some of us worked in a firm where there was a hierarchy of beverage cups – associates were not permitted to use the fancier cups that certain senior partners put their lips to.

These distinctions might seem petty but they symbolised something deeper: a carefully maintained professional order. Studies show how seemingly trivial material signals – access to spaces, differentiated amenities or even who drinks from which cup – can reinforce deeper power inequalities within an organisation.[38] Traditional firms in India have had the tendency to replicate, consciously or otherwise, the hierarchies and exclusionary practices visible in broader society. In the end, the toilet and cup distinctions were only symbols for the professional influence that remained concentrated in the hands of a few.

Young lawyers had limited choice regarding their specialisation. Hiring decisions, even for partners, were tightly controlled, making it difficult to build your own team. Marketing budgets and business development trips were allocated based on status and fealty, rather than opportunity and capability. Building a practice often meant navigating internal political considerations rather than pursuing promising client relationships. Even approaching potential clients could require permission, and the sharing of work internally was often driven by politics and control rather than expertise.

We could see that it was possible to have a decent career, and maybe even make a good living, within these structures. But it was clear that none of us would ever have any meaningful say about policies, practices and other ways in which a firm is run. It felt inevitable that the interests of those controlling these firms would at some point impose a glass ceiling on any individual's aspirations of even reasonably unfettered professional growth.

The Tocqueville Effect in Indian Law Firms

Even back in the 1990s, some law firms' head honchos realised that many of their best lawyers were unhappy with the status quo. In response, some bigger firms started making up more 'partners' from outside the family group. These were almost exclusively salaried partners who did not share ownership. Some were given limited roles in governance, but effective veto powers were retained by the family or individual. This rarely worked to prevent the departure of top partners to set up their own firms.

This reminded me of what Alexis de Tocqueville, the French political philosopher, observed about revolutions – that they often occur not when conditions are at their worst but when they begin to improve. He noted, 'The social order destroyed by a revolution is almost always better than that which immediately preceded it, and experience shows that the most dangerous moment for a bad government is generally that in which it sets about reform.'[39]

In response to growing popular dissatisfaction, unpopular rulers embark on a reformatory drive to placate the more moderate sections of the populace. But they are not able to go all the way to cater to the demands of the radicals. History shows that in general this does not work, and regime change takes place anyway. Something similar seemed to have happened to Indian law firms through the first two decades post liberalisation. Talented lawyers were leaving established practices to set up on their own because insufficient reform made it clear that they would remain second-class citizens if they stayed.

Critically, there was something else that told us that success on our terms would require a different approach. Not only was the traditional model inequitable but, interestingly, the new breakaway firms tended to replicate the same inequities they were running away from. To continue the revolutionary analogy and quote Hannah Arendt, 'The most radical revolutionary will become a conservative the day after the revolution.'

Newer firms, which were themselves spin-offs from older firms had reproduced many of the same hierarchical structures and concentrations of power that their founders had once sought to escape. We were determined not to fall into the same trap, not just because of our personal experiences but also because this model seemed inherently unstable and unsuitable for growth.

So, the motivation of greater freedom was not exclusive to us. However, we had the clear sense, almost as a matter of faith, that the firm we established must be significantly different from the firms we were leaving or choosing not to join. The question was: how would we translate this instinct into something concrete?

Looking Back and Connecting the Dots

While looking back to reflect on these early founding moments, I found it useful to compare our experience with some of the literature on start-ups. But first and foremost, I found myself drawn to this thought of Rick Rubin, the legendary American record producer, from his book *The Creative Act: A Way of Being*, 'Rules direct us to average behaviours. If we're aiming for greatness, rules won't help.'[40]

If we had been setting up Trilegal today, we would probably have scoured the Internet for information on establishing and running law firms. If you Google 'law firm management', suggestions are something along the lines of 'The Top 17 Law Firm Management Books Every Owner Should Read' and 'The Top 10 Books to Grow Your Law Firm'.

I think we were lucky that Internet searches (and AI) didn't exist back then. If they had, each of us would have read these law firm management books and developed our own half-baked, ungrounded-in-reality and inevitably inadequate theories about how to build a law firm. We also didn't have any seniors or mentors in the profession to consult – no one in India had ever set up the sort of firm that we were envisaging.

What happened instead was more along the lines of what Rick Rubin recommends: don't take too much advice, don't try to create the perfect thing. Academic research on start-ups backs up the view that this kind of ignorance can be a blessing. Noam Wasserman describes how too much outside advice or pre-formed theory can lead to rigid thinking in founders, while the most successful ones often shape their structures organically around their founding values and the emotional bonds that develop among them.[41]

Founding Values

In any event, most features of what we wanted our firm to look like were points of departure from what we had experienced in the traditional firms. Boiled down, this translated into the following core values: equality and respect, meritocracy, ambition, client centricity and, critically, firm-mindedness and fraternity. At the time, we did not articulate these values in exactly this way, but looking back, there is little doubt that these were the principles that guided us. As Steve Jobs said in his 2005 Stanford commencement speech, 'You can't connect the dots looking forward; you can only connect them looking backward.'

So, how would these values translate into firm structure and practice?

Equality and Respect

The initial manifestation of this principle was equality among the founders. There were two aspects of this equality in the context of a law firm: equality in decision-making and equality in shares or compensation.

Equality in decision-making was self-evident. Beyond a theoretical belief in the principle, we had come together as a group to co-create the firm and it never occurred to any of us that one person should have a greater say than the others. Also, we didn't know what our relative contributions would look like in the future – equality seemed like the most sensible starting point. Finally, and instinctively, even if we didn't say this out loud, we felt we were more likely to stay together if we treated each other as equals. Howard Aldrich identifies the sense of early solidarity that founders feel as a critical binding force in start-ups. The ideas of sharing and trust, not hierarchy, are often the glue that holds early ventures together.[42] This was the basis for the one partner–one vote principle that we established from Day 1. It was also clear that this principle would apply to any future partners of the firm.

The second key form of equality was in ownership and profit sharing. As we will see, for the first few years Delhi, Mumbai and Bangalore operated on different balance sheets, so this equality of profit share applied to the two founding partners in each location. As a result, Anand and I, Sridhar and Karan, and Rahul and Prem were all on a 50:50 basis inter se.

The decision for the founders to have equal shares also came from a place of trust. Trust and positive emotional engagement among founders in the early days are pivotal in creating a sense of ownership, fraternity and even belief in each other.[43] Additionally, equal shares would be an important signal to others in the firm, and to the outside world.

Over the years, the principle of equality has manifested in other aspects of firm management. Salaries between offices are uniform, and no distinction is made between lawyers hired from different law schools – if you are good enough to be hired at any level, you receive compensation in the same range as anyone else at that level, regardless of your educational background. For freshers straight out of any law school, salaries are exactly the same.

Meritocracy

As we have seen, young lawyers were often hired based on family connections or because they were part of the same social group. In turn, they didn't always demand career progression based on ability or performance. However, the post-liberalisation economic growth – with its exposure to foreign investors and global capital – brought in new workplace dynamics.

This capital brought greater transactional complexity and demanded skills that Indian lawyers hadn't yet had the opportunity to acquire and that legacy firms weren't equipped to provide. To capture this high-quality, high-value work, firms had to hire the best lawyers available. This meant that the principle of meritocracy in a law firm was both sensible and necessary.

We had seen that while legal competence, or the potential to acquire it, was becoming increasingly important to be hired into Indian law firms, this wasn't sufficient to rise up the ranks to the top. Without the incentive to become genuine leaders, the most competent and ambitious lawyers risked losing their motivation. Research shows that meritocracy – like equality – isn't just an operational principle; it can create a deeper emotional alignment among members of a growing organisation.[44] It makes it more likely that ambition is rewarded, which in turn keeps levels of energy high as the organisation grows.

We believed that for us to succeed, competence and merit had to be the criteria for advancement within the firm – potentially all the way to the very top and not just as the price of admission.

Ambition

Outside of individual practitioners who dreamt of becoming senior advocates arguing important constitutional cases before the Supreme Court of India, lawyers in India weren't overtly ambitious back then. This was especially true of transactional lawyers working in law firms. None of the founders can claim with a straight face that our initial ambition included becoming one of the country's top firms in reputation, revenue and size within 25 years. But, precociously, perhaps even with a touch of arrogance, we believed in our ability – that the quality of our work and service delivery would enable us to match the top names in the market. The investor and writer Paul Graham says that many successful founders believe they belong in the major leagues long before the world notices. That belief, he argues, is what sustains founders before external validation arrives. We also believed that setting the bar high for ourselves would drive us harder.

As we began to carve out our space in the legal market, our ambition became sharper and we began to own the belief that our rightful place was at the top end of the market, even at a time when the outside world had barely noticed us. As we will see, in 2017, we formalised our vision statement: 'To be the best, most innovative law firm in India.' But the seeds for this had been planted right at the beginning.

Client Centricity

Here's something obvious: lawyers exist because clients exist.

For a law firm to be client centric may sound self-evident. Fierce competition and rising client expectations have required Indian law firms to become more focused on their clients than ever before. But this was far from true in the 1990s.

Emails and faxes from clients went unanswered for days, sometimes weeks. Answers to clients' questions tended to be long-winded, academic and lacking a commercial approach. Deadlines were taken lightly at best, and ignored completely at worst. Documents were poorly drafted, with loose formatting and typographical errors, partly because lawyers had bad habits from drafting documents for court, where shoddy draftsmanship was acceptable.

We felt that clients had the right to be dissatisfied with the status quo and correcting some of these shortcomings was pretty low-hanging fruit for us. It wasn't rocket science to be responsive to clients, think commercially about the business problems that lay behind the questions they asked and make an effort to produce top-quality documents. Putting the client at the centre of our delivery of legal services would, therefore, be a key component of our values.

Firm-Mindedness and Fraternity

As we have seen, most law firms in India were partnerships in form but not really in substance. One person or a tight family group took key decisions and claimed the lion's share of the financial rewards.

I've often been asked how we have managed to stay together for so long. My short answer has been that each of the founders has at some point given up something – an idea, a preferred approach, a matter or a client – for reasons beyond their immediate self-interest. This came to mean that even when we disagreed sharply on something, we knew that the opposing view was honestly held in the belief that it was in the firm's best interest. This does not mean that individual ambition, or even pride, was absent. This also does not mean that we pulled our punches – differences of opinion have been serious, deep and occasionally even bitter.

Why were we prepared to behave in this way? This is a harder question to answer. My view is that various factors were at play. We had seen the lack of a fraternal feeling in traditional firms, and our relative inexperience and lack of patronage meant we had only each other to rely on. We were careful not to upset one another too much, perhaps motivated by the fear that doing otherwise would tear us apart.

I think we also had a strong instinct that it was in everybody's individual interest to ensure the success of the collective. There was something quite emotional about this. Research on founders suggests that the emotional experience of building something together – a shared sense of passion and collective identity – is one of the most important, yet often overlooked, elements of start-up success. Quite simply, we were bursting with excitement about what we were starting – an excitement that, at key moments, trumped wanting to be right about everything.[45]

This gave us the platform and trust – in the intellectual and emotional journey to build a firm, and later an institution – to create an environment where we supported one another and maintained the sense that we were 'in it together'.

Of all our values, this was the most important.

7
Trilegal Is Born

With the serious matter of establishing our core values and principles done, we faced the practical task of turning them into an operational structure. No small challenge, given that our founding group was not composed of life-long friends or colleagues with decades of shared history.

Rahul, Anand and I overlapped at Dua Associates, though only briefly. Rahul and Prem were classmates from NLS, as were Sridhar and Karan, so they were knew each other pretty well. But before the meeting in his flat at Carter Road, I had only met Sridhar twice: first, incidentally (and drunkenly), in the Oberoi Mumbai after the MAI–Merwanjee Securities closing; and then with Rahul and Anand in the summer of 1999. Moreover, as mentioned before, Anand and I had never met Karan.

The Strength of Weak Ties

In retrospect, our relative unfamiliarity might have been an advantage. The sociologist Mark Granovetter calls this 'the strength of weak ties'.[46] It is the theory that looser, more accidental connections – and not close friends – often bring with them new ideas, opportunities and partnerships. In our case, not being deeply enmeshed with each other created space for flexibility, fewer hard assumptions about how things should be done and an openness to building something together.

The venture we were contemplating carried layered risks. Beyond the inherent challenges of starting any new business – particularly one that was essentially a hydra-headed joint venture – we faced the complexities of a partnership among relative strangers, each with only four to five years of corporate law practice. What if we didn't get along? Even if we did, what if the business didn't take off? There was no guarantee that the venture we were planning to launch would be a success.

Yet, what appeared as risks on paper eventually revealed themselves as potential strengths. We sensed that the same factors that created uncertainty also offered opportunities. Our experience in different practice areas, cities and countries meant we could offer clients a broader range of (growing) expertise. Our presence across Delhi, Mumbai and Bangalore – the three premier economic centres of India's modernising economy – would give us immediate scale and courage.

Each city served different economic sectors. Delhi was important for regulatory and government interactions, key for the energy and infrastructure sectors, and had a substantial industrial footprint. Mumbai was critical for access to banks and other financial institutions, financial regulators and established business groups. Bangalore was in the process of becoming the technological hub of India. Also, the traditional firms we aspired to compete with had (or were planning to open) offices in all three cities. Any ambitious firm would eventually want the same footprint, and we would have it from Day 1.

Now, the immediate question was how to structure such a venture. Also, we needed a name.

What's in a Name?

Back to Sridhar's flat in Bandra. We had made progress on how the firm would be structured and what our initial relationships would look like. It was now 5 p.m. on a Sunday evening and some of us had flights to catch, but we hadn't yet been able to come up with a name.

We had agreed that the firm would not carry our own names. Almost without exception, every significant law firm that existed in 2000 carried the name or initials of its controlling family or founding individuals. The landscape was dominated by Dua Associates, Amarchand Mangaldas, Ajay Bahl & Co. and Jyoti Sagar Associates, with Khaitan & Co, Luthra & Co., Kochhar & Co. and Titus & Co not far behind.

Here was an immediate opportunity for us to make a statement by breaking from this tradition. A name independent of the founders would signal our commitment, from the very beginning, to creating meaningful space for non-founders in our firm. Naming a new venture after an idea can signal an early, deliberate indication that what is being built is an institution, not a private monument.[47]

In any event, we were nobodies in the legal profession, so our names weren't adding any value. Plus, there were too many of us. With time, the last few of the six names on the door would inevitably have dropped off – none of us was humble enough to accept that.

So, a neutral name it was going to be. Hours of racking our brains had thrown up various atrocious options. We found ourselves gravitating towards the idea that the name should hint that we had three offices. Someone suggested 'Trillium Legal', based on the three petals of the eponymous flowering plant. That was discarded as being too pretentious but gave us the 'tri' and the 'legal' to play around with. 'Arre, let's just call it Trilegal,' someone said. And there it was.

A bunch of unimaginative lawyers taking a decision not to use our own names, and having flights to catch, are responsible for the name 'Trilegal'.

When I came back to Delhi, my wife, not one to mince words, told me that we had chosen a 'silly name'. Many others agreed with her. Oh well. Moreover, I wish I had a rupee for every time someone asked me, 'Will you change your name to Quadrilegal if you open a new office?'

Balancing Excitement with Prudence

We had to balance two sets of considerations. On the one hand was the excitement we felt for our new venture, and our instinct that forming a unified firm was the right way forward. On the other was our relative unfamiliarity. The balance we struck was between full commitment and excessive caution – a courtship period, as it were. We adopted policies and structures that would be loose enough for us to go our own ways if things didn't work out, but strong enough for us to feel committed to make the individual and collective effort required for our project to succeed. Research backs up our early instincts: early-stage ventures can thrive in an environment of deliberate flexibility. This gives founders time to learn, adapt and build deeper trust before formalising systems.[48]

This led to the creation of the following structure: Initially, there would technically be three separate firms, with three different sets of accounts and tax filings. The firms would be called 'Hazarika Prasad Jaitly' in Delhi (as mentioned earlier, Upamanyu Hazarika was briefly part of Trilegal), 'Singh and Gorthi' in Mumbai, and 'Matthan and Ayyappa' in Bangalore.

We would use the name 'Trilegal' as the common brand that would literally underline each individual firm, so that, for instance, the Delhi firm would be called:

Hazarika Prasad Jaitly
Trilegal

The Mumbai firm:

Singh & Gorthi
Trilegal

And the Bangalore one:

Matthan & Ayyappa
Trilegal

Our email addresses were all just firstname.lastname@trilegal.com. We would have common collaterals such as firm profiles, stationery and business cards, and the intention was that with time (and if all went well), we would subtly swap the juxtaposition of the names such that it became:

TRILEGAL
Hazarika Prasad Jaitly

So forth for the other two as well.

We thought we should do this so that the outside world, especially clients, would not get the sense that one brand had suddenly disappeared and had been replaced by another. The third step of the process would be to lose the names of the partners altogether and just be called 'Trilegal'.

Looking back, this elaborate branding strategy perhaps reflected a misplaced sense of self-importance. The outside world cared little for our names, much less the 'brand' we thought we were establishing. The only people really invested in these distinctions were us and, at a stretch, our families.

Structural Flexibility

In addition to the flexibility we built into the name, we decided that some prudence was required in the way in which we structured our initial relationship as well. We were aligned on our foundational values but hadn't formed common views on how these values would find expression in the details of day-to-day and year-to-year operations. There were also different perceptions of the degree of risk presented by the new venture; some of us wanted the arrangement to be a looser than others. Therefore, practically, it did not make sense to formalise too much up front.

Having separate balance sheets meant that each firm (office) would take care of its own costs. Each office would invoice its own clients and collect and share profits equally among its partners. Importantly, each office would contribute 10 per cent of its revenue into an account called the 'Common Pool' account, which would be used for joint expenses such as marketing, stationery and staff welfare. We accepted that the benefits of spending this 10 per cent might accrue disproportionately across offices. This had an important psychological effect. Even small acts of sharing can foster a strong sense of collective ownership – a belief that the success of the enterprise is bound up with one's own success – which binds individuals to a common future beyond short-term personal gain.[49]

We also established a referral system for work passed on to other offices: 10 per cent of billings in the first year of a client relationship, reducing to 5 per cent in the second year. The system had obvious gaps: what happens after year two? What about clients referred to multiple offices? As we will see in the next chapter, these elaborate arrangements turned out not to matter too much.

In any event, despite these temporary arrangements, we had breathed life into the idea of Trilegal. It was now time to get started. With our name, initial structure and values in place, we were about to leap into a marketplace that knew nothing of us and had little reason to care.

Part 3

The Early Years

8
One Firm: Testing the Waters

Our initial arrangement had been put into place at the beginning of the FY 2000–01. We had differing views on how long it would take for things to progress towards us integrating into a single entity. We did, however, have a commitment to stress testing the arrangement and making an honest effort to give it the best chance to succeed.

Work and clients were referred between offices. We made regular trips to the other cities to pitch for work together, held joint meetings to evaluate our progress and even ventured overseas. Rahul, Karan and I went on Trilegal's first business development trip, to Singapore, where we met with international law firms and had a good time in each other's company. Notably, we always presented ourselves just as 'Trilegal', downplaying our individual office names. In retrospect, many of these early actions were based on trust alone. Perhaps, this was because we had little to lose, but even at the very beginning, it instinctively felt like we were on to a good thing. This reinforced the idea of 'shared sense of purpose' that Simon Sinek invokes.[50]

Things Are Going Alright

By the end of the calendar year 2000, the results of our experiment were beginning to show. Work was flowing in from various sources, each office was performing better than anticipated, and revenues were easily covering salaries and rent. Most significantly, we were developing stronger personal relationships and working well together. We were beginning to feel more like real partners.

Around the same time, in November 2000, Upamanyu Hazarika decided that he would leave to pursue a career as an independent counsel. This had been on the cards from the beginning and fitted better not just with his own ambitions but also because it left us as a more homogenous group, since he was a few years older and the only litigator among us. That left just Anand and me in Delhi and there was symmetry: two founders in each office.

By early 2001, the six of us began to have the common feeling that closer integration was feasible. Wiser persons might have advised us to wait a little longer to establish a stronger track record of working together, but the gut feeling was strong. Entrepreneurship researchers find that founders often act before perfect knowledge is available, relying on trust, instinct and the belief that the future can be shaped together.[51] It was clear to us that there wasn't anything horrendously wrong with any of the others, so why not deepen the commitment right away?

Our First Partnership Deed

Over the first quarter of 2001, we drafted a partnership deed for Trilegal. Following a few rounds of discussion, the deed was finalized by the end of March and we met in Delhi on 10 May 2001 to sign the actual document.

The deed began by recognising that we were getting along with each other:

> The Partners have been independently practicing law under three separate partnerships in New Delhi, Mumbai and Bangalore and, over a period of approximately 18 months, have been interacting/cooperating with each other on a professional basis.
>
> Based on the positive experience of working together, the Partners have mutually agreed to enter into this Deed with the intention of jointly practicing the legal profession through a partnership.

Another significant extract was, 'The Partnership shall have no head office.'

Reflecting our 'together but apart' strategy that marked the initial phase of our existence, partner compensation was determined by the following arcane looking formula:

$$PPP = \frac{CPS}{NoP} + \frac{L\ rev - L\ exp}{NoLP}$$

In this formula,
- **PPP**: profits per partner
- **CPS**: common pool surplus
- **L rev**: location revenue
- **L exp**: location expense (includes monthly remuneration of location partners and tax to the extent of income accruing in the location)
- **NoP**: number of Trilegal partners
- **NoLP**: number of location partners

In plain English, this meant that each partner's compensation would comprise two components: first, an equal share of any surplus from our common activities (the 10 per cent Common Pool contributions from each office); and second, their proportional share of whatever their office earned after covering its expenses. This allowed us to create a sense of unity through the Common Pool while recognising that the three offices were still generating differing levels of revenue. It was our way of sharing some rewards collectively, while allowing each location to benefit from its own performance.

The deed stated that Common Pool funds could only be spent on common expenses and – to document that we were running away from the hereditary principle – stated that each partner's share in the partnership property was a personal right that would not become the property of his heirs.

Just One Name and the Bangalore Conundrum

Signing the deed also led to our first visible change: at the start of FY 2001–02, we simplified our identity by adopting 'Trilegal' as our sole name. As we finessed our name, the world took a little longer to cotton on. In fact, the Delhi office still receives mail in the name of the non-existent 'Mr Hazarika Prasad Jaitly, Trilegal'. In hindsight, moving to one name was possibly also about creating some jeopardy – if we got rid of our own names, we would be even more invested in the success of the collective.

This was the easy part. Trickier was financial integration. We had, of course, started with the idea of equality among founders and were keen to stick to this principle. However, we were confronted by the different financial realities of each city. While each office was performing quite well, Delhi and Mumbai – as might have been expected, as they were the larger business centres – were doing better financially than Bangalore. At that time, Bangalore had a lower cost base but fee levels were also lower than in the other two cities.

Some disparity existed even between Delhi and Mumbai, with Delhi performing a little better. This, combined with Anand's relative seniority in the profession, initially made him reluctant to accept complete parity among the three offices. Sridhar and I eventually persuaded him to agree to Delhi and Mumbai operating on equal footing, and these two offices integrated financially. Extending the same treatment to Bangalore presented a more significant problem given its significantly lower revenue. When offered to integrate with 20 per cent less equity, Rahul refused and took a principled stance: there would either be equality or the Bangalore office would remain separate until its revenues were in the same ballpark.

Despite this financial separation, we operated as a unified entity in all other ways. We implemented common systems, notably for lawyer evaluation and information technology (which as we will see was Rahul's baby); went on highly enjoyable annual firm retreats; shared leads, work and clients; held partner common meetings and maintained a unified front before our lawyers, staff and the outside world.

These experiences reinforced the idea that there would be benefits to full integration. Essentially, we got along well with each other.

Full Integration, Finally

Within a few short years, Bangalore revenues were on their way up. Some of us were uncomfortable with Bangalore's status; our experiences as partners had been overwhelmingly positive and we strongly felt that we would be better off if Bangalore integrated. Around the same time, Prem decided that he wanted a slightly different career path, for personal reasons, and said that he would step back and take things at a slower pace. He wanted to remain a partner but wanted fewer responsibilities and, in return, was prepared to forsake the financial benefits of being an equity partner. The rest of us wanted him to remain a partner and felt that, as a founder, he had the right to make this choice.

This meant that Bangalore profits were no longer divided between two partners and more would be available to contribute to a common balance sheet. Thus, Bangalore integrated. In hindsight, it was wise of Rahul to stick to his guns. Equal partnerships can be emotionally powerful but structurally fragile. They require conscious acts of principle to be preserved and Rahul's stance cemented the principle of equality among us.

I recall feeling a deep sense of relief when this happened. We no longer had to pussyfoot around the integration issue and the equality principle of our founding vision had finally taken full shape.

While Trilegal's structure has evolved since, the foundational values embedded in that first partnership deed have endured. A symbol of this continuity is the Common Pool account, created in 2000 for our initial 10 per cent contribution towards shared expenses. Now, as our primary bank account, it receives all client fees and disburses all expenses, including salaries. Each month, when I receive my drawings from this account, it serves as a reminder of how far we have come from those first tentative steps towards becoming one firm. Institutions that endure often carry small artefacts from their origins – little reminders of the stories and struggles that built them.[52]

9

Law Firm Structure: Equity and Compensation Choices

Trilegal operates what is called a 'lockstep' system for its partners; there is a lot hiding behind that term. Fundamentally, it means that partners of the firm have an ownership interest in it. To anyone unfamiliar with the legal profession in India, this might sound obvious. Well, it isn't. Trilegal was the first to adopt it and in 2025 remains the only one of the top-tier of law firms to operate this model.

Picking an ownership and compensation model that would work for us was not an obviously simple task. We would have loved to follow examples from closer to home but, in the early years of the twenty-first century, there were no natural domestic role models for us to follow. As we have seen, most of the larger firms that existed at the time were closely held, either by families or by individuals that had established them.

There were other partners in these firms beyond the 'name' partners but, to the best of our knowledge, the vast majority of non-family partners were salaried. This meant that while they functioned as partners in many ways – they led transactions, supervised teams and perhaps even managed some client relationships – they were compensated on the basis of a salary plus a performance-linked bonus. This didn't sit well with us, so we decided to start from scratch and see how law firms outside India worked.

Where Partnership Models Come From

The evolution of professional firms follows a pattern that is consistent across industries. What started as individual practices gradually developed into the sophisticated partnership structures we see today. Take accounting firms, for example. Price and Waterhouse were once separate family businesses before merging and evolving into a professional partnership. The same happened in consulting – McKinsey, which turns 100 next year, grew from an individual practice into the partnership model that became the gold standard for professional services.

Law firms followed a similar trajectory. Most lawyers started as sole practitioners – they would set up their practice, wait for clients to find them, and gradually build their reputation and client base. As these practices grew, the natural first step was to bring in family members. Sons (rarely daughters) would join what then became family firms. Thomson Snell & Passmore, the oldest continuously operating law firm in the world, went through three generations of Hoopers starting in 1570, followed by several generations of Scoonses.

As long as ownership stayed within the family, there wasn't much need to worry about equity structures or profit distribution models. But eventually, these family firms would hit natural limits – descendants who were incompetent, uninterested or simply too few to sustain growth. Any firm with serious growth ambitions eventually would need to look beyond the family.

Separately, a different model evolved. Some lawyers realised that it made sense to share office space and support staff costs while maintaining financially separate practices. Many barristers' chambers in the UK (and some Mumbai law firms still operate this way) would have individual lawyers under one roof, sharing expenses but keeping their own clients and profits.

Over time, as lawyers began specialising, it is easy to imagine these loose associations developing internal client referral arrangements and fee-sharing systems. Eventually, some of these groups would have wondered whether it made more sense to formalise everything into a single profit-sharing entity. This is where things got interesting and complicated. Eventually, these firms would have had to think about how equity would be allocated and how partners would be compensated.

The evolution of compensation models is the continuing story of law firms navigating the tension between the need for institutional cohesion and the recognition of individual achievements. We will see how this has been a key thread through Trilegal's history as well.

Cravath and the Lockstep Model

To understand modern law firm partnerships, a natural place to start is the Cravath System. This framework was pioneered by the New York firm Cravath, Swaine & Moore in the early twentieth century, and it fundamentally shaped how elite law firms think about partnership.

The Cravath approach aimed at institutional excellence and was built around developing internal talent as the primary engine for growth. The firm trained junior associates rigorously and promoted only those who consistently demonstrated both high ability and alignment with the firm's culture. Loyalty to the firm had to come before loyalty to individual ambitions or even individual clients. The most distinctive feature of this system was lockstep compensation. Here's how it works:

> The firm's total equity is divided into points or units. Partners receive a certain number of points based primarily on their seniority (how long they've been a partner). These points form a ladder, say from 10 to 50 points, with the senior-most partners capped at the top. When lawyers become partners, they start at the bottom of the lockstep – in our example, at 10 points. Each year, they move up the ladder, gaining additional points according to a pre-defined scale. After 10 years, assuming they gain four points annually, they'd have 50 points and be at the top of the lockstep, at which stage their points are capped.

Additional points are 'created' each year, to take care of annual points increases and points allocated to new partners. Practically, this involves a sub-division of the existing equity and, in real terms, capped partners at the top of the lockstep see a reduction in the actual percentage of equity their points represent. The firm's distributable profits are divided among all partners in proportion to their points. If the total profit pool is ₹100 crore and all partners collectively hold 1,000 lockstep points, a partner with 50 points receives ₹5 crore.

The system encourages loyalty because it takes years to reach the top, where the big rewards are. It promotes collaboration, since everyone shares from the same profit pool – partners are incentivised to help each other rather than compete internally. Clients tend to become clients of the firm, not just of individual partners. This aligns with the early-twentieth-century view of legal practice as a profession centred on trust and collegiality.

However, lockstep has drawbacks. Underperforming senior partners can earn substantial compensation simply due to their accumulated points, while younger, high-performing partners may feel their progression is too slow and become frustrated. It is not a system that works well for rainmakers – partners who bring in significant business and who might feel that their rewards should reflect their business origination abilities more closely.

In fact, the global financial crisis of 2008 placed significant pressure on lockstep models, as top London-based firms like Clifford Chance and Freshfields grappled with demands from rainmakers for faster rewards, leading to them 'de-equitising' or pushing some partners down the lockstep.

Lockstep vs Eat What You Kill

These tensions led to the emergence of a very different philosophy: the 'eat what you kill' model. This performance-based system rewards partners primarily on the basis of the revenue they generate – billable hours, client origination and other measurable contributions are closely monitored and directly rewarded. By the 1970s, this model had gained traction, particularly among firms with high-stakes litigation and lucrative transactional practices, where individual rainmaking was critical.

The trade-offs were clear to us. While the 'eat what you kill' model incentivises productivity and entrepreneurship, it can foster destructive internal competition and make it difficult to build a cooperative culture. As legal scholar Richard Susskind points out, firms embracing pure performance-based models often struggle to maintain long-term vision and suffer from cultural decay over time.[53]

Two-Tier Partnership

By the 1970s, law firms who did not want to go the 'eat what you kill' route faced a conundrum that still exists – how to reward exceptional individual contributions while preserving the stability and collegiality of lockstep. The solution that many adopted was the two-tier partnership system, distinguishing between equity and non-equity partners. Non-equity or salaried partners received fixed compensation with variable performance bonuses, while equity partners retained ownership stakes and profit-sharing privileges.

This offered flexibility; firms could attract and retain talent without immediately diluting equity. But it created its own problems, including the perception of second-class citizenship among non-equity partners. We had a choice to make and the stakes were high. Get it wrong, and we could either tear ourselves apart through internal competition or stagnate through lack of incentives. Get it right, and we might actually build something of value.

Aligning Rewards with Values

We knew that how we structured equity ownership and compensation could make or break what we were trying to build. There is probably no single decision that shapes a law firm's culture more than how you divide the money. With the wrong structure, our founding values of equality and meritocracy would become empty words.

The organisational behaviour literature confirms what we felt instinctively – reward systems are powerful carriers of organisational values. Since we wanted to create a culture that was recognisably different from the traditional firms dominating the market, this choice would be the key to shaping that culture.[54]

If we had planned for ownership to remain predominantly with the founders, we could have just continued with our equal-sharing structure and stopped there. But we wanted to grow; this would need genuine partners from outside the founding group, not just people earning salaries while being called 'partners'. We saw this as the most obvious way to attract talent away from our competition. And this was one of the main reasons we had set up the firm in the first place.

It took no discussion to reject 'eat what you kill'. This model fundamentally contradicted our foundational values – firm mindedness and fraternity, in particular, would have been dead on arrival. The internal competition it would create could tear us apart. The lockstep model aligned much better with our values. But the idea of compensation being mainly seniority-based was problematic – it didn't adequately incentivise ambition and merit.

We decided to remain flexible about our compensation model and keep testing its effectiveness. Managing the tension between collegiality and meritocracy would be an ongoing challenge, particularly for a firm wanting to maintain a fraternal culture while keeping people properly incentivised. Over the years, this has meant making many tweaks to our model as we've adapted to growth, changing workplace practices, and the increasing success and ambition of our partners.

The Two-Tier Solution

To start, we took the middle path and adopted the two-tier partnership model, with both equity and non-equity partners. Our version had a strong bias towards the equity-owning with lockstep part of it. Here's how it worked:

- Lawyers at about seven years post-qualification experience would be considered for entry into the partnership.
- Candidates would go through an evaluation process conducted by all partners.
- Successful candidates would enter the partnership as salaried partners, where they would stay for two to three years.
- In addition to salary, they would receive a performance bonus.
- During this two to three year period, they had to reach a specific revenue target.
- Upon hitting the target, they would automatically become equity partners.
- No special pools of equity were reserved for founders – there was no 'founder premium' or 'founder equity'. Firm revenues would go into a single pot, from which all expenses would be met. Whatever remained – the total profit pool – would be shared among equity partners based on their profit points or units.

We felt this model stayed true to our foundational values while providing a safety net in the form of an evaluation period for new partners. We could ensure that each salaried partner's performance justified the equity they were going to receive.

What Equity Actually Means at Trilegal

Here's where the Trilegal model became radical. Many still find it hard to believe. Traditional ideas of 'equity' might suggest that new partners should pay something to receive their share, like buying shares in a company. Many law firms around the world require partners to make capital contributions for their equity.

We, however, decided that partners would not have to pay for their equity. As a corollary, leaving or retiring partners would not be paid for their equity when they left. This decision was based on several practical considerations. First, determining the price for equity would require complex valuation exercises each time we made new partners (potentially twice a year). Goodwill is notoriously hard to value. Second, the burden of paying for equity would weigh heavily on entering partners. Since a lockstep gives partners points annually as they progress up the ladder, this burden would persist for several years. Even with discounted credit lines, like many international firms offer, seeing chunks of your earnings go to capital contributions could be demotivating. Third, taking on lateral partners (particularly higher up the lockstep) would become difficult. Once our equity became valuable, the price of entry would scare potential laterals away. Finally, if we had increasing numbers of partners with large equity stakes, we would have to make significant payouts to retiring partners. This could become complicated and expensive, requiring reserves or credit lines that would eat into current profits.

The collapses of venerable American firms (like Dewey & LeBoeuf and Coudert Brothers) are cautionary tales. Dewey imploded under the weight of expensive partner guarantees and retirement obligations. Coudert collapsed when its ageing, expensive equity structure could not handle competition and payouts that became due on the simultaneous retirement of several high-equity partners.

This lead us to a stark conclusion. What our approach means is that holding equity in Trilegal simply entitles a partner to a share of profits representing their units while they are in the firm. When partners leave – *including founder partners* – they get a farewell party and a thank you very much. That's it. This remains a powerful concept within the firm that continues to surprise even sophisticated observers.

Beyond practical considerations, there was an important principle behind our approach. In a country where many lawyers do not come from wealthy backgrounds, making lawyers pay for equity could be seen as a thinly disguised barrier to entry. Susskind argues that removing financial barriers to ownership is essential for democratising elite knowledge-based professions and making opportunity genuinely accessible.[55] We also strongly felt that retaining even a small amount of founder equity would create caste-system-like distinctions among founders and other partners.

Creating an Institution

Looking back, our approach to equity – no founder equity, no payment required and entitlement only to profit shares while at the firm – was key to creating our value system and culture. It showed that the founders did not want to retain any vestiges of the proprietorship attitudes that prevailed in many traditional firms. *We wanted to create an institution.*

We liked the interlocking incentives this created. The system would motivate people to work hard and contribute to the collective while at the firm, since there were no retirement payouts. It would keep founders honest and contributing rather than resting on their laurels. The model was not perfect and we have refined it over the years, but the core principle remains unchanged – true partnership means genuine shared ownership, not just shared titles.

10
Money Matters and Decision-Making

While Trilegal does not charge partners for their equity, the founders did, in a sense, pay for theirs. Each of us contributed initial capital in some form to get the firm off the ground – office fit-outs, security deposits, books and communication systems all cost money. These early financial decisions, though quite basic, helped build habits and patterns of mutual trust and ethical behaviour that would come to define the firm.

Anand had accumulated some savings from his time at Titus & Co., which went towards fitting out our Jaipur Estate office. I contributed approximately £10,000 (₹6 lakh at the 2000 exchange rate) from my Ashurst savings, part of which went into building out my room when I joined the office. Beyond this, Anand and I had sufficient funds to cover six months of salaries and rent – a cushion that helped us sleep better in those uncertain early days.

Rahul brought in savings from his time at Dua Associates as and when needed. The Bangalore office had lower expenses initially, partly owing to savings on rent (for reasons that we will see later). These initial contributions were later formalised in our capital accounts with the firm. Several years later, in the interests of parity with newer partners who had not contributed capital, these initial investments – an important symbolic contribution to our shared future – were repaid to the founders, wiping the capital slate clean.

Rajenbhai

At this point, we must introduce a key character in the Trilegal story – Rajen Gandhi, chartered accountant (CA). 'Rajenbhai' is Trilegal's principal tax and finance advisor, down to the present day.

Rajenbhai first crossed paths with us through Sridhar. Before Trilegal was formed, while still at Lex Inde, Sridhar was advising Alchemy Capital on a SEBI-related matter, and Rajenbhai was their auditor (and still is). They developed a rapport, and Sridhar asked Rajenbhai to handle the tax audit and returns for Singh & Gorthi as well.

Remember that first meeting at Sridhar's flat in Bandra in 2000? Rajenbhai was there too – he came for a couple of hours to give us tax advice and recalls sensing the excitement bubbling among us. His presence would prove more significant than any of us could have imagined at the time.

First-Year Revenues

Our revenue projections for the first year were charmingly naive. Beyond hoping to cover salaries and rent, and have a little left over for ourselves, we had no idea what to expect. Since we operated on separate balance sheets then, each office considered this independently, though we all recognised that quick growth and financial stability would be crucial for the success of our collective venture. I remember an early conversation with Anand where we speculated about the Delhi office's first-year revenue.

'Bhagwan (the affectionate term by which we still refer to each other),' I said to Anand, 'what do you think our revenue will be this year?'

'About ₹60 lakh?' he answered.

I agreed, thinking that was both realistic and rather satisfactory. The actual figure turned out to be more than twice that amount. While I would like to attribute this to our exceptional legal abilities, the reality probably involved a combination of our ignorance about law firm finances, a growing market and a healthy dose of luck. Additionally, perhaps, there was something about our service delivery model, though we didn't fully recognise it yet.

Mumbai's revenues reached about two-thirds of Delhi's figures, while Bangalore achieved slightly less than half. These unexpectedly strong first-year results provided crucial financial stability and enabled us to meet our financial obligations with room to spare.

Clean Books from Day 1

The need for separate books of accounts before financial integration meant that each office needed its own accountants. In Delhi, this led to enlightening, if disconcerting, conversations about how many small businesses in India operated at the time, and still do today.

Neither Anand nor I came from business backgrounds, and some of the suggested tax strategies we encountered were eye-opening, often law-breaking and uniformly unacceptable. Proposals ranged from the patently illegal to the creatively dubious. The most blatant one was to accept cash payments from 'compliant' clients to hide income from taxation – we didn't want any such clients. Another offered to connect us with people who, for a fee, would provide fictitious invoices for various expenses. We would pay these invoices and receive cash back, minus a 2 per cent commission, effectively padding our expenses to reduce taxable income. My favourite, perhaps, was the suggestion that came with the dramatic statement that without creative structuring 'the Government of India would become our firm's largest shareholder' by receiving taxes from us. This involved an elaborate system of recording personal expenses in different coloured pens – black for legitimate business expenses, blue for personal ones –allowing the firm to claim both, while Anand and I settled the personal expense amounts in cash between ourselves.

All these schemes were summarily rejected. We received sage advice from our friend Gopal Rao, who was our personal CA for two decades before he retired. 'You guys are going to be successful,' he told us, 'and very soon your revenues will be so large that the cash generated from these schemes will become unmanageable. Your beds won't be big enough to hide the money under.' This was practical advice that aligned with our moral compass.

At that pivotal meeting at Sridhar's house in Bandra, Rajenbhai had made a similar point. He reminded me recently that he had told us firmly that 'in tax there are only two ways, black or white, no shades of grey'. If we were serious about building something enduring, we had to commit to clean accounts from the outset.

But Rajenbhai wasn't worried about us. He recounted (I have no recollection of this) how we had insisted on issuing a proper receipt even for a ₹5,000 payment – this was normal for us, but unusual enough in the business environment of the time to mark us out as different.

This wasn't just a matter of personal integrity. As we later discovered, it became a commercial advantage. The Enron debacle was around the corner, and in the decades that followed, India witnessed several high-profile corporate scandals.[56] Satyam Computers was an early example, in which 'creative' accounting practices led to catastrophic collapses of otherwise successful corporate groups. More recent allegations against some of India's largest groups have also shown how fragile trust can be when financial practices aren't above board.

No one could have imagined these scandals back in 2000, but avoiding even the smallest compromise on financial transparency allowed us to build a firm capable of withstanding scrutiny from international clients, foreign law firms and tax authorities. Staying within the four-square boundaries of the law became another quiet foundation of our later growth.

Rajenbhai says that our early decision to maintain clean books was 'probably the most momentous decision you all took'. It was made before we had money, reputation or bargaining power, but it shaped the firm's future as much as any decisions on equity structures or compensation models could have. In the end, integrity wasn't a strategic calculation, it was simply the *only way* we could imagine operating.

No Assets in the Firm

Soon after we had set up, Mr Jyoti Sagar, the respected founder of JSA, summoned Karan and Sridhar to his office and gave them some advice that aligned with our view on equity and shaped our financial philosophy.

'Never create assets in the firm,' he told them. 'They'll become a barrier to future partners.' Jyoti explained that he had faced this problem in his uncle's firm – when partnership was offered, prospective partners had to buy into accumulated assets but often didn't have the money to do so.

To this day, we follow that advice scrupulously, with an asset-light approach – we don't own any of our offices and try and lease as much of our equipment, fixtures and fittings as we can.

From Financial Foundations to Governance

However, having sorted out our approach to money, we needed to think about power. It had proved surprisingly easy to agree on values and operating practices up front, but how would we actually make decisions once we were up and running?

One Partner One Vote

As previewed when discussing our founding values, our commitment to equality had deep implications for decision-making. From that first meeting on Sridhar's floor in Bandra, we operated on the principle that each of us would have an equal say. We didn't know this then, but governance norms established early in a firm's life tend to become 'sticky', shaping culture and decision-making far beyond the founding years.[57]

When the partnership consisted solely of the founders, this meant that important decisions were taken collectively by the six of us. When Prem decided to take a step back from an active role, Anand, Karan, Rahul, Sridhar and I shared this responsibility. This laid the foundation for what is our most cherished principles: *one partner, one vote*.

While some professional service firms follow a corporate model where voting rights are tied to shareholding percentages, our version of equality made it essential that each partner's vote carried equal weight. This was much more than just decision-making mechanics; it would prove to be a cornerstone in shaping the firm's culture.

Learning Partnership at Each Office

Practical implementation began at each office, where the two founding partners would make relevant local decisions together. This was not always smooth. In Delhi, for instance, Anand and I found ourselves disagreeing on matters ranging from consequential decisions like choosing premises for our next office to relatively trivial issues such as laptop specifications. Interpersonal dynamics, personal preferences and personality traits matter, and day-to-day decision-making can throw up unforeseen differences of opinion. Karan and Sridhar faced similar challenges.

Working through these disagreements taught us a lot about partnership. We learnt, with varying degrees of individual success, the art of compromise and how to handle not getting our way – invaluable skills as the partnership grew. It helped that the firm was doing much better than we had anticipated – so it made business sense to pull one's punches from time to time and keep things going smoothly.

However, for some decisions, all the structure and organisational theory in the world were useless. Within our first couple of years, we had to ask someone to leave for performance-related reasons. Neither Anand nor I wanted the honour of being the first Trilegal partner to sack someone. We flipped a coin; I won and remember being in my car heading out of Delhi for a holiday when I got a call from Anand saying, 'Bhagwan, I did it.' (This respite was temporary – I have had to ask tens of people to leave over the past 25 years and it is never a nice thing to have to do.)

Post Integration: The Coordination Committee

As we evolved into a single partnership and contemplated the idea of admitting new partners, it became clear that we needed to streamline our decision-making processes. We remained committed to universal suffrage among partners, but it was increasingly impractical for every partner to be involved in all decisions, particularly day-to-day operational matters. The obvious solution would have been to appoint a senior partner or managing partner, perhaps with a board for oversight. However, this posed several challenges.

First, any departure from our principle of equality would be difficult to implement. It would create a 'first among equals' dynamic among the founders – a hierarchy that none of us were ready to accept yet. Second, none of us wanted the responsibility of making decisions on behalf of the other founders. Third, we were still relatively young and inexperienced in management. Collective decision-making, despite being a bit clunky, seemed better with its inherent checks and balances. Professional firms usually function best when leadership is distributed – independent-minded lawyers tend to be allergic to rigid hierarchies.[58] Finally, we were operating in three offices of equal status, each requiring local governance while maintaining our commitment to operating as a unified firm.

These considerations led to the creation of the 'Coordination Committee', comprising Karan, Rahul and myself. We self-selected by simply putting our hands up for the job. True to its name, the Committee was not granted specific authority but rather took on the responsibility of ensuring that partnership decisions were implemented consistently across all offices.

This was not unusual – if formal hierarchy appears too difficult or cumbersome, organisations naturally develop informal ways to coordinate work efficiently. The celebrated economist Ronald Coase wrote about this phenomenon, and we were unconsciously following an established pattern.[59]

The Committee's role encompassed various operational matters: coordinating salary and bonus decisions, organising business development trips and overseeing approved budget expenditures. We spoke to each other often, keeping tabs on what was going on in the other offices and consulted the other founders for even halfway-significant matters.

Long-Term Consequences

This decision-making structure had several significant long-term consequences for the firm's development. Having to consult each other on decisions fostered more frequent communication among offices than we might have otherwise had. This surfaced viewpoints from different offices and, without quite realising it, cultivated a culture of considering other perspectives in decision-making.

We also learnt valuable lessons about the well-known challenges of having responsibility without corresponding authority. While the Coordination Committee helped promote alignment, it exposed the limits of informal influence when formal decision-making power was absent. This was possibly necessary at the time, but it took longer than we would have liked to evolve beyond this approach.

Finally, and most enduringly, we developed deep skills in building consensus through conversation and persuasion. This is what organisational experts call 'deliberative collaboration', where agreement emerges through dialogue and negotiation rather than executive authority.[60] Even with more formal management structures today, this approach to decision-making is a defining characteristic of Trilegal's management style and a dominant theme of the firm's culture.

11

Delhi: Early Deals and Clients

I had specific plans for my personal life for the period between our first discussions in Mumbai on firm structure and our formal launch on 1 April 2000, the beginning of the new financial year. My wife had never lived in India and I had promised her that I would spend this time introducing her to my friends and helping her settle down in an unfamiliar city. Little did I know that the firm's first transaction would consume my life and upend these plans.

Telesystems International Wireless

Trilegal hadn't formally launched yet when my friend from Oxford, Vinay Ganga, who was with the London office of a US law firm called Cadwalader, Wickersham & Taft, called. It was early March 2000 and our conversation began something like this:

>**Vinay:** Have you guys opened for business yet?
>**Me:** Why do you ask?
>**Vinay:** Because I have a deal for you.
>**Me [struggling to hide my excitement]:** Well yes, then we're open.

What followed was an all-consuming transaction that would define our first months. The pace of the deal was brutal – meetings at the Maurya Sheraton during the day and late-night document-drafting sessions in our basement office in Nizamuddin, with fractious negotiations providing an occasional (almost welcome) interruption to our non-stop desk work.

The client was Telesystems International Wireless (TIW), a listed Canadian telecom company embroiled in a complex standoff with Shyam Telecom, a Delhi-based telecom company. Together with Telecommunications Consultants India Limited, a public-sector company, they had a three-party joint venture which held a cellular licence for the state of Rajasthan. Anand and I approached the matter with what would become our modus operandi in the early years: working exceptionally long hours to understand the issues, which were related to telecom regulation and complex company law matters, and reviewing each other's work to ensure quality and comprehensiveness.

After two intense months, there was a brief lull in the transaction. Not having many other clients, we had time on our hands, and Anand and I kept ourselves out of trouble with head massages at Delight Hair Salon and preparing our first client invoice.

Given the number of hours we had invested on the matter, we had accumulated an impressive billable amount, even at our then-modest rates. Somewhat insecure about the value of our work, we crafted detailed narratives of the work done, trying hard to make the invoice look professional. A week of drafting and redrafting produced what we considered a bill of sublime beauty, which we promptly despatched to Shaun Parmar, the client.

He paid within a week, God bless him. To celebrate, Anand and I bought matching dark green Ford Ikons, upgrading from a Gypsy for him and a Zen for me.

When Shaun visited next, we went out for dinner together in one of our shiny new cars. 'Did I pay for this car?' he asked cheekily.

'Yes!' we replied in chorus.

'Then you're paying for dinner,' he said, laughing.

Our pleasure entirely, Shaun.

Telesystems International Wireless was key for us because it showed us that relationships could deliver work even when brand recognition was absent. It taught us early that working hard and delivering consistently could trump reputation, at least for a while.

Petronet LNG

Our next significant client was Petronet LNG Ltd, a newly established company formed by four public sector oil and gas giants: Indian Oil, Bharat Petroleum Corporation Ltd, Hindustan Petroleum Corporation Limited and Gas Authority of India Ltd. By any measure, we had little right to expect their business. They were a company with grand growth plans and securing them as a client would have been a coup for any law firm, let alone a piddly little firm like ours. We had heard that Amarchand Mangaldas was already advising them on some matters.

Our initial attempts to secure a meeting were unsuccessful. In a moment of desperation, I went to my father, a senior government officer, with a request. It was difficult for him, I'm sure, to say what he did: 'Beta, I'm telling everyone in town that my son is part of setting up a new law firm and he hasn't asked me for any help to get work. Let me continue saying that.' A chastening and, at the time, disappointing moment, but in hindsight an early and valuable lesson in not leaning on family for favours and learning to stand on my own feet. A lesson that did a lot for my confidence in pitching for and acquiring work and clients in the future.

Eventually, we managed to secure a meeting. A senior official tossed a contract in our direction, casually remarking, 'This has already been reviewed and approved. Take a look and tell us what you think.'

We had nothing to lose. Anand and I pulled an all-nighter reviewing the contract, generating over three dozen comments on how to improve it, most particularly highlighting a significant issue that arguably made the contract difficult to enforce. We submitted our analysis and were met with a couple of days of silence.

After a few days, they called us in for a meeting. We were appointed to take the contract forward to signing – this was the beginning of a decade-long relationship. Our work with Petronet subsequently encompassed negotiations with Gaz de France (during their acquisition of a stake in Petronet), project-financing documents, shipping contracts, LNG sale and purchase agreements, gas supply agreements and, eventually, a stock market listing.

Perhaps, more importantly, it kickstarted our oil and gas and energy practices, which turned out to be key elements of the firm's initial growth and remain a bedrock of our current service offering.

Power Grid Corporation of India Ltd

In early summer of 2000, Rahul got an email from his college classmate and good friend Malavika Jayaram. At the time, she was an associate at Allen & Overy (A&O; now A&O Shearman) in London and worked with Chris Watson, a top telecoms partner. She asked whether Trilegal would like to pitch to work as Indian counsel alongside A&O on a project which involved the Power Grid Corporation of India Ltd (PGCIL), the national electricity transmission utility. Of course we said yes, and after a brief beauty contest (shorthand for selection process), Chris hired us.

This project was one of a kind and envisaged PGCIL wrapping fibre optic cables around its power transmission lines. The work involved creating a complex transaction structure navigating a number of different legislations, including three venerable statutes from India's colonial past – the Indian Telegraph Act; the Indian Electricity Act, 1910; and the Indian Easements Act, 1882. The project was complicated and exciting.

We prepared meticulously, analysing the legal and regulatory framework and developing potential transaction structures. Chris arrived in Delhi, kicking off a week of sustained, sharp and intense work. Days were 12–16 hours long; many long and complicated contracts were drafted, reviewed and redrafted. Many, many pizzas were eaten. At the end of the week, a suite of high-quality contracts was close to completion. Our young and inexperienced team had impressed Chris. His praise was generous: 'I'm not sure if my own team at A&O would have pulled out the stops and delivered as you guys have.'

Then, Chris told us that he had to leave early for London, before the work was over. This was surprising, even mildly alarming, as there was a lot of work left to be done and, as the senior member of this inexperienced team, his inputs remained critical. He promised to provide comments from afar but explained that he had an urgent family commitment relating to one of his children.

'You see,' he said, 'my eldest daughter recently auditioned successfully for a role in a film and shooting starts next week. I have to chaperone her.' The film? *Harry Potter and the Philosopher's Stone*. His daughter's name? Emma. Yes, *that* Emma Watson.

The transaction was important from many perspectives. It was a first of its kind, a unique intellectual challenge requiring innovative thinking. It provided many of our lawyers with invaluable experience of law and regulation in two key sectors – electricity and telecoms – and showed them that they could meet the high standards of a top international law firm.

Most importantly, it also gave us a glimpse into the power of two of our founding values – trust and fraternity. Rahul simply passed on the work to Anand and me, even though under our structure at the time he did not stand to derive much financial benefit from it. It wasn't a grand, conscious decision to live out our founding values; it just seemed to be the obvious thing to do. But looking back, it was exactly the kind of collaborative instinct we had hoped we would develop.

12

Mumbai: Early Deals and Clients

While Delhi was establishing its early rhythm with telecom and energy clients, Mumbai was carving out its own path in the financial capital. It took a very different set of skills to build business in Mumbai. While Sridhar and Karan approached client development with the same combination of persistence and opportunity that characterised our early Delhi efforts, their approaches were different.

As a slightly more reserved person, Karan was more drawn to institutional clients and international law firm relationships, whose slightly more formal working styles lent themselves to more measured engagement. Sridhar, on the other hand, was always more outgoing. He had (and still has) the ability to strike the right chord with Indian business leaders, with a combination of legal nous and an intuitive understanding of the business concerns of such clients. As a combination, this worked well for our Mumbai office.

Godrej: Working with a Major Corporate

Among our earliest and most formative client relationships was one that Sridhar built with Godrej. We were beginning to develop a reputation as a 'new age' law firm, one that understood the emerging technology-driven business models catalysed by the Internet, particularly in areas like outsourcing and medical transcription, which were gaining traction (and, as we will see, were being serviced by our Bangalore office). Godrej was planning to enter this domain and was looking for legal advisors who could understand these new businesses.

'One of the people we had worked with in a previous role had joined this new business line at Godrej,' Sridhar recalls. 'We were brought in to assist on outsourcing contracts because it was felt that the traditional firms didn't really grasp the nuances of this new model.'

This initial engagement led to a deepening relationship with the Godrej legal team, particularly with their general counsel, S.K. Bhatt. He appreciated the speed, responsiveness and precision of our support – qualities he found were different from some of the older firms that had traditionally served Godrej, including established legacy Mumbai firms with partners sitting on the boards of various Godrej companies. This opened the door to bigger opportunities.

The pivotal moment came around 2003–04, when Godrej was preparing to make a significant acquisition in London. Bhatt entrusted Sridhar with a dual mandate: to work alongside a UK law firm for local law matters and to also manage costs by retaining as much control in India as possible. 'We ended up taking a pretty substantial lead role on that deal,' Sridhar recalls. 'And the success of that deal triggered a spree of acquisitions.'

Over the next few years, Trilegal supported Godrej on seven or eight international acquisitions, in jurisdictions as diverse as South Africa, Argentina and Indonesia, as well as in India. The work spanned due diligence, negotiation, documentation and deal execution, and gave Sridhar invaluable lessons in multi-jurisdictional coordination.

He recalls the rigour of these cross-border transactions, saying, 'We would sit in all-day negotiations in London. Every night, I'd return to the hotel, type out a detailed update, print it at the business centre and slide it under Mr Bhatt's door so he had it first thing in the morning. This sort of dedication helped us build deep trust with him.'

These were pre-digital due diligence days; data rooms were physical, and the team was often on-site in locations as varied as Durban, Jakarta and Coimbatore, poring through files with local lawyers, building diligence reports and identifying deal risks. Sridhar also had the opportunity to collaborate with major international firms, including Deneys Reitz Inc. (South Africa), Mishcon de Reya (London) and Ginting & Reksodiputro (a leading firm in Indonesia which later became part of A&O). These experiences helped us show international firms that we could 'bring clients to the table' and, more importantly, execute complex international deals.

Ultimately, Godrej's acquisition spree slowed, but the relationship had been established. Moreover, the work had served another purpose – it was early proof of our capability to handle cross-border mergers and acquisitions (M&A) with zero prior experience.

Reliance Infocomm Limited Financing

This 2004 transaction was among the largest financings (US $750 million) that Reliance Industries Limited had undertaken in its corporate history. The financing was intended to enable a mobile network rollout in 5,000 towns and cities, and provide the financial strength to plan a broadband rollout.

We had to win a beauty contest that included India's leading firms to be appointed as lenders' counsel. The firm was only in its fifth year and we were relatively young professionals, particularly in the context of the stellar cast of parties involved and international lawyers engaged. Our counterpart as international lenders' counsel was the US firm Milbank Tweed, a giant in international project finance, and the relationship partner handling the matter had been Glenn Gerstell, widely regarded as a leading authority in the field. 'We went on to become friends and do a lot of work together with him and Milbank after this transaction,' Karan recalls.

This transaction was important for establishing our reputation with large institutional clients and to be taken seriously in the banking world. But it was much more than that. 'To me, there was something that emerged from this mandate that was even more important,' Karan reflects. The initial request for proposal (RFP) had come to him. Months earlier, before the deal had been on the horizon, Karan had written an email to Glenn Gerstell saying that he had read his book on project finance and found it particularly helpful. Karan had read it to prepare for a pitch on another matter that he had failed to land. This earlier email had prompted Glenn to write to Karan with an RFP on the Reliance financing – an early example of playing the long game on business development.

The excitement of receiving the RFP was accompanied by apprehension about how to manage the pitch and win the mandate. The Delhi office had just done the TIW and Power Grid matters, and Karan felt it would be strategic to bring in Anand to help with the pitch.

This collaboration worked well, showing the client that we were not only competent to handle the matter but were also a firm keen to serve the client's interests by putting together a cross-practice, multi-office team with the (recently acquired) skills and telecoms experience needed to execute the transaction. This was standard practice in more developed legal markets but stood out in India and, again, showed that trust and collaboration were crucial for us to compete and grow.

Rajesh Kapadia and the Rahejas: The Power of Relationships

Another defining relationship in Sridhar's early career – and for Trilegal more broadly – was with Rajesh Kapadia, managing partner of G.M. Kapadia & Co., a storied and deeply respected Mumbai chartered accountancy firm established in 1938. In a neat coincidence, Kapadia (as a representative of Udayan Bose) had been involved in the MAI–Merwanjee Securities deal that first brought Rahul and me together in 1996.

The relationship began over a small transaction, in which Kapadia was conducting financial diligence and Sridhar had prepared the legal due diligence report. 'He called me to his office and said, "This is one of the clearest and most well-drafted diligence reports I've seen. I want to work with you,"' Sridhar recalls.

Kapadia was as good as his word. He personally introduced Sridhar to the Raheja Group – including the promoter, Rajan Raheja himself – and involved him in the negotiation of one of their most complex deals: an acquisition relating to the ING–Vysya Life Insurance joint venture.

At the time, the Rahejas, via Exide, were negotiating to buy out GMR Group's stake in the joint venture. The deal, by all measures, was a stretch for a young firm like ours. 'There is no way that a law firm with three years of experience should have been advising on a deal of that size or complexity,' Sridhar notes. 'But we were there – at the table, negotiating every clause.'

The deal was intermittently on and off for nearly two years, reflecting the complexity of the transaction and the strategic stakes involved. The patience and persistence required to steer the matter to completion helped build credibility in the insurance sector and as an M&A advisor. 'That deal laid the foundation for what is today the largest insurance M&A practice in the country,' Sridhar observes.

The story came full circle earlier this year (2025), when Sridhar was appointed chairman of the Board of Exide Industries, a Raheja Group company where Rajesh Kapadia had previously been chairman. This was a testament to the depth and longevity of the relationship that began with Kapadia's faith in a young firm. Sridhar observed, 'It was entirely on account of Mr Kapadia. He just took me under his wing. He said, "I will trust you." And what he did was extraordinary.' Sadly, Mr Kapadia passed away in 2016, but for Sridhar, his influence on our early growth cannot be overstated.

What emerged from these early Mumbai engagements was a pattern that would define much of our subsequent growth – the power of doing quality work on smaller matters to earn opportunities on larger ones, the importance of cross-office collaboration and the value of building genuine relationships rather than just transactional ones.

13

Bangalore: Early Deals and Clients

The Bangalore office's early client relationships shared some similarities with those in Delhi and Mumbai, particularly in how the telecoms work across different offices fed off of each other to create a strong, market-leading practice. We will see how all this came together in the next chapter. Sure there was regular corporate work – company setup, joint ventures and acquisitions and the like – but some of the work we did out of Bangalore was more interesting for the way it differed from what was keeping our other offices busy.

While our other offices focused on more traditional practices – such as M&A transactions, financing, and energy and infrastructure – some of the early work in Bangalore was at the exciting intersection of research, technology and innovation. The clients we worked with here weren't just building businesses, they were technological innovators and pioneering new models of entrepreneurship while taking entirely different sorts of risks. Crucially, this early work set the tone for the Bangalore office's approach towards building its practice.

Strand Life Sciences: Creating India's First Academic-Industry Framework

Our relationship with Strand Life Sciences represents one of India's most innovative early forays into academic–industry collaboration. The company emerged from the Indian Institute of Science (IISc), where a group of four professors from the computer science laboratory decided they wanted to be entrepreneurs and build businesses out of their research. Innovation-led businesses coming out of top institutions like the IITs is more standard today, but in 2000 the idea was path-breaking.

There were significant regulatory challenges to overcome. As Rahul recalls, 'In the US, you have the Bayh-Dole Act, which allows academics to also do entrepreneurship. India had no such thing. And, so, when these four guys said they wanted to set up, we had to create the equivalent of the Bayh-Dole Act for the Institute of Science.'

The legal work was unlike anything we had done before. We weren't just documenting a business transaction – we were creating policy. We negotiated with IISc to create a framework that would allow professors to maintain their academic positions, while founding and running commercial ventures. Fundamental questions of intellectual property ownership, conflict of interest and the role of academic institutions in commercial enterprise needed to be resolved. 'We created a framework that's now the template for academic entrepreneurship in the country because that was the first time we did this at the Institute of Science. Everyone follows that model now,' Rahul explains.

Rahul first started working with these brilliant scientists in 2000 when he was just getting his feet wet in technology law. 'I was the founding director of their company,' he recalls. 'I did a lot of work with them, went through all the funding rounds.' The relationship continued when Kosturi Ghosh became a partner and took over much of the ongoing work.

Twenty-five years later, Strand has been acquired by Reliance and they are currently pioneers in something called liquid biopsy. As Rahul describes it, 'From a blood draw they can tell you whether you have cancer and what cancer it is. So no PET scan, no nothing – just tiny fragments of some part of the tumour which has flaked off and is in your blood.' It is the kind of breakthrough that validates the early bet we took on supporting academic innovation.

PicoPeta and the Simputer

The same professors from Strand Life Sciences created a second company called Pico Peta, which built the 'Simputer'. The Simputer was essentially a proto-smartphone before anyone used the word – a handheld computing device with intuitive interfaces and connectivity.

Time magazine highlighted it as a significant technological innovation in 2001, recognising its ambition to bridge the digital divide in India. The device was praised for being a low-cost multilingual Linux-based handheld computer, designed to make computing accessible to the masses, especially in developing countries. Bruce Sterling, writing for the *New York Times*, captured its essence like this: Computing 'as it would have looked if Gandhi had invented it, then used Steve Jobs for his ad campaign', emphasising its blend of social vision and technological innovation.[61]

The Simputer was way ahead of its time, featuring several technological firsts: the first commercial handheld computer to run Linux, an open hardware licence, smart card support for secure multi-user access, a full motion sensor and text-to-speech in multiple Indian languages. As Rahul puts it, 'It didn't succeed commercially. But these brilliant guys built an iPhone before there was an iPhone.'

The Simputer story captures something essential about the Bangalore technology ecosystem and the general environment in India to support hardware innovation in the early 2000s. There was incredible innovation taking place, with world-class thinking and engineering, but market timing and commercial execution could be challenging and the regulations could be clunky.

Working with these academic entrepreneurs taught us that legal innovation often had to match technological innovation. There were no existing templates to apply; we had to think creatively about structures, relationships and risk allocation in ways that supported genuine innovation. This became a defining characteristic of our Bangalore-based tech practice.

National Spatial Data Infrastructure

Sometimes significant opportunities come from unexpected places. At some point in 2001–02, I was at my sister's (Aditi's) dance guru Leela Samson's house for a dinner where I met Amitabh Pande, the then joint secretary in the Department of Science and Technology (DST). Pande knew my family and, on hearing that I was a lawyer, casually asked if I could help him with some legal issues he was grappling with. This was not long after Rahul had written what he calls 'the publication I'm most proud of' – an article in the August 2000 edition of *Current Science*, the preeminent scientific journal, on whether there was a legal basis for a fundamental right to access geographical data in India.[62]

Pande was leading a project that aimed to help the government rationalise its approach to geospatial data by funnelling the mapping activities of various disparate state agencies into a single coherent national policy. For this, he wanted us to draft a law on geospatial data, because he felt that the Ministry of Law and Justice would not be open enough in its approach to deregulate what was considered a sensitive area of public policy with potential national security considerations.

This was Trilegal's first 'public policy' assignment with the government and would provide an early foundation for an area of work that would become increasingly important as the firm grew. We were offered the modest sum of ₹50,000 to do this work, which we were told might take a year or two. We leapt at it because of both the legal and policy challenge, and the fact that it could potentially be of national significance.

What followed was years of patient work trying to get 30-plus agencies – as diverse as the Department of Meteorology and the Indian Army – to agree to geospatial data sharing. Some of the security concerns were hard to understand: the defence forces wanted to retain classified status for data that was available through free satellite images on the Internet. Initially both of us, and later Rahul on his own, spent much more time than originally envisaged on this matter. The work was high quality and deeply interesting, but the law that Amitabh Pande dreamt of was never to pass (or so it seemed at the time).

What started as a small advisory engagement with an uncertain future grew into extensive involvement in India's spatial data infrastructure. The Bangalore office developed a long history of geospatial work, including representing TomTom, which was then a global leader in mapping technology. This Dutch company became a significant client and the connections continued when Apple became a client and TomTom's maps became part of Apple Maps.

The story came full circle when Rahul played a key behind-the-scenes role in reforms that were introduced in 2021 that transformed India's geospatial data regulations. The detailed story of this journey is explored in Rahul's blog *Ex Machina*.[63] As you can see there, the early work that we did in the early 2000s was finally vindicated 20 years after Rahul first wrote about geographical data rights. Sometimes it takes that long for deep reform to take place.

What these early Bangalore relationships taught us was that technology law was not just about applying existing legal frameworks to new business models. It required understanding the technology itself, anticipating regulatory challenges and even helping to create the legal infrastructure that would support new industries. The clients we worked with in Bangalore – academic entrepreneurs, hardware innovators, policy pioneers – required a different approach from traditional corporate clients. They needed lawyers who could think like engineers and policymakers, who could work with incomplete precedents and uncertain regulatory frameworks. These engagements established patterns that continue to define our technology practice today – deep technical understanding, policy engagement, long-term thinking and a willingness to create legal solutions for new technological realities. These relationships required us to be comfortable with ambiguity, since much of our early work was about building frameworks and capabilities that would pay dividends years later.

14

Lessons in Collaboration: Building the Telecoms Practice

After the TIW and Power Grid deals that Anand and I worked on, I moved on to other types of work while the telecoms practice continued to grow in ways we could not have imagined. When I sat down with Rahul recently to review how that growth happened, what emerged was one of the clearest examples of how our collaborative principles actually worked.

Perhaps more vividly than any other practice, telecoms showed us how individual deals could compound into something larger – a serious practice with market recognition. What began with foundational work in a technical sector eventually led to being instructed on some of the largest and most complex telecoms transactions in India – deals that would have been remarkable for any firm, let alone one still finding its feet. The path from those early engagements to billion-dollar transactions could never have been planned, but it followed a logic that would become central to how we approached building other practices: start with hard work, pass work around, leverage relationships and don't be afraid to take on work that pushes you well beyond your comfort zone.

First Steps: Building Technical Credibility

The foundation for our telecoms expertise was laid by the Power Grid work, where we navigated the intersection of electricity and telecommunications law; and the TIW deal, which gave us a front-row view of how telecoms regulations constrained and shaped corporate arrangements between Indian and overseas joint-venture partners. These early Delhi office matters provided something invaluable for a young firm: credibility in a highly regulated technical sector. However, what transformed this into a firm-wide capability was an example of our 'one firm' approach and collaborative spirit working across offices, even when we weren't yet on the same balance sheet.

The Reliance Infocomm Rollout

An opportunity arose to second some lawyers to Reliance for several months to help with the rollout of an entire telecommunications network. This became one of our first examples of true multi-office collaboration, with lawyers from Delhi, Mumbai and Bangalore all part of the seconded team. The work was intense and comprehensive. 'We seconded four people there and I was the relationship partner,' Rahul recalls. 'So they were working on the ground, and I was the guy who had to deal with management, do the firefighting and have the back of the team doing the work, who were coming under immense pressure.'

The scope was vast – drafting a complete suite of contracts for the hardware, software and services needed to build out a brand-new telecoms network, effectively helping design the entire legal and contractual framework for the project. This was the Dhirubhai Ambani-era Reliance, before the eventual split between the Ambani brothers that would come after the patriarch's death. For our young lawyers, the experience was transformative. They were embedded in one of India's most ambitious infrastructure projects, working alongside business and technical teams. The intensity and scale made this a crash course in understanding the commercial and technical realities that drove legal requirements.

As Rahul explained recently, the engagement provided credibility that went beyond our telecoms expertise. He said, 'That [the engagement with Reliance] then gave us the credibility of having actually rolled out a telecom system – all the contracts for towers, equipment, software. We did the works.' More importantly, it demonstrated our willingness to commit resources and take risks for clients.

Building on this foundation, we were later appointed to the US $750 million Reliance Infocomm financing, which was the largest in Reliance Industries' corporate history at that time. We have already seen how this financing provided another example of our collaborative approach across offices, with Karan from Mumbai bringing in Anand from Delhi to help. Reliance had even waived conflicts of interest for us to act for their lenders – a sign of the trust we had built through the rollout work.

The Headline-Making Deal: Vodafone

The Reliance credentials opened doors we could never have imagined. 'That allowed us to pitch to Linklaters [a major London-based international firm], to be their Indian law firm partner on the Vodafone deal,' Rahul reminded me recently. 'We did a lot of pitching and finally, we got it. Vodafone is, I would say, one of the marquee deals that really put us on the map.'

The Vodafone matter involved the acquisition of Hutchison Whampoa's stake in Hutchison Essar Limited. 'Linklaters batted very strongly for us, and we did that deal all the way through from the bidding stage to the end,' Rahul recalls. The deal held personal significance for Rahul too. He observes, 'Vodafone won the bid to buy Hutchinson's stake on the day my son was born – I got the call about the win when I was in the hospital.'

This was a massive transaction. Vodafone agreed to buy a 67 per cent controlling stake in Hutchison Essar for approximately $11.1–11.7 billion, with an additional assumption of about $2 billion in debt, valuing the entire company at around $18.8 billion.[64] This marked Vodafone's entry into the fast-growing Indian mobile telephony market and became notable not only for its size but also for what would become the infamous Vodafone tax dispute with Indian authorities over the taxation of indirect share transfers between foreign entities.

But beyond the headlines, the work involved regulatory innovation that would reshape the industry. 'There was the roaming issue, where they had taken a call that you could do 3G roaming within the context of the existing licence,' Rahul explains. 'Up until then, you had to get a licence for every circle that you operated in. But for that auction, all the telcos took a call that if they didn't win a licence, they would do roaming in that circle, which had never been done before.' This regulatory strategy had industry-wide implications. As Rahul explains: 'The reason why the price for the 3G auction went so high was because the bidders chose to bid and put all their money only in some circles, trusting that in the other circles they could roam on someone else's network.'

Creating Industry Infrastructure: Indus Towers

The Vodafone work led to industry-changing innovations that went beyond the immediate transaction. 'Vodafone was part of creating Indus, which was the first tower company in the country,' Rahul explains.

Indus Towers Limited was established in November 2007 as a joint venture among Bharti Infratel, Vodafone Essar and Idea Cellular. The goal was to merge their passive infrastructure assets across 16 telecom circles, providing shared infrastructure to all operators. This was not just a business arrangement; it was a response to the Indian government's push for greater tele-density and the telecom regulator's recommendations for infrastructure sharing.

The creation of Indus Towers required navigating entirely uncharted regulatory territory. As Rahul recalls, 'I remember speaking to the regulatory team in Vodafone, saying, "Look, this has never been done, but there's no reason why you can't do it, because this is certainly something that would work for the country." And then eventually we moved to passive sharing and the whole system was built.'

Discussions with regulators ultimately led to industry-wide adoption of passive sharing, which became a model for efficient, cost-effective network expansion across India. Indus Towers' success set a global benchmark for the telecom tower industry, demonstrating how infrastructure sharing could drive innovation, reduce costs and improve service coverage. The regulatory changes it inspired remain a key example of how industry innovation and regulatory collaboration can transform a sector.

Today, Indus Towers is one of the largest mobile tower infrastructure operators in the world, with nationwide coverage and a broad customer base. The company's creation and the regulatory framework we helped establish became a template that influenced tower sharing models globally – an early example of how innovation in India's complex market could create solutions with worldwide application.

Telenor: Investment, Disputes and Regional Work

The Vodafone success generated immediate opportunities. After Vodafone, Rahul got a call from an A&O partner, Ian Ferguson: 'Look, I was on the train with this guy from a Norwegian company called Telenor. They're looking to come into the next telecom auction in India. Will you do it?'

Of course, the answer was yes.

Telenor's entry into the Indian market was through a joint venture with Unitech, forming Uninor. The initial investment was substantial – over ₹6,100 crore for access to 22 telecom licences. But when the 2G spectrum corruption scandal erupted and the Supreme Court cancelled all 122 licences issued in 2008, including those held by Uninor, Telenor's relationship with Unitech deteriorated rapidly.

We advised Telenor through the bitter disputes that followed, as the company sought to protect its massive investment and accused Unitech of misrepresenting the legality of the licences. The disputes were complex and multifaceted, involving corporate restructuring, joint venture exit negotiations and extensive litigation. As Rahul described it to me recently, the Telenor work showcased our capabilities in different ways. He said, 'On the one hand, we did the joint venture and the 2G litigation work for them. On the other hand, we created a business model where they owned absolutely nothing – they just rented everything, which got them really cheap rates.'

The depth and complexity of the work provided invaluable experience for our team, particularly Nikhil Narendran from the technology practice and Ashish Bhan from disputes, and played a role in both of them becoming partners later. The success also expanded our geographic reach. Impressed with our work, Telenor deployed their Indian business model in Southeast Asia and started using us for outsourcing contracts throughout the region. As Rahul recalls, 'And it was on the back of that work that Nikhil Narendran eventually became a partner. Some of Nikhil's associates were sitting in Thailand for six months just doing these regional contracts.'

The Key: Building Regulatory Expertise

The telecommunications work gave the firm deep regulatory expertise that would prove valuable far beyond the telecom sector itself. Through the Reliance engagement, we learnt to navigate India's complex telecoms regulatory environment, but it was the Vodafone work that truly tested our capabilities. We found ourselves pushing regulatory boundaries in ways that had never been attempted before; some approaches had been tried in European markets, but others were entirely unprecedented.

India's sheer scale and complexity created unique learning opportunities. Dan Lloyd, Vodafone's regulatory head, told Rahul something about his career progression that stuck with him. After running regulatory affairs for Vodafone in India, managing European operations felt surprisingly familiar. Each Indian telecom circle presented challenges equivalent to managing an entire European country – the regulatory differences, varying local requirements and complex approval processes had prepared him for anything Europe might offer. This revealed something important about our early telecoms work that we hadn't realised – India's complexity and scale provided an unparalleled training ground for regulatory professionals, both our own team and the international clients we worked alongside.

The Power of Collaboration

What becomes clear when you trace this progression is how naturally work flowed among offices. The Power Grid and TIW work gave us telecom credentials; those credentials won us Reliance; Reliance opened doors to Vodafone; Vodafone led to Telenor and regional work.

None of this followed a grand plan – it emerged from the practical application of our founding principles, which became embedded behaviour. Trust enabled partners to share opportunities across offices.

When Rahul simply passed work to Anand and me without thinking about financial implications, it felt natural because our founding principles had become embedded behaviour.

For a firm still in its early years, the scale of these transactions was significant. We were working on multi-billion-dollar deals alongside established international law firms, competing through technical expertise and strategic relationship building.

The telecoms practice validated something we'd hoped for but weren't sure would work: our founding principles weren't just idealistic notions but also genuine business advantages. The pattern we established here became our template for other practices – build credentials through excellent work, leverage relationships for larger opportunities and collaborate across offices to maximise capabilities. We didn't plan it this way, but it just worked.

15

'How Do You Get Your Work?'

The telecoms practice that grew from Power Grid and TIW into billion-dollar transactions for Vodafone might suggest that building our business followed a sophisticated formula of collaborative thinking, relationship building and technical expertise. This might have become true over time, but the reality of our early business development efforts was far more colourful.

'But how do you get your work?' was a question I was often asked in the early days. Back then, our answers were a lot more audacious and interesting than the systematic relationship management that would come years later.

Learning on the Job

Personal contacts and well-wishers count, of course, but those alone can't sustain a firm's practice over time. And even those could not be relied on – my father had refused to find us a connection to Petronet LNG, as mentioned before. We discovered that growing the business of a young firm required a mix of strategy, creativity and persistence. Additionally, as with much of the other firm-building work we did in our initial years, it required a willingness to make it up as we went along.

In March 2000, just before our formal launch, Anand and I met with Manzer Ijaz of the London firm Linklaters at the Regent Hotel (now Lands End Hotel) in Mumbai. The lobby was a building site, with the floor dug up and power drills rattling, and we were telling him how great the firm that we hadn't quite set up would be. He must have chuckled to himself but put on a good show of trying to be interested. He was probably headed to a fancy dinner with Cyril Shroff of Amarchand Mangaldas.

Some attempts to build work in our early days reflected a more 'creative' side of our entrepreneurial spirit. Saket Shukla, a senior associate at the time, and I created a fictitious email address – ajay.sagar@hotmail.com (an amalgam of Ajay Bahl and Jyoti Sagar, two prominent lawyers after whom law firms were named, don't ask why). From this address, we wrote to *The Lawyer* magazine in London, suggesting that they might be interested in the news (?) that a former Ashurst associate (me) had been involved in setting up a new firm in India.

Imagine our shocked delight when, a few weeks later, they called the office asking to interview me. A few weeks after that, the interview appeared in print. Even further shock hit when, within days, Trowers & Hamlins, a London firm, called saying that they had seen the article and wanted to send us a deal – acting for Vivendi Universal on a potential transaction in the entertainment sector. The deal didn't close but we did build a relationship with Trowers.

A similar example of initiative, as mentioned earlier, was Karan writing to Glenn Gerstell of Milbank Tweed praising his project finance book, which helped us land the Reliance Infocomm financing sometime later.

The Constraints We Faced (and Continue to Face)

It is useful to understand the context in which we were operating. Indian lawyers are not allowed to solicit work or to advertise. For years there was a debate as to whether we were even allowed to have websites. This was finally permitted, on the condition that these were used strictly to provide information about what the firm did. This rule constrains Indian firms from seeking work in the same way as our UK or US counterparts are able to, and disadvantages Indian firms who might want to compete internationally.

So Indian law firms have to adopt different (less publicity driven) approaches towards building their practices – personal contacts with sources of work, attending conferences and seminars to display knowledge and build networks, and simply being really good at their work. Within these constraints, we had to be creative.

Adventures in International Business Development

Our early business development trips were exercises in naïve optimism. The first one we did formally as Trilegal was to Singapore, with Rahul, Karan and I representing our three locations. The trip turned out to be as much about building internal camaraderie as building relationships with international firms.

No hotels for us; we didn't have the money for them. We stayed with my cousin Udai, who himself was sharing a flat with some school friends in their first jobs out of university. We walked around downtown Singapore, from one law firm to another in the sweltering heat, armed with our shiny new Trilegal business cards and firm profiles, on which the cheap silver printing on the cover page was already smudging off. We would tell whoever we met that we were young and enthusiastic lawyers from this new law firm in India that had three offices and a fresh approach to delivering legal services to its clients. Tall claims, but we believed in what we were saying. I don't remember if we got any work out of that trip, but we were making a few folks aware of our existence. It would take many trips over many years for us to become a regular option for Singapore-based law firms to consider, but the firms we met on that first trip remain close relationships for us today.

A highlight was a night when the three of us ended up at a latenight bar where we were introduced to 'dentist's chair' cocktails and 'upside-down' margaritas. When the festivities began, Karan yelled 'Bombay!' and ran to the stage to be the first to down one of these lethal drinks – an early form of competition among our offices.

Our first trip to meet law firms in London, in 2001, was also hotelfree. Anand and I slept on my friend Paddy Boyle's sofas. He was an associate at Ashurst then, a friend from my time in Tokyo, and now a senior partner in their projects practice.

A similar Californian expedition by Karan, Rahul and Anand had a genuine 'Wild West' feel to it. Starting off in a dodgy $30 motel in San Francisco, they heard gunshots at night and decided their lives were worth more than that, immediately upgrading their accommodation to something borderline unaffordable. They finally ended up staying with a cousin of Anand's 70 miles outside the city.

These early travels brought some important revelations – not just about potential clients and partners, but sometimes about ourselves. Soon after we had named the firm, we noticed something unexpected. If we searched for 'Trilegal' online, the results were full of Brazilian sites that clearly had nothing to do with us. While we had registered 'trilegal.com', the mystery of the Brazilian connection remained. The answer was revealed in Lisbon, at a conference of the Union Internationale des Avocats in 2003. I was introduced to a group of Brazilian lawyers, and when I said I was from an Indian firm called Trilegal, they asked me to spell it. I did, and they burst out laughing. In a Portuguese dialect from the south of Brazil, they explained, the prefix 'tri' means 'very' or 'extremely' and 'legal' is slang for 'cool'. In other words, in that part of the world our firm's name translates to 'very cool'. We agreed.

Strategic Evolution: Working with Intermediaries

As we moved beyond pure survival mode, our approach became more strategic. I remember following two key strategies back then. The first was getting close to other types of consultants – CAs, investment bankers and the like. As these intermediaries encounter numerous clients and deals, if they liked us, they might recommend us to their clients. Sridhar developed strong relationships with investment banking outfits who would later recommend us for their clients' legal work. Similarly, Karan's connections with banks and funds in Mumbai led to a stream of mandates.

The same logic applied to relationships we sought to build with international law firms, particularly those with a longer-term interest in developing India-related work. These firms were a gateway to cross-border work. As a new firm founded by first-generation lawyers without established domestic corporate relationships, we prioritised international work and consequently international business development. International firms and their clients were less concerned with the legacy and pedigree of the traditional firms, and more with how they thought we would handle their work.

Steve Hirschfeld, who selected us as the Indian member of the Employment Law Alliance in 2001–02, recalls that Trilegal stood out among five Indian firms being 'test driven' for inclusion. A piece of work was sent to each firm. He says that what distinguished us was our commercial sensibility, responsiveness and clarity – qualities that aligned with global clients' expectations of concise, solution-oriented advice. He said, 'What was different about your firm was that, rather than writing a very long legal memo, you just answered the question – which is the way an American firm would do it. That was very unusual for the time.'

Being Hired by the Other Side

As we gained experience, we discovered that the most sustainable and legally permitted way to advertise our knowledge was simply doing good work. In addition to keeping clients happy, impressing the folks on the opposite side of a transaction, can often lead to future instructions.

When we were acting for Petronet LNG against GDF Suez (now Engie), my ability to speak to the counterparty in French and understand their most important concerns helped establish a connection. Some years later, GDF Suez became a long-standing client of the firm.

One of Sridhar and the firm's best relationships, with the Shriram Group from Chennai, began similarly. Sridhar recalls, 'We were advising a US fund on a potential investment in one of Shriram's smaller group companies. Whilst that deal didn't materialise, the Shriram group CFO liked our approach and asked us to support them with vendor diligence on their next transaction. Since then, we've advised them on several billion dollars' worth of M&A deals.'

Jumping ahead, in 2018 we acted for Ant Financial (an Alibaba affiliate) on its US $200 million investment into Zomato. Years later, in 2024, we represented Zomato itself on the acquisition of Paytm's events and ticketing business, steering the competition clearance. There are many more similar examples.

I'm not sure exactly when these early efforts evolved from creative hustle into the systematic relationship-building we practise today. What I do know is that while we no longer create fake email addresses or sleep on friends' sofas, echoes of the entrepreneurial spirit that prompted those early adventures remain part of how we build business today.

16

Our Early Offices (and How They Shaped Us)

Two things marked the offices of our first few years – our aspirations were bigger than our reality, and rapid growth kept requiring us to move because we could not afford offices large enough for us to grow into.

We knew that attractive, high-quality offices would be important for the image we wanted to project, and had seen some stunning law-firm offices overseas. But our financial priority was paying our associates the best salaries we could afford, which meant our offices had to reflect our ambition through creativity and distinctiveness rather than budget.

Delhi: From 'Lower Ground Floor' to a Boat in the Reception

Our first Delhi office was a basement in Jaipur Estate, Nizamuddin East. We had rented the space from Sandeep Dikshit, an old school and college senior, who later became a member of Parliament from Delhi. Another college friend – Samir Kuckreja, later managing director of Nirula's and Yum Foods (Pizza Hut etc.) – lived on the ground floor above us with his wife and newborn twin daughters. It was a little cocoon of familiarity.

We had been told that our address should appear on our business cards as a 'lower ground floor' – that is how brokers dress up a basement. Anand and Upamanyu Hazarika had already moved in and, when Trilegal started, we carved out a little cabin for me in a corner. Close family friend and brilliant architect, the late Pradeep Sachdeva, who later designed Dilli Haat, gave me an unusual, curved office desk as an office-warming present. This was lucky, as a rectangular one of the same size would not have allowed me to shut the door of my little cubbyhole.

This basement office saw some memorable client visits. We had secured a role as legal counsel for a first-of-its-kind public–private water management project in Bangalore. The project would involve handing over the operation and management of parts of Bangalore's water system to two French water giants, Vivendi (now Veolia) and GDF Suez. The appointment itself was something of a miracle for a firm barely a year old. These companies, globally renowned as fierce competitors (think Coke vs Pepsi), had agreed to share legal counsel for the first time in anyone's memory.

Our key client contact for the project was Victoria Rigby (now Delmon), Vicky, who was with Vivendi and we were keen to impress. Some way into the transaction, Vicky decided that she wanted to visit our office. As luck would have it, our single toilet was undergoing major renovation – it was *literally* a hole in the ground. Our temporary solution was an arrangement with the friendly Kashmiri carpet seller across the corridor to use his facilities.

In each of our early offices, we tried to shepherd clients towards meetings in five-star hotels, where the amenities better matched our aspirations. This time, our subtle nudges to hold the meetings elsewhere failed; Vicky insisted on visiting us. The details of her visit are fuzzy, but two things are true. One of our first international clients used the Kashmiri carpet seller's toilet and, 25 years later, we still represent Vivendi.

By year-end, we had outgrown the space. Still unable to afford commercial office space, we moved to another residential colony, Panchsheel Enclave, where we rented a house. With some innovative design work, we created a double-height reception which we hoped would impress our clients.

Head massage habits die hard, and for some months Anand and I continued to summon Dharampal, our talented masseuse from Nizamuddin, for inspiration – *'band akal ka tala kholne ke liye* (to unlock our closed brains)'. This continued until our new lateral partner Sumanto Basu (to be introduced shortly) told us that this was inappropriate behaviour for partners of a law firm and we sheepishly had to end Dharampal's visits.

By 2004, we ran out of space again. We found a building in Greater Kailash-II and my architect friend Ambrish Arora helped design the first of three offices that he was to create for us. For the first time, we could afford to spend some money on design and aesthetics. Ambrish's eye for detail and skill in reimagining existing spaces yielded a smart, modern and functional office, with lots of natural light and an exposed red brick and glass look. We stayed here for a few happy years before moving to our first fully commercial office on Mathura Road. This office had our most flamboyant design gesture ever to grace a Trilegal office – an entire wooden Kerala racing boat as the centrepiece of our reception.

Mumbai: Learning to Make Do

In the first few years, Mumbai was an exercise in micro-office management. Our first office was a travel agency's old premises in Dalamal Towers, Nariman Point. It was already fully done up – reception, furniture, etc. – so we didn't have to spend much. Rent was ₹50,000 a month, with a six-month deposit of ₹3 lakh.

The conference room was so small that we joked that if we tried to seat more than three people in it, everyone would have to have their legs in the air. To spare our clients such acrobatics, Sridhar and Karan would suggest that meetings be held in a hotel, like Anand and I did in Delhi.

Karan's wife Malini paid for the deposit and Alchemy Ventures, an early venture capital fund client, also helped out. Sridhar was doing most of Alchemy's work and Lashit Sanghvi (the principal there) had been a client of Sridhar's from his Lex Inde days. When Sridhar told him he was setting up on his own, Lashit said, 'Tell me what you need.' Sridhar asked for a retainer of ₹25,000 a month and got a six-month advance – priceless seed capital.

Within a year, like in Delhi, the Mumbai office had run out of space. This time we hired an interior designer to do up a new office, still in Nariman Point. Tejal Mathur went on to design our first five or six offices as her practice grew alongside ours, and she has since become a prominent designer in her own right. In this office, Sridhar recalls her installing a blue and orange light combination as an artistic gesture. Karan felt it made the office look like a disco and pushed back, leading to a small standoff between him and Sridhar about creative freedom. Karan prevailed and the blue light was removed; funny how some minor details stick in the memory.

We then moved to an office in the Phoenix Mills's premises, which was next to a mall. Everyone recalls this as an awful office, though it was conveniently located next to eBay, which became a big client. After that, the office moved to a charming building, Madhuli, in Worli. I remember this as a beautiful space, with a garden and a parking lot by the sea – an excellent spot to hang out and smoke a cigarette – a place with a view, a breeze and perhaps a sense that we had already travelled some distance.

Bangalore: The Home Office Advantage

Our first Bangalore office was rent-free – it was in Rahul's house. Taking advantage of the fact that his parents had moved to Chennai, he commandeered the ground floor of his family home. 'Working from home', if you like.

The physical setup was improvised. Rahul's memory is clear because he still lives in this house. He recalls, 'I had a table, our current TV room was the conference room and the current dining room was my office. Above my left shoulder was the bar my dad had built which still had a bunch of alcohol in it.' Johnny (Pinto) served as office boy and receptionist, positioned at the front door. When Prem joined, Rahul just added another table opposite his own. He says,

'That's where the bar currently is. There was no place for anyone else.' Johnny is still with the firm today and we will hear more of him later.

The office's first associate was Beena Rajagopal – who later became a film star and is now married to Cisco's general counsel, Navneet Hrishikesan. During her interview in Trilegal's home office, Rahul told her she would join in a new office that we were about to move to. Kartik Kumar, currently at Khaitan & Co, was the second associate taken on board.

The first rented Bangalore office was a two-bedroom house on Nandi Durga Road, owned by a friend of Rahul's, Praveen Lekhraj. (In a nice little coincidence, Praveen later married Piusha Bose, daughter of Udayan Bose – the investment banker and protagonist from the MAI deal that first brought Rahul and me together.) In another tenuous and irrelevant film-world connection, this office's immediate neighbour was the actor Kabir Bedi's brother.

Associates sat in the living room, while Prem and Rahul shared the master bedroom for their office. The standout feature was a conference room that Rahul designed, with sandwiched glass panels providing views of the Jai Mahal Palace grounds. He said, 'I had a blackout blind that could be switched on to come down between the glass panels, so the front glass became reflective and functioned as a whiteboard.' Rahul recalls the oversized pride with which he introduced this feature – something he now considers entirely unnecessary.

When Ajay Raghavan and Kosturi Ghosh were hired straight out of law school (both of them eventually became partners), space became critical again. The office expanded to take up the third floor. After the firm moved out of this building, Prem bought the property and still lives there.

The move to Ratna Avenue marked another step up – this was a large residential house with a garden. Rahul's office was unusually spacious; he claims it was because 'it was just a badly designed house', though he converted the balcony into an extension of his room. Important HR decisions were made in this office; Kosturi was prepared for her partnership interview during walks with Rahul up and down Ratna Avenue.

From here, the office moved to its first commercial space at a swanky building called 'The Residency', just round the corner from the first Bangalore office in Rahul's house.

Learning What Really Mattered

Our frequent office moves taught us some lessons about creating spaces that reflected how we thought about ourselves. First impressions matter, but substance trumps style. Clients expect professionalism, but Chris Watson rolling up his sleeves on Power Grid and Vicky's willingness to use the carpet seller's toilet showed us that what you lack in facilities can be compensated for with attitude. Natural light is essential; our Delhi basement showed us that natural light beats artificial lighting, every time. Space allocation reflects values – we gave associates significantly more space than was common and founders had (and still have) the same sized rooms as any other partners.

Dharampal's massage visits, the minuscule conference room in Mumbai, Rahul's blackout blinds – these are part of the many early experiences that have become part of our firm's storytelling. Our early offices were more than just places to work – they shaped who we became, teaching us the flexibility we would apply to how we ran the firm.

17
Opening Up the Partnership

By 2002–03, less than three years in, we were discovering that growth creates its own pressures – we needed more senior lawyers. From telecoms to financing to M&A, we were stretched. We needed to expand the partnership and we had two ways to do this – bringing in lateral partners who could add immediate expertise and promoting the home-grown talent we'd been developing since our early days.

First Laterals

Sumanto Basu had briefly been a colleague of Anand's and mine at Dua Associates in 1997. After Dua he went to Arent Fox (now ArentFox Schiff), a firm in Washington DC, where he specialised in oil and gas transactions. This aligned well with our growing practice. Our oil and gas work was showing potential beyond our initial work with Petronet LNG and we had been invited to pitch to National Thermal Power Corporation (NTPC), the country's largest power generator, to draft a suite of documents for a major gas purchase tender.

We did not have the credentials for the more complex LNG contracting work that this engagement would require. Sumanto introduced us to his mentor at Arent Fox, Eugene Massey (a well-known oil and gas lawyer), whom we in turn introduced to Petronet LNG. During this period, Sumanto decided to come back to India. Anand and I felt that there was value to his US contacts and sector expertise and recommended his admission as a partner, which materialised in 2002. Sumanto spent about four years with the firm, leaving in 2006.

Sudipto Routh was (and remains) one of Sridhar's closest friends from NLS. He joined us in Mumbai in 2003, becoming a partner in 2005. In 2007, he left, deciding to go to London to join Clifford Chance, and is now a partner with Luthra & Luthra in Mumbai.

While lateral partners brought immediate expertise, the heart of our growth came from the associates who had entrusted their fledgling careers to us early on – young lawyers who shared our vision and had grown with the firm.

Home-Grown Talent

Sawant Singh was only two years behind Karan and Sridhar at NLS. During his third year, Sawant was in the running for being named best athlete. Through the complex workings of a points standings system that sounds as arcane as the new UEFA Champions League format, this somehow required Sridhar to win the javelin event, which he duly did. To thank him, Sawant took him drinking at a dive bar (what his student budget permitted) – the first of many drinking sessions involving the two of them.

Later, while interning at a labour lawyer's office, Sawant accepted Sridhar's offer to intern at Lex Inde, with the encouragement of Sawant's then boss (who didn't see a future for him in employment litigation). The internship led to a job offer, which was accepted, and Sawant joined Karan and Sridhar at Lex Inde. When plans for Trilegal were taking shape, Sawant inevitably became part of them and became the first senior associate of the Mumbai office in early 2000.

It wasn't easy for Sawant to quit Lex Inde. He was reluctant (scared) to admit to his boss there, Akshay Chudasama, that he was leaving to join the nascent Trilegal. To avoid embarrassment, he came up with a cunning plan – he would tell Akshay that he was leaving the legal profession to become (of all things) an actor! Shockingly, the ploy worked – he was allowed to leave without too much fuss.

Perhaps Akshay thought that the legal profession's loss would be Bollywood's gain?

The amusing postscript to this came a few months later, once Singh & Gorthi was up and running. Sridhar and Karan were out meeting potential clients. There was no support staff and Sawant was manning the phones. The phone rang. Sawant picked up and said 'Trilegal'. 'Sawant?!!' yelled the voice on the other side, which belonged to Akshay. This story has become the stuff of legend – retold whenever Sawant and Akshay are out together.

Towards the end of my secondment to Dua Associates (in late 1997), Omnicom, the global media giant, was negotiating to purchase a stake in Anthem Communications, a Delhi-based advertising company that I was representing. Omnicom's lawyers were Kochhar & Co. Most of the heavy lifting on the deal was being done by a young associate called Saket Shukla. Saket turned out to be the cousin of my close friend from college, Amitabh Tripathi. Towards the end of the deal, I mentioned that I was planning to come back to India in a few years' time to set up a new law firm. Saket said, 'Give me a call when you do.' In March 2000, I did. We needed associates to work on the TIW transaction and within a month Saket had joined us.

The ease with which Sawant and Saket moved mirrored the dissatisfaction the Trilegal founders had felt with the firms where they previously worked. Sawant had seen what Sridhar and Karan had experienced at Lex Inde. Saket, much like Rahul at Dua Associates, had been promised various things – a secondment to Tokyo, a conference in South Africa – that hadn't materialised.

A few months after Saket joined, we were engaged by Petronet LNG and needed more hands on deck. Saket introduced his law school classmate Abhishek Saxena to us. Abhishek was working in a public sector company and was looking to move to a law firm. It took no time for him to come on board – he was serious, super smart and the fact that he was also from St. Stephen's College gave him additional points with me.

Saket, Sawant and Abhishek were pillars of the early Trilegal. Not only were they clever young lawyers with a great work ethic, but they also seemed aligned with what we were trying to build. They became friends – Sawant and Saket in particular were close to Sridhar and me, respectively. But we were careful to separate personal loyalty from professional judgement – friendly acquaintance opened the door, but performance and fit kept it open.

The First Partnership Evaluations

In 2004, within four years of setting up the firm, Saket and Sawant became partners, with Abhishek following in 2005. But despite the closeness, they had to earn their partnership.

When I cast my mind back to those first partnership evaluations, I realise we were essentially asking ourselves two questions: Could they do the job and could we work with them for the next 20 years? The first question was about technical ability – legal knowledge, client management, team leadership. The second was more personal – would they fit into the culture we were trying to build?

I can see now that we were instinctively testing for what mattered. Could they handle the pressure? Would they be able to think like owners? Would clients trust them? Could they disagree with us respectfully? These weren't formal criteria then, but they became the template for future partner selection.

As our system envisaged that our partners would eventually own part of the firm, it was essential to select the right people. In a lockstep, which relies on fraternity and a collegiate environment, cultural fit is critical. In a small firm, even one misfit stands out like a sore thumb. Also, if we liked the new partner and believed in their capability, we would be more motivated to pass on work and clients, and to provide mentorship.

While each candidate had worked with the partners in their office, partners in other offices were not as familiar with their work. Consequently, we decided to do a partnership selection interview, comprising a two-part presentation. Each candidate would discuss a legal topic in an area of their choice and present a personal SWOT (strengths, weaknesses, opportunities and threats) analysis, discussing the areas of law they wanted to specialise in.

Saket chose telecom – he had been a key member of the team seconded to Reliance Infocomm, working closely with Mukesh Ambani's team. Intense exposure to high-stakes transactions in a sunrise sector led him to believe that there was a future for him as a telecoms lawyer. He recalls that Sumanto wasn't convinced of his candidature, feeling that Saket could be a bit casual (even brattish) in his manner, and feared that this attitude would carry across to his approach to clients and practice of law itself. Anand and I, on the other hand, had worked closely with Saket for four years, and were convinced that he had what we wanted from a Trilegal partner. To ensure maximum diligence, we checked with Eugene Massey, who had worked with Saket on the NTPC tender. Eugene gave the green light and Sumanto's objections were addressed.

On the basis of work done for Citibank on the new SARFAESI Act, more about which later, Sawant presented on securitisation models and transaction opportunities thrown up by the new legislation. Sawant was convinced that because the rest of us (other than Karan) were ignorant about the new legislation, we didn't really know what he was talking about. Also, on the flimsy basis of having taken a Spanish course with his wife Archana (in which she had come first and he had come last) he spoke of developing business in the Latin American and Spanish markets. We suspended our disbelief about his Spanish skills and relied on our knowledge of his legal ability to wave him through to partnership.

Abhishek's partnership evaluation was conducted the night we were taking a train to Rishikesh for a firm retreat. He had a long and detailed presentation, which we were desperate for him to finish so that we could get to New Delhi Railway Station on time. An excellent senior associate with a great future, voted in as well.

All three of them, following our model, began with salaried partnership, with the intention that they would get equity shares in the firm after two to three years of performance evaluation.

Setting the Template

Our partnership evaluation approach served various purposes. First, we gathered feedback from multiple sources, including inputs from outside the firm. Second, it forced candidates to reflect upon what they would specialise in if they got through, which would give them some direction once they made partner. Third, it ensured that partners from other offices would get to know the candidates (their future partners) better. Overall, it created the broadest possible buy-in from existing partners about each partner promotion – critical for a young firm with a small but growing partnership.

Trilegal has a complex, detailed and rigorous partnership evaluation process today, in that it has evolved significantly from 2004–05 but remains a palimpsest of our first partnership evaluation. As I often say (only partly in jest), I'm not entirely sure if I would make it through Trilegal's partnership evaluation process today.

Part 4

Growing Up

18
Taking Stock

By 2008, we found ourselves in a position we would have struggled to imagine when we started. The firm had grown steadily with healthy revenues and, rather satisfyingly, some of India's most established law firms were taking notice. We had achieved meaningful early success that validated many of our founding principles, allowing us to invest in important aspects of our practice – information technology systems, better offices, regular firm retreats and focused business development efforts.

Most importantly, the founding partners had grown closer through our shared experience. We had developed simple but effective decision-making practices and were learning how to accommodate each other's views. Success in building our practices enabled us to take on lateral partners and promote partners from within our ranks, freeing up the founders' time to seek out new types of work and clients.

With minimum fuss, our market position relative to firms we considered competitors had strengthened. We were winning mandates in competition with more established firms. Our client roster was impressive for a firm of our size and vintage, with names such as Citibank, Godrej, Reliance and Vodafone in it, among others. We had established excellent working relationships with many international law firms, who not only took us on as co-counsel on large transactions but increasingly passed on their clients to us directly.

We had begun to make our mark in the legal landscape and started appearing in some legal industry rankings. However, our market reputation hadn't quite reached the level we believed the quality of our work deserved. This reflected a broader phenomenon – reputation is a 'trailing indicator' and often lags behind reality. As legal market observer Reena SenGupta notes, 'It can take a decade for a law firm's real capabilities to be recognised externally. Consistent client service is the slow but sure route to reputation.'

Being Taken Seriously

Perhaps the clearest indication that we were being noticed came in the form of approaches from two well-established Indian law firms exploring our appetite for a merger.

The first, as early as 2002, came from a firm that a few of us were quite familiar with. Having established a market-leading position in the late 1990s and early 2000s, the managing partner had a formidable roster of international clients and good relationships with both US general counsel and international firms across the globe. Flattered by the interest, in a meeting in our Delhi office we set out in detail what we had achieved so far and what our vision for the firm was. He listened, or perhaps he didn't. He came back to us with a proposal that ignored the essence of what we had told him about ourselves. One firm, a lockstep, real equity ownership and a culture of partnership – all of it seemed to pass him by. And he had completely missed our ambition. His offer: merge our practice into his firm, become salaried partners (!) and after a period of evaluation he would consider moving us towards equity. Perhaps we should have felt insulted; instead, we laughed, wondered what on earth he was thinking and got on with our lives. Incidentally, this gentleman came back to us twice with merger offers, the last as recently as 2018 – still without appreciating what our firm was about.

The second approach, which came in 2005, was from another top firm, through our friend Upamanyu Hazarika. Anand and I were invited by the senior partners for a charming private dinner, during which we were treated with the utmost respect while we waxed eloquent about the shape and size of our firm, and what we thought we had achieved. These folks were classy – they listened carefully to what we had to say, and after a lovely evening we went on our way and never heard from them again.

We speculated that our hosts had read between the lines, where these upstarts had spelt out the level of their ambition and shown an independent spirit. This, coupled with the fact that our firm (with about 50 lawyers) was of a decent size, told them that it would be impossible for them to absorb us into what was essentially a family-run law firm.

The truth was, we were quietly thrilled. Being courted by firms the market looked up to was flattering; people at the very top of the Indian law firm world were taking us seriously.

The merger approaches confirmed what we had hoped: our founding principles were working in practice. Our initial strategic choices had been sound, particularly three key propositions we had started with. First, our decision to operate as one firm with three integrated offices had provided us with the scale, reach and depth that gave us the look and feel of a more substantial firm than we actually were. Second, our lockstep model and the principle of sharing from a common pot had fostered the kind of cooperative behaviour we sought. Matters, clients and even relationships were being freely passed around the firm. Finally, because of the stability afforded by these two factors, our partners were free to focus on their clients and begin to develop specialisations, rather than protecting their turf from their own colleagues. This made it easier for us to put clients at the centre of what we did. People would mention our client-centricity and commercial approach to legal advice.

The Broader Market Context

The merger approaches also confirmed what we knew about the broader Indian legal market. Partners who managed the traditional firms maintained tight control over both management and ownership, partly because non-family lawyers had few alternatives. This had created problematic incentive structures in many firms. Even the most talented lawyers faced glass ceilings – the same issue that had led to the creation of Trilegal in the first place.

This was unfortunate because India had, and continues to have, plenty of highly talented lawyers. However, this individual excellence hadn't translated into creating excellent institutions, as many firms struggled to become the best versions of themselves.

Looking Ahead

Looking back from 2008, we could see that early wins with clients and growing revenue was only the beginning. Building resilience and further growth would demand learning, evolution and reinvention.

Moving up a few notches would require us to improve how we ran our firm's operations. Our management practices and back-office systems were adequate but rudimentary. Working alongside international law firms on transactions had given us glimpses of sophisticated financial and knowledge management (KM) systems, advanced IT infrastructure, modern HR practices and systematic approaches to managing client relationships, which underpinned their approach to the practice of law. We saw how this enabled our counterparts in those firms to function at higher levels of efficiency than we were capable of.

We had proved that we could create and sustain a different kind of law firm. Now we needed better tools to run one at scale.

19
Allen & Overy: Making Best Friends

On 15 February 2008, Trilegal and A&O, an international law firm, announced that they were entering into a 'non-exclusive referral' arrangement. While many people (even within our own firm) weren't quite sure what this meant, it was pretty big news, surprising many in law-firm circles in India and the UK.

The announcement sent ripples through law-firm circles in both countries. What was a globally renowned, market-leading firm – with 77 years of history and 3,000 lawyers – doing aligning itself with an eight-year-old Indian law firm whose oldest partner was just about 40 years old? For context, A&O wasn't just any international firm, they were one of the 'Magic Circle' – the handful of elite London-based law firms that, along with some US firms, dominated global legal services.

The move was especially striking given what came shortly after. In 2009, Clifford Chance, also a Magic Circle firm, entered into a 'best friends' arrangement with AZB – one of India's most reputed firms at the time. That too generated industry buzz and was understood as part of broader positioning in anticipation of the Indian legal market eventually opening to foreign firms.[65] In contrast, our relationship with A&O had no such heavyweight domestic market footprint to lean on. As David Morley, former A&O's senior partner, later said, it was 'a bet on quality and alignment, not just size'.

To many in the Indian and UK legal markets, this felt like it had come from left field. They were wrong. The seeds of this development had been sown in our very first year and the path to this announcement was more logical than it appeared.

Chris Watson and the Outsourcing Boom

The story began with Chris Watson's engagement with us in Delhi on the Power Grid telecoms work back in 2000. The positive impression he carried from working with 'the boys from the Nizamuddin basement' would have far-reaching consequences.

The timing of this connection couldn't have been better. India's nascent information technology industry, liberated by the 1991 economic reforms, had established its credentials in dealing with the 'Y2K Challenge' in 1999–2000. For readers unfamiliar with this episode, the 'Millennium Bug' represented what was considered an existential technological threat. The practice of using two-digit year representations in computer systems (e.g.: '99' for 1999) had created widespread concern that digital systems would misinterpret '00' as 1900, potentially triggering catastrophic failures across banking, utilities and government operations.

While global remediation efforts prevented major disruptions, the episode had an unintended positive consequence for India: it showcased the country's technical capabilities to the world. As a low-cost technology centre, India – particularly Bangalore – played a crucial role in reprogramming software for thousands of global businesses. Once Y2K passed without incident, these companies, impressed by Indian software engineers and programmers, began exploring other ways to leverage this skilled, cost-effective resource pool.

The dot-com crash of 2000–01, which wiped billions of dollars off tech businesses, accelerated the trend towards cost-reduction, contributing to India's outsourcing boom. Companies worldwide, particularly in the English-speaking world, sought to reduce costs by relocating non-core functions to lower-cost jurisdictions. India's English-language skills, along with favourable government policies creating relatively regulation-light environments for companies exporting these services, made it an obvious destination.

Allen & Overy had a stellar reputation as the pre-eminent banking law firm in London, with many major banks and financial institutions as clients. These organisations were large, often overstaffed, with employees in non-core back-office functions that were ripe to be relocated overseas. Allen & Overy's banking clients were inundating them with projects to move call centres and subsequently accounting, software development, payroll and myriad other functions to India.

Building the Relationship

Thanks initially to Chris Watson, a growing stream of outsourcing work found its way to us. We were also getting similar work from other sources, including many of A&O's competitors, but the A&O connection felt different – more systematic and substantial.

To build on this opportunity, Ameya Khandge, then a young associate in our Mumbai office, was seconded to A&O in London. Rahul and his team usually led on IT and IT-enabled services matters, while Karan, as our banking and finance partner, was also often involved. Together, they built a relationship with the idiosyncratic Lawrence Jacobs, who split his time between London and Tel Aviv and led A&O's outsourcing work.

A collateral benefit of working on these projects was raising our profile with lawyers in the general counsel's offices at British banks and financial institutions. Once these lawyers gained confidence in us, we found ourselves considered for transactions in their core business areas – loans and other debt-related work. This dovetailed with our growing banking practice, which was already handling work for Citibank and the US Export–Import Bank.

The Broader Landscape

Allen & Overy wasn't the only UK-based international firm we worked alongside. My old firm, Ashurst, had referred a stream of excellent clients to us, including Mitsui & Co., Abbey National Bank and others. We had also cultivated strong ties with a number of other firms, including Norton Rose (now Norton Rose Fulbright) – particularly through Mike Rebello, who headed their technology practice and had developed a friendship with Rahul. Kosturi Ghosh was seconded to them, and as she put it: 'It was great to see how another firm, a global one, operated. And I made friends there that I'm still in touch with.'

Through this period, the prospect of India opening its legal market to foreign firms remained a constant backdrop. The UK-based international firms, constrained by limited domestic growth opportunities, showed particular interest, along with several internationally-oriented US firms. Delegations from the Law Society of England and Wales made visits to India, meeting with the Bar Council of India, the Ministry of Law & Justice and groups of Indian lawyers.

Anticipating potential market liberalisation, we had been in intermittent discussions about closer ties with Ashurst from as early as 2001. This was through my good friend Jeremy Sheldon, who had spent time in Ashurst's Delhi liaison office, and Geoffrey Picton-Turbervill and Ian Scott (two of my former bosses). Initial discussions had been cordial and showed promise, but we felt that Ashurst's internal circumstances at the time – they had undergone management changes and their growth wasn't matching their peers' – meant that deeper engagement with an Indian firm under uncertain regulatory conditions wasn't a top priority for them.

Opportunity Knocks

Allen & Overy was easily the biggest name firm we were close to, and we sensed that a closer relationship with them could be transformational. In mid-2007, Karan was invited by A&O to speak at a conference on outsourcing for the banking and finance sector. On the way to the event, he called me from the back of a cab. 'I'm on the way to this thing,' he said, 'anything that I should mention to them?'

'Ask them if they're interested in exploring a more focused relationship with us, the sort that we've been speaking to Ashurst about,' I replied.

'Right,' he said, and we were off to the races.

Right Place, Right Time

Timing, once again, worked in our favour. Soon after that phone call between Karan and me, A&O's leadership decided to give the Indian market a closer look. Alex Pease – a seasoned A&O banking partner who had spent considerable time in Tokyo and was familiar with the Asian market – was dispatched to India in the second half of 2007 to assess possibilities.

We were one of several firms Alex visited during what seems to have been an eye-opening tour of the Indian legal landscape. By the time he reached us, he had sat through meetings where certain law-firm managing partners described their dual books of accounts and off-the-record cash earnings – the very practices we had steered clear of from our early days. (Alex, being a thorough gentleman, never named names, and became a vicar after retirement so his discretion was doubly understandable.) Our straightforward approach to firm finances stood out.

I remember being shocked when Alex told us about the questionable financial practices he had encountered elsewhere. We just gave him our standard pitch about being a young, dynamic and ambitious firm with a lockstep partnership structure and a commitment to one partner, one vote. We had no founding family or single figurehead to navigate around, and were a tight-knit group who got on with our work and enjoyed each other's company.

Clearly something resonated. Soon after Alex returned to London, Guy Beringer (then A&O's outgoing senior partner) came to Delhi on what felt like a diplomatic mission. He was accompanied by Matthew Fleming, former England cricketer and Ian Fleming's nephew, who later headed the Marylebone Cricket Club (MCC). I remember Guy giving me a stack of *Wisden*s[66] (as he did to all the Trilegal partners he met), and our conversation being about how we had built the firm, what we wanted to achieve and what our client base looked like (and cricket).

The Changing of the Guard

By this time, A&O was in the midst of its internal elections, which would lead to significant changes at the top. Wim Dejonghe had been the head of the corporate department and David Morley had been managing partner for five years, having previously headed banking. David would soon be elected senior partner and Wim managing partner – taking over their new roles in spring 2008. The two were aligned on several issues, including the need to build out the firm internationally.

For us, the timing was excellent. We were dealing with A&O's future leadership rather than a departing regime, which meant any relationship we built would have continuity and commitment from the top.

Dinner in Mumbai

David and Wim travelled to India to meet the five of us as founding partners (Prem having stepped back by now, as mentioned earlier). Wim had played a key role in integrating parts of his old firm Loeff Claeys Verbeke into A&O some years earlier. He understood the importance of cultural compatibility and personal relationships as part of an integration process and was the ideal person from A&O's perspective to engage with us. After initially dipping toes in the water with Alex Pease and Guy Beringer, it was time to meet the decision makers who would lead A&O for the foreseeable future.

Our first meeting with David and Wim took place over dinner at a restaurant in Mumbai, and we all recall that the chemistry was immediate. For us, this was simultaneously thrilling and surreal – here we were, eight years after starting in basements and parents' homes, having dinner with the leadership of one of the world's most prestigious law firms. David recalls the connection forming almost instantly: 'I remember thinking, that's a good start, because of your personalities and your special sort of energy.' Recently, David told me that he and Wim made up their minds almost immediately after that evening. 'You reminded us,' he said, 'of what A&O must have been like in its earliest days.'

Wim's recollection was that it happened even faster: 'I think from the first few minutes, we got along. We understood your philosophy, which suited us well.' He recalled that he and David exchanged a quiet word during dinner, saying 'these are the guys'.

The green signal was given for formal discussions to proceed. I remember feeling a mix of excitement and disbelief – were we really being courted by A&O?

Nuts and Bolts

We approached the engagement with seriousness but without becoming overly formal. There were many meetings in India and London. I remember sitting in the A&O office in Spitalfields, listening to descriptions of global practice groups, offices worldwide and management boards, comparing our modest firm with the complexity of the A&O network. I remember thinking to myself, 'This is pretty cool…'

Allen & Overy sent Xavier Thalasso, their financial controller from Belgium, to understand our books and financial processes. Xavier was close to Wim and had worked on the Loeff Claeys Verbeke integration. From our side, his main counterpart was Rajenbhai, who vividly remembers the experience. Xavier went through our financials line by line, repeatedly asking the same question: 'Is there anything else?' He kept asking and Rajenbhai kept providing more documents, until there were no more to give.

Later, once we had concluded the agreement, Xavier told Rajenbhai that this was code for asking whether there were hidden accounts or undisclosed financial arrangements. Rajenbhai later told me, with an amused smile, 'He was convinced there had to be something missing.' But there wasn't. Our 'single books' approach was working in our favour again.

There were internal debates at A&O. Some partners were uncomfortable about opening their systems to us, and particularly sharing their invaluable bank of precedent documents with, a small, relatively unknown Indian firm. One apparently asked, 'Why are we giving away the crown jewels?' But David and Wim held their ground. Their belief was that if we were going to be treated as future partners, it made no sense to withhold anything.

As David told us later, 'If we couldn't trust you with our knowledge, how could we ever contemplate a deeper relationship in the future?' This approach impressed us. We were being treated as equals, not as junior members of a business relationship.

What Impressed Them about Us

Several aspects of our approach impressed A&O's leadership. First was our institutional mindset; despite being relatively young (around 12–13 years into our careers then), we spoke with one voice about building an enduring institution rather than just a vehicle for personal enrichment.

They valued our commitment to a lockstep system and meritocracy – rare in the Indian legal market. The balanced dynamic among us founders also stood out. We presented a cohesive team with diverse but complementary skills and personalities – what David called 'the magic formula'.

Jonathan Brayne, another A&O veteran who became key to the relationship, described his first impressions of us as 'young, ambitious, but cosmopolitan and congenial people trying to build a firm that was quite different from the established leading firms in India'. He also appreciated that we were 'unapologetic about admitting that you needed all the help you could get from us'.

The Signing and Beyond

After further discussions, including a visit to London where we had dinner at David Morley's house, an agreement documenting the formal 'non-exclusive referral arrangement' was signed in Dubai. Everyone in the market referred to it as a 'best friends' relationship.

The signing dinner in Dubai stands out in my memory. David gave a speech declaring that it would be 'a day that everyone would remember in the history of A&O' – words that mattered hugely to us as the founders of a not-yet-10-year-old law firm. I have no recollection of what I said in my response speech, but a light-hearted moment stands out when Anand, characteristically, stated that his motivation for the alliance was that he wanted one day to be the managing partner of an international firm, not just an Indian firm.

This wasn't a formal merger or equity tie-up. For regulatory reasons, there could be no financial arrangement between the firms. But the vision was ambitious. Wim explained A&O's thinking: 'Originally, the idea was, let's get into an alliance. As soon as the law allows it, we'll integrate Trilegal into A&O.' While we didn't fix a specific timeframe, the expectation was that integration might take three to five years, depending on when the Indian legal market opened up. How wrong we were.

Just before the alliance was announced, I thought it right to call my old boss and mentor Ian Scott at Ashurst, so he would hear about it directly from me rather than in the press. As mentioned, we had previously had conversations with them about a similar relationship. 'Is it too late for us to throw our hat in the ring?' he asked. I was embarrassed and flattered, but by then matters had advanced too far and A&O was the right fit for us.

What It Meant for Us

The alliance provided us with a potential solution to our need to overhaul management systems and support functions to scale our practice. The prospect of partnering with a Magic Circle firm offered not just referrals and enhanced visibility, but, crucially, guidance on building an institution. It was also validation on an international scale. One of the world's most prestigious law firms was choosing to bet on us. Our excitement was palpable – we envisaged ourselves playing on an international stage, learning best practices and building friendships with lawyers who operated at the highest levels of the profession.

At its heart, though, beyond all the strategic considerations, our relationship began as many meaningful ones do – a few chaps getting along over drinks, good conversation and a shared meal. The technical and strategic benefits would follow; the personal connection came first.

20

Pantone 484

Our relationship with A&O transformed how we operated, touched nearly every aspect of our firm and created friendships that have lasted to this day. What began as a strategic alliance became a bespoke training programme in management law firm.

Aligning Our Identities

A key element of the relationship was aligning our visual identities. While we remained financially independent, we wanted to capitalise on the strength of the A&O brand and establish that we were as close as regulations permitted. This meant adopting A&O's distinctive red – Pantone 484 – as part of our livery and ensuring our collaterals and externally distributed materials visually represented our alignment. A joint client newsletter was developed and a cooperation committee was established, comprising the Trilegal founders and A&O partners in London, Singapore and Hong Kong, with regular calls on various topics.

Not only did the A&O leadership have deep experience in running a large and successful firm, they also had a reputation for innovation in law firm management, and the resources and vision to implement measures that were ahead of their time. While we didn't have the financial heft to make large investments in firm management, there were many areas in which we could learn from their experience. The knowledge transfer was systematic and generous.

Refining Our Lockstep

One of the first things we did was formalise and refine our lockstep. Allen & Overy had a system similar to what we had envisaged, which made it easy to look at their approach and adapt it.

The A&O lockstep went from 10 to 50 points. Following partnership evaluation not unlike ours, new partners entered as 'one-point' partners, essentially salaried partners. After a two- to three-year period, they would enter equity at 10 points, then accrue three points annually until reaching the 50-point cap. Unlike our system, equity had to be purchased, with A&O facilitating discounted credit lines to help partners.

We decided on a flatter structure – our equity ladder would be shorter and run from 10 to 40 points. Salaried partners entering equity would start at 10 points and the most senior equity partners (at that time, the founders) were capped at 40 points. We maintained the three-points-per-year progression.

As part of these changes, we inducted Saket, Sawant and Abhishek into equity at 10 points. They had been salaried partners for a couple of years and were performing well. This was significant – it marked the beginning of founder equity dilution.

Updating (and Humanising) Our Partnership Selection Process

Alongside lockstep changes, we re-evaluated how we selected new partners. Jonathan Brayne, who was to become embedded in our selection process for the next few years, sat in on our partnership selection interviews and gave us direct, valuable and, at times, embarrassing feedback. To reciprocate, Sridhar was invited to participate in A&O partnership evaluations.

It turned out that the process we had developed independently was similar to A&O's – technical presentations, self-assessments, partnership-wide votes. But there were differences. Allen & Overy used a three-partner committee while we involved everyone. With only 10 partners in 2008, this was manageable and we wanted to prevent the founders from dominating the process. We also asked candidates to do a SWOT analysis of the firm (in addition to one on themselves) to help them start thinking like a partner and had role-playing exercises simulating challenging client interactions. We adopted A&O's terminology, and called it the Partnership Selection Committee or PSC – which has now become part of our internal DNA.

The problem was that our process had become unnecessarily brutal, mainly because every Trilegal partner participated in partnership interviews, and Jonathan remembers watching as we collectively grilled Kosturi Ghosh in 2010. He was visibly shocked. 'My gosh, that's a lot more intense than anything we do at A&O,' he said – his polite English way of telling us we were too aggressive. Kosturi herself looks back at it as baptism by fire: 'Being grilled by 18 partners and Jonathan - that was the most daunting experience of my life. I'm proud to say I survived and still tell people about it!'

Charandeep Kaur, who became partner a year earlier, recalls similar intensity: 'Madness! At the time I thought, "Good Lord, these people don't want me to make partner!"' The client simulation exercise was particularly daunting. She said, 'I was completely baffled… I thought I did well on technical and on the SWOT – but on the client exercise, I was struggling.' Looking back, she appreciated the rigour: 'It was a solid system, even back then. It's not a profession for the faint-hearted and the PSC is a very good testing ground.'

Of another candidate who delivered a dry, tedious presentation, Jonathan uttered the classic line: 'I nearly lost the will to live' – a phrase that lives on in firm lore. As a consequence of his advice, our partnership interviews gradually moved from an adversarial model to one that's far more balanced and supportive – less trial by fire, more a constructive conversation about readiness for partnership.

One of his favourite things about participating in our process, Jonathan said, was getting to know the next generation of Trilegal leaders. These relationships became lasting friendships enriching both firms.

Building Professional Systems

In other areas, A&O helped us develop capabilities we realised we desperately needed. Xavier and his team worked closely with Rajenbhai and Karan to develop our financial systems. Terms like 'busyness', 'WIP (work in progress)', 'invoice ageing' and 'debtor days' entered our partnership's consciousness. Our intuitive management processes based on rough financial indicators were moving towards becoming systematic analyses of firm performance.

Sridhar worked with A&O's head of HR, Genevieve Tennant, to implement modern HR policies. Their team shared templates and strategies reflecting international best practices, with emphasis on lawyer appraisals and performance management. We also made a significant jump in business acceptance (client KYC) and conflict-of-interest management. Allen & Overy had highly developed processes for managing potential conflicts, a major step up from what we were doing.

We initially explored developing a scaled-down version of A&O's IT systems but decided against direct adoption – it would have required spending money we didn't quite have and we wanted independence in the long term. But even in choosing our own technology, discussions with A&O helped us think more clearly about what we needed (and didn't) and why.

Aimi Hodiwala-Rale, then a senior lawyer in our Mumbai office, and I led efforts to build our KM function. Allen & Overy generously shared precedents and training manuals, and we developed pathways for our lawyers to participate in their training programmes. We also began a multi-year process adapting some of their precedents for the Indian market.

Joint Endeavours and Shared Experiences

We ran joint business development pitches, presenting ourselves as a seamless team to clients. This helped us access decision makers we might not have reached otherwise – A&O's brand had its own pull and their credibility gave us immediate legitimacy with new categories of clients.

Joint recruitment drives at top Indian law schools produced mixed results. Jonathan recalls that confused students sometimes didn't know whether they were applying to A&O or us, or what the relationship really meant. Still, the symbolism was important – Trilegal was showing up as part of a global alliance, which impressed students who had previously only heard about the traditional firms.

External training was another collaboration area. A highlight was a joint project finance training course we ran at NLS for several years. I did one edition with Andrew Digges (an A&O finance partner) which was both educational and great fun.

Then there were the events. Our tenth anniversary celebration in 2010 at the lovely Taj Mansingh Hotel's terrace in Delhi stands out. Jonathan gave a thoughtful speech to our clients and contacts that evening, praising what we had achieved – a great endorsement for a young firm. A similar joint event in Mumbai featured Nandan Nilekani as keynote speaker. As a founder himself, he compared our emergence to the Infosys story; something that gave us great pride at a relatively early stage of our journey.

We were invited to various A&O events – partner meetings and practice retreats at evocative locations like Barcelona, Monaco, Lisbon and elsewhere. These were slick, well-designed affairs with excellent cocktails and dinners, trapeze artists in museums, live cartoonists and early use of technology for instant polling. Karan was asked to join a panel moderated by BBC anchor Mishal Husain. Speakers included the former Attorney General of Ireland and maverick American lawyer Alan Dershowitz. We participated in focus groups and practice area discussions – exciting opportunities that made us feel we were playing on an international stage.

But the heart of the relationship between the firms was the human connections we formed. The alliance worked because we genuinely liked each other, and that meant there was real fun to be had in each other's company. There were conversations about the profession's future, and war stories were shared – not just about work, but about life and family.

Some of the best memories come from personal moments. I was invited to A&O's annual European cycling trip, organised by the irrepressible Simon Roberts, requiring us to traverse alpine passes on pedal power. Wim and David were regular participants. The friendships we built went far beyond professional collaboration.

Karan and I planned a business development trip to coincide with Wim's '49-and-a-half year birthday' in Flanders. We landed in Brussels, rented a car and found ourselves in beautiful coastal Belgium. We had booked a meal at Fox's – a highly rated local restaurant – and unwittingly decided to stop at a couple of bars on the way to sample some dangerously strong Belgian beers. Add the wine at the meal, and we arrived back at the hotel at 5 p.m., rather tipsy and in dire need of a nap. Waking with a start at 9 p.m., we dashed to the party at Wim's rambling house, where the DJ was the former head of international tax at Deloitte Belgium. These are the unexpected moments that transform business trips into stories you will bore your younger colleagues with.

Market Reaction and Validation

The domestic reaction to our A&O alliance was mixed but telling. There was grudging respect from competitors who recognised the significance of a Magic Circle firm choosing us, coupled with scepticism about what it really meant. Legal industry observers questioned whether we could maintain our independence or if we would eventually be absorbed.

We never felt concerned about independence because A&O's approach was consistently light-touch while being open-hearted. They shared knowledge generously but never imposed their ways of doing things. The relationship enhanced our capabilities without constraining our autonomy – exactly what we had hoped for.

In February 2011, we extended the relationship indefinitely. What began as a three-year experiment was working well. We had gained international exposure, implemented better systems and built credibility with new clients and potential recruits. The alliance confirmed what we were already learning from our relationships within the firm – that collaboration was a valid path for growth.

Most of all, the A&O relationship gave us confidence that we had the personal and professional qualities to operate at a high level. That validation would prove crucial as new challenges emerged to test everything we had built.

21

Crisis in 2008 (No, Not That One)

The year 2008 marked the first major crisis in the firm's fledgling existence. Thousands of organisations around the world, not to mention millions of individuals, faced difficult times that year but our main challenge was not related to the most severe financial downturn the world had seen since the Great Depression. In fact, while the world's economies reeled under the effects of the global financial crisis (GFC), India proved relatively resilient.

It wasn't that the GFC didn't affect India. Financial institutions worldwide were collapsing, credit markets were freezing and even the largest economies were sliding into what would become the deepest recession since the 1930s. As economic liberalisation had deepened our connections with the global economy, India felt the tremors as well. GDP growth dipped from an average of 8.8 per cent during 2003–08 to 6.7 per cent in 2008–09 – a significant decline, but not the precipitous fall that many other economies experienced. Our exports suffered, dropping by about 18 per cent in the latter half of 2008–09, and the Indian rupee came under pressure as capital flows reversed.[67]

For once, India's conservative financial policies and relative insulation from global capital came to its assistance. Our banking sector had limited exposure to toxic assets like subprime debt that had triggered the global meltdown. The government and Reserve Bank of India took action, implementing fiscal stimulus packages and monetary easing measures to ensure credit continued flowing to industry. Still, businesses were cautious and we could feel that deal flow was affected.

Business levels, for law firms focused on transactional work, ordinarily track overall economic activity. However, we found that Trilegal was somewhat cushioned from the impact, partly as a consequence of the dynamism of our recent growth. Perhaps our recently established relationship with A&O helped too, elevating our profile and helping us maintain momentum despite economic turbulence.

However, an internal crisis was brewing – one that, for the founders, would prove to be traumatic and far more challenging than any external economic pressure.

The Departure Announcement

In September 2008, our first home-grown partners – Saket, Sawant and Abhishek – announced that they were leaving to set up on their own. These three were part of our close circle, colleagues who had worked with us from the firm's formative years. We had celebrated their elevations to partnership only a few years earlier – the genuine pride we felt in making up our first cohort of non-founder partners was fresh in our memory. Now, they were walking away to set up Phoenix Legal.

It felt like much more than an ordinary organisational setback. For me personally, and for the other founders, it raised questions about whether the firm we were building actually aligned with our founding vision. Their departures would test not only our client servicing capability, as they handled many key transactions, but also our image of what we believed Trilegal could become.

Understanding the Roots of Discontent

Trouble had been brewing for months. The roots of their dissatisfaction lay primarily in our newly formalised lockstep system, which ran from 10 to 40 points. We had placed them at the bottom of the equity ladder, believing this was the natural starting point for salaried partners entering equity. However, they saw it differently. Having been with us from the very early days and being close to us in age, they considered themselves something of a second founding generation. Waiting as long as 13 years after making partner to reach the founders' level felt unfair to them.

But the issue was more nuanced. Our relationship with A&O had created additional, unanticipated tensions. The agreement specified that A&O could reconsider the arrangement if any founders left and it had been signed by the founders alone. Allen & Overy had been clear that they were entering the relationship primarily due to the founders' reputations and we did not want to make the arrangement vulnerable to any other partner leaving. To the three departing partners, this sharply highlighted the distinction between the founders and themselves.

They also had their individual emotional calculations. For Saket, leaving was not his preferred option. He had felt a mounting sense of negativity and disconnection, an erosion in communication that allowed smaller issues to fester. He described a gradual buildup of resentment, fuelled by a sense of isolation and his perception of growing distance between him and me, personally. Saket acknowledges that his own tendency to over-analyse might have contributed to the communication gap. He also believed that I was dealing with personal challenges at the time – the impending arrival of a second set of twins and renovating a house – which made me distant and less accessible.

An unfortunate but casual joke about equity distribution had stuck with him in that context. Someone had remarked that they would be given 'just enough equity that they would not be able to either swallow it or spit it out'. In the atmosphere of uncertain communication and rising negativity, what was intended as humour struck a blow.

According to Saket, he urged caution among the three – pointing out that it was the founders bringing in clients and suggesting they wait to see how things played out. But Sawant and Abhishek felt differently. They believed that given their contributions, the equity levels being offered weren't commensurate with their value to the firm. For Saket, it was more personal and emotional, complicated by his concerns about the A&O relationship and whether he could keep pace with what he saw as the founders' increasing sophistication.

Sawant claims his view was more straightforward, though I recall an emotional aspect – he believed that his long-term friends hadn't been fair to him. The position he was offered in the lockstep simply didn't align with his vision of himself in the Trilegal partnership. He had always been driven by entrepreneurial ambition. As he put it, 'I was never going anywhere else – if not Trilegal, I would have to build something of my own.'

Difficult Conversations

Anand and I had multiple meetings with Saket and Abhishek in Delhi. I don't recall the precise words anymore, but I remember feeling almost overwhelmed by the emotional weight of those discussions. Sawant describes how, because of his closeness to Sridhar, he was afraid of speaking with him – he felt it would be easier to speak to Karan. When it was done, the message was clear: they were leaving and there was no changing their minds.

For Sridhar, the emotional impact was particularly hard. Sawant wasn't just a colleague but a close friend whom he had brought into the firm from Lex Inde. Sridhar learnt of Sawant's decision through an email with the subject 'Moving On', received while halfway up Mount Kilimanjaro. 'I cried that night in the tent,' he recalls. Upon returning, he discovered that not only had Sawant left but he had also convinced some associates to join him.

Existential Questions

Rahul, echoing what all of us felt, said that the Phoenix departure was 'questioning the idea that we're building something different from the other firms. To have them leave felt like they didn't believe in the vision.' This was an existential challenge – had we got something fundamental badly wrong? Would 'our grand project' be able to scale? We had consciously set out to create something significantly different from the traditional Indian law firm model. Yet, here were the very people we had invested in most heavily, feeling let down by that vision as it played out in real life.

The crisis tested us on many levels. Beyond the philosophical questions, there were immediate practical concerns about the client load these partners carried. Unlike other smaller crises we might have faced, which tended to affect just one partner or office, this one hit us all simultaneously, removing our usual support structure. 'Here, all of us were having to deal with this, at the same time, in different ways,' Rahul recalls.

Finding Our Way Through

Several factors helped us navigate this challenging period. First, we closed ranks. Eight years of working together had shown us the power of being a closely-knit collective and that solidarity proved crucial now. Second, we received an excellent response from the lawyers just below the departing three. Our people stepped up, assuring us of their commitment and willingness to fulfil client obligations. Charandeep, for example, flew back early from a trip to Berlin to help out. Third, A&O's response was deeply reassuring. As experienced law firm hands who had seen many partners come and go, they reaffirmed their faith in us and our vision.

The most relatable perspective came from A&O's Wim Dejonghe, who had encountered challenges in his professional journey that resonated deeply. In 2000, just as Trilegal was being established, his previous firm Loeff Claeys Verbeke's Amsterdam, Brussels and Luxembourg offices had merged with A&O. Wim told us how their next-in-line partners had also departed following the merger and that an exit of this sort was almost inevitable in first-generation firms.

The parallel was striking – close personal relationships among partners at different levels had paradoxically made it harder for the younger partners to accept significant differences in status. It was their experience of the A&O relationship and where they were placed on the lockstep that created this status differential. Being left out from being named in the A&O agreement had highlighted this, and the three younger partners felt excluded from the core of the relationship, despite being welcomed to A&O events like the Barcelona conference.

Institution Building vs Accommodation

Looking back, I wonder if we could have handled things differently. While he might have appeared less accommodating at the time, Karan recently wondered if we could have found middle ground – maybe moving them up a few notches on the lockstep would have been enough. After all, the youngest of the three was barely three years younger than our youngest founder, and they had been pillars of the firm in those critical early days.

However, Rahul disagreed strongly. There was a fundamental difference between the risk we founders took in establishing the firm and our central role in bringing in work. Would a few extra lockstep points really have solved the deeper issues? There is no way of knowing.

What I do know is that we perceived a choice that felt fundamental to the institution we were trying to build: accommodate our friends or stick to our principles. Karan viewed it as 'the first real test of our capacity to think of and build an institution'. As he saw it then: 'If we don't maintain our principles now, we'll be cutting special deals for people all the time. We won't be consistent, transparent or fair.' Our decision also provided what Karan describes as 'great confidence that all of us [the founders] were aligned' and demonstrated to the next generation who stuck with us that 'these founders were for real'.

After they left, the five of us got together at a restaurant in Delhi to take stock and reaffirm our commitment to and support for each other. We drank many bottles of Châteauneuf-du-Pape – the same wine Rahul and I had shared that night in Mumbai when we first discussed starting the firm. By the end of the evening, the wine and solidarity made our situation feel more like the beginning of a new phase rather than the end of an old one.

The Lingering Impact

But the pain of their departure lingered. It wasn't just about losing colleagues and friends – it felt like a rejection of us personally and the firm we were trying to build. While we succeeded in maintaining our vision and principles, it took time to restore our belief in what we were doing. We were left with some lasting insecurities about how our own people felt about our model, possibly making us more careful about our interactions with junior colleagues and younger partners.

Today, Sridhar believes that it was a blessing in disguise, allowing the firm to consolidate under the founders and implement structural changes without internal friction. There was a clear seniority gap with the generation of partners following the three, and they were not vying for parity, enabling decisive implementation of new systems.

I wonder if a reason for the inability to find middle ground stemmed from the founders not sensing overt appreciation from the three of them for the platform we had created and the opportunity it afforded them. But the mounting negativity and breakdown in communication had created the perfect storm and prevented us from having the conversations that might have bridged the gap.

Reconciliation and Lessons Learnt

For me personally, true closure came only while writing this chapter, through conversations with Saket and Sawant. Their generosity – both with their time and their perspectives – helped me fill in the blanks. Saket's reflections were particularly poignant. He spoke about how Anand and my close supervision of his work, while providing him professional space, instilled a self-belief that had shaped his entire professional journey. The assurance of having support when needed, particularly early in his career, built a confidence that still guides him today.

Despite the hurt and emotion when the departure happened, the personal relationships never fell apart. Given the number of messy fallouts that the Indian law firm world has witnessed over the past two decades, we can give ourselves some credit for that. Even now, Saket occasionally calls for a chat and contacts Anand for advice on firm management.

Saket, Sawant and Abhishek went on to found Phoenix Legal immediately after leaving in August 2008. Today, Phoenix is well established with a good reputation, and our three former partners have carved out excellent names for themselves. Their genuine pride in Trilegal's achievements reflects a generosity of spirit that helps square the circle.

The departure taught us how delicate managing a partnership could be, while at the same time clarifying our values. We learnt that growth brings challenges, that even close colleagues might see the world differently and that sometimes holding to your principles means accepting painful losses. But it also showed us something else: that the foundations we had built were stronger than we had realised.

22
New Partners and Tweaking Compensation

The period following the Phoenix Legal departures marked significant expansion in our partnership. The firm's growth and improving reputation meant that work was continuing to stream in. This created dual pressures: we needed more partners to lead transactions, and our commitment to the lockstep model meant that the next round of partners had to be both excellent and become an enduring part of the firm's future.

Looking Within: Our Home-Grown Partners

Our first choice for new partners was to look within. This strategy served multiple purposes – rewarding performance while setting clear incentives for others in the system. 'Work hard and do well, and partnership is on the cards' needed to be the clear message. Also, it was hard for us to bring in laterals. Partners in other firms whom we considered highly competent and a good fit with our distinctive culture weren't necessarily rushing to join what was still, in the eyes of much of the legal market, a relatively unproven firm. Moreover, lateral partner movement between Indian firms was still quite rare.

We had also adopted a strict rule, one that still exists – we would not take someone on as partner if they weren't already a partner in another firm. This didn't mean that someone who hadn't yet made partner somewhere else couldn't become a partner at Trilegal – it just meant that they would have to join at a level below partner and then go through our selection process.

Internally, Amit Tambe (who had joined from Desai & Dewanji in 2005) and Nishant Parikh (who came aboard a year later from DSK), were at the front of the queue with seven and six years of experience, respectively. Their selection interviews took place at the Claridges Hotel in Delhi – we felt that taking the process out of the office would provide greater gravitas than our still relatively modest offices. Both made it through, becoming partners in October 2008.

For Nishant, this was the first significant milestone in what has become a remarkably successful career at the firm. He was always an exceptional lawyer and, as we'll see later, he had been earmarked early for leadership. By becoming partner at just over six years qualified, he remains the lawyer with the shortest track to partnership in Trilegal's history – a record that won't be broken given how much the bar for partnership has risen (it now takes 10 years).

In April 2011, three years after making partner, both Nishant and Amit met the revenue targets and other criteria that qualified them to receive equity in the firm, entering at 10 points in our lockstep system. Nishant's precocious confidence was striking when he remarked: 'There are quantitative as well as qualitative parameters to make it to equity which are fairly transparent to people in the larger partnership. Given the environment and market conditions I don't think these are very difficult parameters to meet.'

Shortly after the Phoenix departures, we had introduced a new 'counsel' designation, similar to managing associate or principal associate roles in other firms. Charandeep Kaur, Ameya Khandge, Ajay Raghavan and Delano Furtado, senior associates at the time, were made counsels and placed on partner track. All four made partner in 2009, marking a watershed moment in Trilegal's evolution. Charandeep became our first woman partner – a milestone that was overdue but deeply significant when it happened. Kosturi followed her in 2010. The infamous Trilegal 'boys club' had finally been breached.

It took time for all of us, and Charandeep, to realise the significance of this. She says: 'I must confess that at the time, I didn't think of it as a big thing... but I realised later how symbolic it was – it became a turning point, because people saw that this is what leadership could look like at Trilegal.'

Bringing in Laterals

Growing from within had its limits. While we aspired to be a 'full-service' corporate law firm, there were significant gaps in our offering. A major hole was that we did not have a dedicated disputes practice. While we had handled some high-profile cases for clients such as Telenor, leveraging Anand's past experience as a litigator, our disputes offering paled compared to the firms leading the legal market.

Here, our old friend Upamanyu Hazarika came to our help, introducing us to Sitesh Mukherjee, then a partner at Hemant Sahai Associates. Sitesh had built a strong reputation, primarily as an electricity sector litigator, which we saw as complementary to our growing energy and infrastructure practice. Our energy sector clients often needed litigation support, and in a heavily regulated sector, a regulatory disputes lawyer's insights would enhance our transactional work. I remember meeting him in the Club Bar at the Oberoi and feeling an immediate sense of comfort with him. Sitesh joined us in February 2009, entering directly into equity. By the time he left, 11 years later, to become an independent counsel, he had established himself as our most successful lateral partner by some distance.

Our A&O relationship yielded another benefit in August of the same year. Srinivas Parthasarathy (Partha) – Sridhar and Karan's NLS classmate and former colleague at Lex Inde – was now a financing and capital markets partner in A&O's Singapore office. While we had acted on NTPC's IPO (initial public offering) in 2004, we hadn't succeeded in building on that and had no capital markets practice to speak of.

In 2006, we felt this lack quite sharply, when Cairn India – a UK oil and gas company with significant plans for India, and a key client for almost five years – sensibly chose to go to S&R Associates (a specialist capital markets firm) for their IPO. This led to the loosening of our ties with Cairn, which was exacerbated by a change in management there and the fact that S&R did a good job for them. We never quite restored this relationship and wanted to prevent similar situations with other clients seeking to access the public markets.

Partha was looking to return to India, and both firms saw value in having someone trusted by both organisations join Trilegal. As Jonathan Brayne noted in our joint press release: 'This is a very positive move for the A&O–Trilegal relationship. […] Partha has been a key member of our India Group and his move will substantially enhance the collaboration between Allen & Overy and Trilegal.'

With Partha's arrival, we could finally claim to have a capital markets practice. Anand took it a bit further in his characteristic style. While acknowledging that our capital markets practice left a lot to be desired, he also laid out the scale of our ambition: 'The plan is to have an extremely robust capital markets practice sometime in the next year-and-a-half to two years and ultimately to be a top tier capital markets practice that competes with Amarchand Mangaldas or S&R.'

It took a good few years longer than that, but Trilegal's capital markets practice is one of the top two or three in the market today.

Compensation Needs Fine Tuning

By 2011, we were pleased with how our partnership model had evolved, but tensions were emerging. Some younger partners were generating substantially more business than their more senior peers and our lockstep system wasn't designed to recognise these outliers. The discrepancy was creating exactly the kind of friction we had hoped to avoid.

This forced us back into that fundamental tension we had wrestled with from the beginning – how do you balance fraternity with meritocracy? Differences of opinion emerged even among the founders. Some of us wanted to preserve the pure lockstep at all costs, believing that the sense of equality and collegiality it fostered was central to who we were. Others argued that ignoring performance differences completely went against our commitment to rewarding merit.

Rather than the founders deciding, we opened it up to the whole partnership for discussion. What emerged was reassuring: every partner believed in the lockstep model and wanted to preserve it, but there was also consensus that exceptional performance deserved recognition.

The solution we developed – a one-time level jump for partners who consistently demonstrated exceptional performance over three years – was a compromise that seemed to honour both our values. This wouldn't create dramatic disparities and the high performers weren't actively seeking disproportionate rewards. Equally important, most other partners felt a genuine responsibility towards their high-performing colleagues and wanted to acknowledge their contributions.

This represented the first significant evolution of our compensation system since founding the firm. It wouldn't be the last, or the most consequential. With growing numbers of partners beyond the founders, we began thinking about how our lawyers could absorb the collaborative ethos and professional standards that had emerged organically in our early years. One way to do this could be through how we trained our young lawyers.

23

The Neemrana Sessions and Other Ways to Learn

Most knowledge in the legal profession is accumulated by observing and doing – working on actual transactions and cases. Law firms supplement this through formal training. But beyond building legal knowledge, KM can be a tool to preserve institutional memory – the culture, values and stories that define how a firm operates and thinks about itself.

Making It Up as We Went Along

Trilegal's 'Form & Style Manual' was our first attempt to codify institutional knowledge. The template was 'borrowed' and adapted from the one I used at Ashurst. Over many weeks in our first year, Sridhar, Rahul and I worked on it in our spare time. We created standards for everything from document structure to line spacing (multiple, at 1.1) to paragraph numbering (1., 1.1., 1.1(a), 1.1(a)(i)). This wasn't just about making things look pretty – I had often heard international lawyers say about documents from Indian firms, 'If they can't even format it properly, how do we trust the legal advice it contains?'

The Manual contained other guidance – active not passive voice, short sentences, how to structure a memo, write emails thinking of who was going to read them and such other things. A Trilegal document has always had a clear, crisp identity and serves as a subtle (and legal) form of advertisement. Lawyers in the firm and those long gone often say how they struggle to work with any badly formatted documents they encounter.

But beyond this, we had no formal mechanisms to capture and disseminate knowledge. We were young, smart and hard-working, but when we ran 'training' sessions – legal updates, deal debriefs – they were ad hoc, sometimes on Saturday mornings. In Delhi, I called in my personal CA to run sessions on how to read a balance sheet.

We did try to build a KM function back in 2004. Biraj Tiwari joined us to set it up but left after a couple of years, partly due to lack of support from partners – we were working hard to build our practices and didn't have time for what we then thought of as only a 'nice to have'. She left to head the KM function at Amarchand Mangaldas, probably thinking (correctly) that she would get greater support and resources at the preeminent firm of the time.

One Person's Initiative

The real KM function kicked off in 2009, but its seeds had been sown some years earlier.

In an alternate universe, Aimi Hodiwala-Rale might have become our first woman partner. But she decided to step away. 'I was enjoying the work I was doing,' she said. 'But the whole business development aspect – client networking, the pressure to go out and bring in work – that wasn't me.' Instead, she went to Karan and Sridhar with a proposal: Why not start a proper KM function within the firm? She had always been interested in 'the knowledge side of things' – the back-end, the research.

Building the KM function with Aimi made sense. She was one of our first campus recruits in Mumbai and knew the firm intimately. 'I hadn't even seen the inside of a law firm before joining. You were just thrown in. Your workplace was your learning ground,' she said. One of her earliest assignments was helping draft a contract for Sawant's father's cook!

So, Aimi understood our scrappy roots and cared deeply for the firm. 'Trilegal reminds me of Hogwarts,' she said recently, 'not for the magic, but because it gives you space to be who you are and shapes you into a better version of yourself.'

Unlike many jurisdictions, India doesn't mandate continuing legal education. But we thought formal internal training requirements were a good idea. Having seen how A&O ran training programmes for their lawyers to fulfil Law Society requirements, we decided to adopt something similar with their help. Our first attempt was what we called ITP – the cheekily named Insider Training Programme.

To begin with, Aimi was her own boss and her own assistant. In 2025, KM includes a team of eight lawyers and two support staff, but back then it was just her, figuring it out as she went along.

The Neemrana Sessions: Building Culture

Around 2008, we decided that our joining graduates needed a proper induction programme. This was probably the first induction programme a law firm in India did for freshers. Based on how much fun we had at firm retreats, why not do it offsite, I thought – and we ended up in Neemrana, the fort-palace turned heritage hotel halfway from Delhi to Jaipur. The choice of venue was deliberate, providing a distinctive, evocative setting, not corporate and hotel-like, and quite informal. We wanted it to reflect how we saw ourselves as a firm – serious about the quality of our work but prepared to have fun doing it.

Rahul, Sridhar, Aimi and I designed and ran the Neemrana Sessions for many years, conceiving of them not as an admin exercise but as providing a crash course in our culture and 'one firm' approach. As founders, we knew the importance of cohesion among peers and wanted our cohorts of freshers to get an early opportunity to start building something similar for themselves.

We tried to balance practical information with cultural nudges. Sessions included introductions to the various practice areas, policies and systems, writing and research skills, and what new lawyers could expect in their first year. We ran chatty sessions about firm history and values. To ensure this wasn't a whitewash job full of corporate spiel, there was a retrospective session – freshers from the previous year, from each office, having a no-filters conversation about their first job and life in the firm.

Team-building activities included egg-and-spoon races in Neemrana's amphitheatre at sunset, impromptu plays, egg drops, ziplining and various ice-breaking challenges. Light-hearted stuff that generally achieved what it was supposed to – people getting to know each other better. Many partners would make the trip from Delhi for the evening drinks and dinner, sharing tales about the firm – the informal storytelling that helps new lawyers understand what we do, how we do it and why.

Gautam Chawla, who attended the 2011 sessions and is now a partner, explained how this worked: 'You got deep insight into what the firm and its people were like in just two days.' There was a conscious choice to put people from different offices together, in cars on the way there and as roommates. 'Some of the people I met in the Neemrana Sessions are among the people closest to me in the firm today,' Gautam recalled. Three others from his cohort – Jyotsna Jayaram, Kabeer Mathur and Niharika Puri – are also partners today.

For 23-year-old law graduates, access to senior partners in a relaxed setting meant something. As Gautam put it: 'There you were…drinking alongside a founder who was strumming a guitar and telling you about the firm… It changed how you acted and made you confident about accessing senior people from day one.'

As Aimi observed: 'We didn't want it to be just a couple of presentations in a conference room. It had to feel like you were being welcomed into something. Freshers all tell us the same thing – it helped them feel like they belonged to something.'

Those early Neemrana Sessions were great fun, a shortcut to getting to know younger folks well in a relaxed context. Once the booze flowed, the initially slightly awed freshers often lost their inhibitions. I remember Megha Kaladharan arguing animatedly with me about whether The Shins were a good band, and Mohit Rastogi and Riyaz Bhagat inventing fairy tales about how Manchester United was a bigger club than Liverpool. They are all partners today.

As cohorts expanded from 10–12 lawyers in 2008 to much larger numbers today, we've had to adapt, moving to the hotels we originally avoided. The challenge is different now with more formal systems and larger groups, though some of the old elements remain. At the last one, in July 2005, I did a session on the firm's history and Sridhar spoke about values and culture. The informal moments often matter as much as the formal training – that's when people actually get to know each other and start to feel part of something.

Part 5

Building an Institution

24

Calling Time on the A&O Relationship

On 27 September 2012, A&O and Trilegal released the following joint statement: 'Unfortunately, the lack of progress towards legal sector liberalisation in India has led both firms to conclude their existing arrangement is restricting their ability fully to exploit the growing opportunities in India.'[68]

And with that, our almost five-year-old 'best friends' relationship with the Magic Circle firm came to an end. This statement was as understated as the one that had announced our tie-up back in February 2008. The news was reported quite widely in the legal industry press, with *The Lawyer* noting we had 'ended our best friends relationship, citing the lack of progress in liberalising the Indian legal market'.

Jonathan commented in the joint press release: 'We have the highest opinion of Trilegal and we look forward to continuing to work with them when the opportunity presents itself, but also to collaborating with other Indian law firms.'

For our part, Anand stated: 'We believe our relationship with Allen & Overy has been of great benefit to both firms. But both sides agree that, in the absence of liberalisation, each firm stands a better chance of increasing its market share by broadening our options for collaboration in the market.'

Behind these polite, politically correct public announcements lay a complex reality and a difficult decision.

What Had Gone Right

It is hard to overstate how much the A&O relationship had transformed us. We had internalised many of their systems, approaches and professional standards. The partnership evaluation processes, financial metrics, precedents and training materials had become part of our institutional makeup. The human benefits were equally important – our lawyers had gained exposure to global best practices and built relationships that extended well beyond the alliance itself.

But perhaps most importantly, the relationship had given us a deep legitimacy. When potential clients or lateral partners looked at us, they saw a firm that had been endorsed by one of the world's elite law firms.

Why It Ended

So, if the relationship had been so great, why end it? Much of the answer lay in how much we had changed as a firm during those five years.

When we tied up with A&O in 2008, we were a 10-partner firm with about 60 lawyers. By 2012, we had grown to 25 partners and 150 lawyers and were significantly better known. Many of our new partners had their own networks with international firms – former classmates, colleagues or contacts they had developed over their careers. The problem was they couldn't capitalise on these relationships.

While our relationship with A&O was technically non-exclusive, the outside world didn't see it that way. Firms that competed with A&O had mostly stopped referring work to us, viewing us as too closely allied with their rivals. While our international referral income hadn't changed much, its profile had shifted dramatically. We were getting more work from A&O and their network, but significantly less from others. All too often, we were hearing 'we'd love to send you work but you're seen as too close to A&O'.

From the viewpoint both of our younger partners who wanted to develop their practices through their own contacts, as well as for the overall growth of the firm, our enlarged partnership was feeling constrained by what had been our greatest asset just five years ago.

Another factor was the lack of progress in liberalising India's legal market. When we entered the relationship in 2008, there were genuine signs that India might open up to foreign law firms. Our expectation had been that deeper integration with A&O might happen within three to five years. By 2012, not only had no progress been made, but opposition to market opening had become stronger. Without liberalisation, we couldn't see how our relationship could evolve into the deeper integration we had envisaged.

Allen & Overy faced challenges too. We hadn't yet developed the deep links with Indian business houses that both firms had hoped for. Major Indian outbound deals – Tata's acquisition of Corus Steel and Land Rover, Bharti's acquisition of Zain Telecom, Mahindra's SsangYong stake – all happened without our involvement. We simply weren't delivering the high-value India-outbound referral work that both firms had hoped for.

Despite these limitations, David confirmed to me recently what we had sensed then – that A&O would have been content to continue. He said, 'From our point of view, we were perfectly happy to carry on as we were. Yes, our fundamental rationale for the relationship – a future merger when the regulations permitted – had eroded, but we were still happy with the work and the relationship.' The reality was that the constraints were affecting Trilegal more than A&O. So we took the first step.

The Weight of the Decision

We had invested enormous amounts of time and effort in the relationship – not just the formal systems and processes but the personal connections we had built. The idea of being part of an international community of lawyers, of having colleagues and friends across the globe, had become something many of us valued. The cycling trips, the joint events, the informal conversations about legal practice and firm management – these had enriched our professional lives in ways that went far beyond just client referrals.

The debate within our partnership was animated but democratic. I was among those who would have continued the relationship, at least for a while. The benefits still felt substantial to me, and I wasn't convinced the constraints were as limiting as some of my partners believed. But I wasn't affected as much by the lack of referrals from other international firms as some of my partners were, since most work in my practice (energy and infrastructure) was generated either directly from international clients or domestically.

In the end, the collective view was that our growth and ambitions required the flexibility to work with a broader range of international firms.

A Difficult Conversation

David recently recalled when Karan and Rahul went to London to meet him: 'I remember the moment when Karan told me that you wanted to go your separate way. It had become obvious that the market opening rules were not going to change anytime soon – a closer integration wasn't going to be possible. Through no fault of anyone's – it just wasn't happening.'

We weren't alone in facing these challenges. Clifford Chance and AZB had broken off their relationship after only a year, citing similar reasons, as had Clyde & Co. and ALMT Legal a few months after that. The pattern was clear: the 'best friends' model worked only if it led to something deeper, and regulatory reality was making that impossible.

David recalls:

> Karan was very straightforward when he broke the news. He just said, 'We love you guys, but we can't just rely on A&O referrals anymore. There are so many other firms entering the market, and our younger partners have their own international relationships.'

And he didn't try to excuse it or soften it – he just said it plainly and respectfully, which is exactly how that kind of message should be delivered.

Wim similarly described the parting as 'a shame' but that it happened 'in a very gentleman-like way and very rationally'.

David also told us how other partners at A&O responded at the time:

> There were a few grumbles – mostly emotional responses – for instance about the sharing of precedents, about how much we'd invested in the relationship. But it didn't gather any steam. There was no real pushback or resentment. You didn't surprise us with anything unpleasant. You handled it like professionals. You could have dragged it out, or tried to quietly step back, or let it fizzle out. But were open and honest. That tells me something about your culture.

Kind words about a difficult time.

The Aftermath

Once the decision was made, we had substantial practical work to do. We redesigned our branding and marketing materials, removing references to being A&O's 'best friend' in India. Bye-bye Pantone 484, the distinctive red colour that had become part of our visual identity. I have to admit, I was fond of that dark red, but it had to go. It wasn't easy but we weren't anxious. We were confident we had built something strong enough to stand and thrive on its own.

The legal grapevine buzzed with theories about why the relationship had ended. Some hit the mark – speculation about A&O's disappointment with India-outbound referrals (they were), suggestions that Trilegal's increasing independence had created constraints (it had) and observations about regulatory uncertainty (right again). Others predicted Trilegal's imminent downfall for various reasons.

Looking Back, Moving Forward

We have always acknowledged that the A&O relationship had been invaluable for us. Despite the formal separation, we often work with A&O on specific matters. Many of their partners remain close friends, and until 2020, when Covid-19 brought an end to it, I continued to go on their annual partners' cycling trip. In 2022, Harsh Pais, then the co-head of our corporate practice, left Trilegal amicably to relocate to London and join A&O as a partner. He works regularly on joint mandates with his former colleagues at Trilegal.

As Ajay Raghavan observed: 'When A&O came along, it gave us greater capacity to think about our practice in a structured way – and also validated a lot of what you all [the founders] had started to think about. It pushed us to communicate more effectively, think more professionally.' While the A&O relationship had given us a tremendous boost at a crucial stage in our development, by 2012 – a bit like an impatient teenager – we needed the freedom to establish our own identity and relationships.

The end of the relationship also gave us the opportunity to re-evaluate where we were as a partnership and what we wanted to become. This exercise would trigger a series of events which meant that while our decision to part ways with A&O was perhaps the most difficult decision we took that year, in the long run, it wasn't the most consequential.

25
We Get Served Some Brutal Facts

In late 2011, even before the A&O split, we had begun a process that would lead to the most significant change to our partnership and compensation model since the firm's founding, and would provide the architecture and incentive systems that shape the behaviours of our partnership to this day. When we began, we had no idea of how significant this process would turn out to be.

We were always aware that our firm's culture would be shaped by its equity ownership and compensation model. As discussed earlier, we had rejected 'eat what you kill' in favour of a lockstep for this reason. But the firm had changed significantly. Notably, many non-founders were now partners. The initial model had served us well through our first decade, but we felt, almost instinctively, that founding principles – no matter how sound in principle – needed to evolve in their practical application.

Growing Pains and Troubling Patterns

While we believed our two-tier partnership was a fair system, offering a genuine path to equity, we didn't quite know what our salaried partners thought about it. And we had observed some worrying trends.

First, troubling patterns were emerging in partner decision-making. When new technology or office improvements were proposed, there was scepticism from our salaried partners. The subtext was clear – this money could have gone towards their bonuses instead.

Second, lockstep equity partners had an incentive to share work with each other based on subject matter expertise, geography and workload. But salaried partners, to meet their financial targets for entry into equity, were developing a tendency to grab any work they could get – regardless of whether they were best placed to do it. This was the opposite of the collaborative behaviour we were trying to foster.

Also, the tension between collegiality and meritocracy had raised its head again. As mentioned, tweaks like introducing equity jumps for consistently exceptional partners had addressed some of this tension, but they hadn't resolved the fundamental divide between salaried and equity partners, which led to these unwanted behaviours.

Seeking External Advice, and Initial Scepticism

We decided that the best way forward was to get external assistance, for three reasons: we lacked detailed knowledge of compensation systems; confirmation bias might be clouding our judgement; and, following the Phoenix departures, we were wary about how founder-driven ideas would be received. We needed a process in which partners could speak openly without worrying about founders' reactions.

We engaged Reena SenGupta of RSGI and Moray Mclaren of Redstone, who became Trilegal's first ever consultants. Our brief was simple: get honest opinions from partners about what was working and what was not.

In December 2011, the founders met with the consultants to think systematically about our firm. We thought about the future constantly, but in a disjointed, reactive manner. Here, we had the chance to build a coherent vision – forcing us busy practitioners to step back and distil what we had learnt.

Management consultants, with their 'frameworks', 'paradigms' and other buzzwords, often seem to dress up common sense in jargon, so we were a bit sceptical of the process. But hiding in that jargon was something useful – a framework to surface new ideas. As the process unfolded, we felt empowered, even excited; patterns emerged from our lived experience that we could imagine channelling into structure.

Our Competitive Advantage

We covered a lot of ground – strengths, weaknesses, competitors and what made us different. We hadn't done this systematically before and it was actually quite good fun. We embraced the idea that our differences with most law firms in India – founding values and lockstep, a collaborative ethos in a traditional market, efficient delivery of high-quality work, youth and energy (the oldest partner at 43) – were our main advantages. These differences added up to our culture, or simply: 'the way we do things around here'.

Reena and Moray had been impressed by our willingness to give equity to the next generation – something unprecedented in India. This squared with what David told me recently: 'You had a sense of integrity… a mission… that went well beyond just making money for yourselves… That's unusual in my experience.'

But to take advantage of what we had created, we needed to take the next step. For our model to work long-term, we could no longer rely on founder authority. We needed formal structures that would outlast us. This set the framework for what came next – individual partner interviews feeding into survey results, shared first with founders and then with everyone, followed by open discussion about the way forward.

The Brutal Facts

On 9 January 2012, with some trepidation, the founders sat around a conference room to receive feedback from Reena and Moray on what the partners had said. The results contained some validation but mainly a bunch of hard truths. Moray referred to the session as a 'hefty dose of tough love'. As Jim Collins wrote in *Good to Great*, 'You absolutely cannot make a series of good decisions without first confronting the brutal facts.' Well, this was one of those moments. We were going to be served up some brutal facts.

What Was Working

But first, the good news.

There were many things that partners thought the firm was doing right. They were proud of the quality of our work for clients, our professionalism, high standards and positive work culture. We were attracting good lawyers and developing strong senior talent. They believed the firm offered a unique value proposition in the Indian legal market, providing an alternative vision for younger lawyers, while achieving growth.

This was strong validation. We had built a foundation of quality with motivated colleagues. Our culture of inclusion, transparency and empowerment had taken root. There was continued faith in and respect for the founders. This felt good – we were being told that we had built something that people were proud to be part of.

What Wasn't Working: The Governance Problem

Much less expected, the feedback revealed big governance problems. Sitting in that conference room, listening to the survey results was a bit of a jolt – I was actually wincing. Our partners were telling us a sobering story about their engagement with firm governance and that they wanted change: 82 per cent felt our management structures were inadequate, 85 per cent thought decision-making had to change, 59 per cent wanted a managing partner and 76 per cent supported a management committee.

We had thought that we were inclusive and collaborative across the board, but it seemed that this was sometimes more in our heads than in reality. The qualitative comments on governance were equally revealing:

> 'We lack strategic direction and we need one. Three or four years ago we had a clear vision but we are not there today. There is a lack of time and focus. As a collective group we do not have that vision.'

'Each of us has our own views as to what we need to do in our own practice areas. But there are no Ten Commandments and I think it would be good to have them.'

'The firm does have a strategy and we are quite focused. But now, it's gone a bit haywire – I'm seeing competition between partners which never used to exist.'

'We are not overly democratic, though we need to be seen as such.'

'We act as an inner circle...' (This was one of the founders)

'I am not sure what my roles and responsibilities in the firm are.'

The Half-Pant Problem

Beyond governance, the survey revealed stark issues with our partnership structure: 65 per cent didn't believe the firm operated as a true democracy, 59 per cent felt the partnership lacked proper integration among equity and salaried partners and 53 per cent didn't feel sufficiently consulted.

Three issues about our two-tier structure stood out, and they were more serious than we had realised. First, and most importantly, salaried partners felt they weren't true partners. The jokey term for this – 'half-pant' – was humorous on the surface, but reflected a sense of being second-class citizens. The nomenclature was self-deprecating and light, but the underlying sentiment was serious. Second, they felt that 15 years was too long to reach the top of the lockstep – this could be demotivating. Finally, they believed that having revenue targets to move from salaried partnership into equity created too much pressure. They felt unwanted competitiveness with each other, something they saw that the founders didn't have to deal with. They had seen the closeness among us and wanted a piece of that for themselves.

It would have been tempting (and self-serving) to dismiss these as excessive demands. After all, which other firm was even holding open the possibility of genuine partnership, with actual equity shares as a real possibility and an equal vote for non-founders? But on reflection, the lack of alignment was obvious. These aspirations didn't reflect ingratitude or greed – this was a way to seek greater alignment. In a way, it was a form of validation; these requests came out of a desire for more equality and fraternity, the very principles we had set up with.

The Collaboration Problem

Our consultants confirmed that the salaried partner model was actively harming collaboration. Lawyers were prioritising individual billings over firm success because the financial targets for entry into equity were encouraging an 'eat what you kill' mentality for salaried partners – the very approach we had explicitly rejected. The salaried partners didn't like this any more than we did; one said that 'the salaried partner stage is creating a culture which is different from the founders' DNA'.

The result? One of our main supposed differentiators from our competitors, our cherished lockstep, wasn't acting as the motivator it was supposed to be. Charles Handy had made the point that if people are not genuinely treated as partners, they will behave like employees.[69] This is particularly true of lawyers, who take great pride in their professional autonomy. The system was reducing their sense of belonging to and investment in the firm.

Growing beyond the Founders

We were also facing the classic challenge of moving from founder-led leadership to institutional governance. We had been operating as a founder-driven firm. As assertive, successful founders, there was an acceptance of our authority. This was necessary for early growth – our purpose, energy and drive was critical to get things off the ground. But the very things that had driven us forward initially were beginning to hold us back.

Our management style was informal because we were full-time practitioners with no training as managers. Our leadership was strong and generally fair, but inconsistent. Our communication practices – friendly and casual – had defined our positive culture early on, but were falling short now. They created the impression of a clique and didn't fulfil other partners' need for formal transparency.

Larry Greiner seemed to be describing us when he observed that the practices that fuel early success – informality, individualism and creative chaos – eventually become liabilities.[70] We had entrepreneurial mindsets and expected similar levels of self-motivation from others. We were also financially more comfortable. These factors enabled a cavalier approach to decision-making that wasn't shared by others. Our missionary spirit meant that sometimes we rode roughshod over others without realising it.

No one appeared to question our intentions, but there was an obvious gap between what we intended and how we were acting. There's an old saying: 'The things that got you there are seldom those that keep you there.' We would encounter this principle again later in the firm's journey.

The Choice Ahead

We took the criticism on board, recognising it as a genuine desire for deeper participation in a collective that people liked to be part of. The feedback wasn't a rejection of what we had built, but an honest request to be more fully part of it. Trilegal needed to evolve from a founder-controlled firm to a more structured, sustainable institution. As Larry Greiner observed, organisations evolve through phases, each challenged by a particular kind of crisis – often of leadership or autonomy. We were showing aspects of both.

The strength of the feedback and our own risk-taking history were pushing us towards a fundamental choice: *Should we make incremental adjustments to patch up the problems or fundamentally reimagine what partnership at Trilegal could look like?*

Given the depth of concerns raised and our risk-taking history, we were heading towards the more radical choice. After all, we hadn't built the firm by playing it safe or accepting conventional wisdom. It was time to take a deep breath and take the conversation to the entire partnership.

26

Refresh! Going All Equity

We were scheduled to be in Dubai over the 26 January 2012 weekend for a firm retreat, and decided that it would be the right time for a partners' meeting to consider the findings of the consultants. The theme for the retreat was 'Refresh', chosen because the whole firm had gone through a period of exceptional busyness – our lawyers were exhausted and needed a break. 'Refresh' was also exactly what our partners' meeting would be about.

The brutal facts from our partner survey had made clear that we needed to resolve two fundamental issues. First, redefine our equity structure to align partner incentives with the firm's long-term health. Second, give partners clarity on career progression and their futures.

The Case for Ownership

Before its 1999 IPO, Goldman Sachs operated as a private partnership. This created a culture in which partners thought long-term about the firm's future and saw themselves as stewards. This meant that partners had a direct stake in the firm's success and were incentivised to train, retain and promote top talent. Their IPO changed everything – now the firm had to prioritise short-term performance for public shareholders rather than focusing on what was best for the partnership. We were like the pre-IPO Goldman and wanted our partners to think like founders about the firm's long-term growth. But we had realised that a key ingredient was preventing them from doing so: a genuine sense of ownership.

Reena and Moray's main suggestion was striking: *Get rid of the salaried partnership category altogether and introduce the lockstep from day one.* All partners would become equity owners immediately, with objective performance standards and criteria for progression through the lockstep.

Boom.

Going All-Equity

We surprised ourselves by adopting the radical solution of making all partners owners of the firm. The mechanics were straightforward when we worked out the numbers. We looked at what salaried partners were earning annually and determined that this sum corresponded to approximately 5 points on the existing equity lockstep. So why not have the lockstep start at 5 points, with partners becoming equity holders from their first day as partners?

This was unprecedented in the Indian legal market. While most established firms jealously guarded equity, we were essentially saying, 'Prove you belong here as a partner, and you immediately become an owner.'

Managing the Lockstep

We decided that the Trilegal lockstep would be a managed lockstep with four 'gateways' at 10, 16, 22 and 31 points respectively. A partner would be entitled to 10 units if they met the performance standards at 8.33 units; 16 units if they met the standards at 13 units and so on. Annual performance in non-gateway years would be monitored, but additional points would be allocated anyway. We didn't want partners to face performance pressure every year.

Partners who met both financial and other performance standards in a gateway year would pass through normally. But we built in flexibility for life's realities – if someone didn't meet either the financial or performance standards at a gateway, they could still pass through at the discretion of the soon-to-be-formed Management

Committee, provided there were circumstances that compensated for the shortfall. If a partner didn't make it through a gateway, they would be held there for a maximum of two years.

Beyond Financial Metrics

We discussed non-financial criteria for partners to progress through the lockstep, driven by our values of client focus and firm-mindedness. Partners would have to promote senior lawyers from within their teams for partnership, and support their practices by passing on work and helping them develop new clients.

The logic was that sustained growth in a lockstep depends on new partners coming into the system, and leadership means training younger lawyers to transition from just executing work to managing teams, transactions and, eventually, clients and practices. Spreading relationships across more lawyers and practices in the firm would encourage an institutional mindset towards client relationships – an attitude of 'our' client rather than 'my' client.

Consistent exceptional performance over a four-year period would be rewarded by allocating three additional units of equity, once in a partner's career.

Fixing How We Ran the Firm: The Management Committee

Changing our ownership structure was only part of the battle. Partner feedback had made it clear that if we were going to make everyone owners from day one, we also needed to overhaul how we managed the firm.

We identified three stages in law firm governance evolution: founder-led (where we'd been), committee management and elected managing partners. We needed to move from Stage 1 towards Stage 2, while maintaining our non-hierarchical culture.

Extensive discussions surfaced the consensus that we weren't ready for a managing partner – none of us wanted to set aside our practices for full-time management and we wanted equal office representation. We also didn't want a 'first among equals' dynamic among the founders. Instead, we created a Management Committee comprising three founding partners: Anand, Karan and Rahul. The Management Committee would handle day-to-day management, with a short list of matters requiring full partnership approval. It was exciting to approve the text of the email that would make this decision-making real – I could imagine the positivity it would spread. On 24 May 2012, everyone in the firm received this message:

> As the firm grows in size and stature, we have increasingly felt the need to put in place a more formal system of professional management in order to help us achieve our strategic objectives. With that in mind, the partnership has decided to entrust the management of the firm to a management committee. This management committee has been empowered by the partnership to take decisions on behalf of the partnership on various aspects of firm management and will report and be responsible to the partnership. The management committee will initially comprise the following partners: Anand Prasad, Karan Singh and Rahul Matthan. We trust that you will extend the new management committee all the support and assistance that it requires.

I had decided not to join the Management Committee. I had been happy being part of our Coordination Committee, but as we moved to formal management, I was uncomfortable with the idea of evaluating other partners. Also, I thought that Anand's typically strong views on many issues would be best accommodated with him having to take official responsibility for them. I also trusted my co-founders to do the right thing and take my advice whenever appropriate.

The Management Committee would have a three-year tenure, with younger partners involved in sub-committees (HR, finance, campus recruitment, technology, etc.) to create pathways for future leadership. For accountability and transparency, the Management Committee would send monthly reports to the partnership.

We envisaged a transition from a three-person committee to a two-person structure in the future – we were aware that our governance model, like our compensation system, would have to evolve. Circumstances would conspire to make this look like an even more foresighted decision than it might have been then.

With all partners now equity owners, we needed more robust partner evaluation processes – this would be a key aspect of the Management Committee's work. Evaluations would focus on multiple dimensions: revenue and profitability, of course, but also client development, people management and mentorship, support for firm strategy, and overall behaviour and collaboration.

A Transformation

It is hard to explain how significant the governance reforms and moving to all-equity partnership were. The Dubai meeting had produced changes far more sweeping than any of us had expected. We had created the foundation for the most widely dispersed equity in Indian law-firm partnerships, and a management model that had the potential to survive the eventual departure of the founders while supporting the firm's growth.

I remember the process as being tremendously exciting. It just made sense to us emotionally, and in terms of our values, to open things up. There was little anxiety about implementing something unprecedented. On the contrary, we felt energised in the belief that all our partners were now on the same page. I believe these changes set us on a path towards a more resilient, sustainable institution and made it easier to weather the end of the A&O relationship and thrive as a fully independent firm. The timing, as it turned out, couldn't have been better.

Because things were about to be turned upside down in the staid and stable Indian law firm world.

27

The Amarchand Mangaldas Split and Lateral Movement

Our new equity and management structures faced their first test a few years later when the biggest firm in the country split dramatically into two, leading to unprecedented flux in the Indian legal market.

The Split

It has now (2025) been 10 years since India's then-largest law firm, Amarchand Mangaldas, became two separate entities in May 2015. This division was the culmination of a family dispute between the Shroff brothers, Shardul and Cyril, each of whom had been managing different regional operations of the firm.

The *Business Standard* reported it like this: 'India's largest law firm... will dissolve for separate businesses to be started by its managing partners and brothers Shardul Shroff and Cyril.'[71]

Given the size and influence of the legacy firm at the time, and the events that unfolded afterwards, this is the most significant single event to have hit the Indian law-firm world, down to the present day. The split not only reshaped the destiny of Amarchand Mangaldas, but also had a deep impact on the broader Indian legal market, including for us at Trilegal.

Why It Happened

As we have seen, the origins of Amarchand Mangaldas trace back to 1917. Over the decades, it evolved into one of India's premier law firms, and by 2014 had over 600 lawyers and a presence in multiple cities. Following the death of their father, Suresh Shroff, in 1994, Shardul and Cyril assumed leadership roles. Shardul managed the Delhi operations, overseeing offices in Gurgaon, Kolkata and Ahmedabad; while Cyril Shroff headed the Mumbai branch, with responsibility for the firm's South India offices in Bengaluru, Hyderabad and Chennai.

The passing of the family matriarch Bharati Shroff in August 2014, who held the largest single share in the firm, was the catalyst for the firm's division and a dispute between her sons in relation to her will.

The dispute escalated to the Bombay High Court in November 2014. Wisely, probably recognising the potential ramifications on the firm's reputation and operations, both parties consented to mediation. A panel comprising former Supreme Court judge B.N. Srikrishna, senior counsel Harish Salve and investment banker Nimesh Kampani facilitated the discussions. After nearly six months, a settlement was reached. The agreement allowed for the probate of Bharati Shroff's will, with Cyril agreeing not to contest its provisions, leading to the formal division of the firm into two independent entities.

Post settlement, the firm reorganised itself along the line of the existing regional management structure. Shardul Amarchand Mangaldas (SAM), the new firm led by Shardul Shroff, took charge of the Delhi, Gurgaon, Kolkata and Ahmedabad offices. Cyril Amarchand Mangaldas (CAM), under Cyril Shroff's leadership, managed the existing Mumbai, Bengaluru, Hyderabad and Chennai offices.

I offer no view on the merits of the positions of the two brothers or on the final outcome of the settlement. What is relevant for us is to look at the effect that the split had on the rest of the Indian law firm market.

The Lateral Explosion

The Amarchand Mangaldas split was the origin of meaningful lateral partner mobility within the Indian law firm world. Sure, the odd partner occasionally moved from one firm to another and at times a group of partners might leave to set up a firm, but this was unlike anything the market had ever seen.

The recruitment war played out on multiple fronts. Both SAM and CAM needed to establish credibility in each other's traditional strongholds – SAM had to build a presence in Mumbai and CAM in Delhi. This led to the most focused and aggressive partner recruiting the Indian market had ever witnessed.

SAM moved quickly to build its Mumbai presence, recruiting Akshay Chudasama as Mumbai managing partner (from JSA) and Shuva Mandal (a senior M&A partner from AZB). This shattered the age-old unofficial no-poach agreement that was rumoured to exist between the erstwhile Amarchand Mangaldas and AZB.

CAM was even more aggressive. Within a few months, Cyril stated that offers had been made to and accepted by close to 100 (!) partners from various law firms. The recruitment included Percival Billimoria (from AZB) to lead their Delhi office, the effective acquisition of Delhi-based MNK Law Offices (bringing four senior partners) and a broad sweep across the market: four more partners from Kochhar & Co., Harsh Kumar from Khaitan & Co, Piyush Mishra from Luthra & Luthra and litigation partners from various firms.

The ripple effect was immediate: AZB struck back by recruiting Ashwath Rau, an Amarchand Mangaldas old-timer who left the newly formed CAM, bringing Anu Tiwari, Dhruv Singh, Ganesh Rao, Nisha Kaur Oberoi and V.P. Singh with him.

But beyond these specific moves, something fundamental had changed forever. Ganesh Rao, one of Ashwath's colleagues who later joined us at Trilegal, puts it quite simply: 'It wasn't in anybody's imagination that you could move somewhere … until the split.' The Indian market for senior legal talent had transformed overnight from a traditional, conservative environment where lawyers stayed at firms for decades, to a more fluid one with the sort of partner poaching that took place in New York and London.

Broader Market Changes

The disruption went beyond partner movements. Some clients were shaken loose from long-term relationships, partly because they realised that apparent market certainties like the existence of a single Amarchand Mangaldas couldn't be taken for granted. To hedge against future disruptions, some clients decided to diversify their portfolios of legal advisers.

While most of Shardul's and Cyril's clients remained loyal after the split, the market had become more open to exploring options. Sensing opportunity, firms like Khaitan & Co deployed aggressive client and talent acquisition strategies. This wasn't just happening at the top end – mid-sized and boutique firms also saw chances to grab market share.

This competition for talent arguably fostered a more dynamic and diversified legal market. With this unprecedented reshuffling of legal talent and loosening of client relationships, every firm had to reassess its position and strategy, us included.

Our Response: Patience

We weren't indifferent to what was going on; it was just that we didn't really need to do anything. For the most part, we watched all this furious action from the sidelines.

From all accounts, many of our partners received offers not just from SAM and CAM but also from other firms caught in the crossfire. Unlike every other firm of any consequence in the market, none – zero – of our partners left. We felt quietly confident about the role of our partnership model in keeping our partners happy. With all our partners now owners of the firm, they had little reason to subject themselves to the uncertainty of unfamiliar people, structures and hierarchies at other top-tier firms.

Further vindication came from the fact that we actually attracted talent amid the chaos, instead of losing partners. Ravi Bandhakavi, a senior corporate partner in the undivided Amarchand Mangaldas, joined us with Vaibhav Kothari (who had previously been an associate with us).

Strategic Gaps and Opportunities

For the first decade and a half of our history, we had remarkably few laterals – Sumanto Basu, Sitesh Mukherjee, Srinivas Parthasarathy, Himanshu Sinha (who used to be with me at St. Stephen's and joined from Deloitte to lead our tax practice, having previously been in the Indian Revenue Service) and Yogesh Bhattarai (from AZB) comprised this exclusive club. Post 2015, several factors conspired to change this, with the Amarchand Mangaldas split being only one of them. We began making more deliberate moves to fill gaps in our service offering and add depth to existing practices.

Bhakta Patnaik (August 2016) joined from S&R Associates to head our capital markets practice. An NLS classmate of Nishant Parikh and Harsh Pais, he had built a strong reputation on high-profile IPOs and felt he needed a bigger platform. With Srinivas Parthasarathy taking a break from the law in 2018 to relocate to the Philippines, Bhakta had primary responsibility to build what has become a leading capital markets practices.

Nisha Kaur Uberoi (June 2017) gave us a competition law practice overnight. With a growing reputation in this specialised field, created by the Competition Act 2002 (which took practical effect in 2009), she brought experience in merger control filings and Competition Commission investigations from her time at CAM and AZB. This led to representations for Schneider Electric and the Aditya Birla Group.

Kannan Rahul (October 2017) from JSA strengthened our banking practice, bringing relationships with major domestic and international banks like Goldman Sachs, Standard Chartered and Edelweiss, plus valuable in-house experience from ICICI that gave him a client-side perspective.

Ganesh Rao and Aditya Jha (July 2018) from AZB filled another gap – we lacked a specialised funds practice. Their arrival brought relationships with large private equity and venture capital funds, including Morgan Stanley, ICICI Group and the International Finance Corporation. As we shall see, their importance to the partnership would extend well beyond their practice area.

More new capabilities were added by Rahul Arora (July 2019), who brought 15+ years in real estate transactions mainly in infrastructure and Kunal Gupta (December 2019) who established our investigations and white-collar crime practice with unique forensic investigation capabilities, reflecting growing government and corporate focus on compliance and whistleblowing.

Arjun Ghose (corporate, Bengaluru, February 2019), Harsh Maggon (corporate, Mumbai, September 2019) and Joseph Jimmy (banking, Mumbai, February 2020) were quality practitioners adding depth to existing practices – as we grew, depth became as important as breadth.

A Shifting Dynamic: From Outlier to Destination

Beginning with Bhakta and gathering pace, well-regarded partners from quality firms were interested in joining us. What had once been rare was becoming, if not common, at least no longer surprising.

We had to be selective. It was essential not to favour laterals over loyal home-grown lawyers who had put in years of effort with us and had legitimate partnership expectations. We took younger laterals only when we lacked internal candidates in specific practice areas that needed new partners for growing work volumes. Getting this balance right was crucial. Looking back, this was perhaps a 'moment in time'. Since 2020, we have generally promoted new partners from within rather than looking outside for younger partners.

The market was beginning to understand our model better. Home-grown and lateral partners were telling law school friends and colleagues in other firms that what we said about our structure and culture was (shockingly) true. This word-of-mouth validation was to prove critical in a close-knit legal community, where firms' internal workings are typically shrouded in mystery.

Finally, we were approaching critical mass. Our firm was now reaching a scale that allowed us to integrate new partners without disruption.

The Longer-Term Impact

The Amarchand Mangaldas split had shown that even the most established institutions could face disruption, that partner loyalty wasn't guaranteed by tradition or size, and that lawyers were willing to move for the right opportunity and culture. Our unique approach was beginning to look less like youthful idealism and more like smart, sustainable business practice. We had long thought we were the right platform for high-quality, independent-minded lawyers. The post-Amarchand Mangaldas split world was making that platform seem more viable to the outside world as well.

The timing of our Dubai restructuring (completed just three years earlier) now looked prescient. We had strengthened just before the market's biggest-ever disruption released a swathe of laterals into the market. As they say, sometimes good preparation looks like good luck.

While the number of laterals in the Trilegal system was becoming significant, it was no portent for what was to come in the 2020s. The lateral door that had cracked ajar would soon swing wide open.

28

The Long Kiss Goodbye

Few events in the life of a start-up have the potential to test institutional growth and resilience like the departure of a founder. For many firms, built around the personalities, chemistry and client relationships of their founding partners, such exits can signal decay, chaos or outright collapse. Which is why what happened at Trilegal in 2016–17 was significant – for the utter lack of drama that accompanied Anand leaving the firm.

A Restless Maverick

Anand had always been a maverick. Starting with his unusual route to the law as we saw in Chapter 3, his journey hadn't followed a conventional path. Those of us who worked alongside him for years came to appreciate – and occasionally brace ourselves for (!) – his distinctive qualities.

There was his booming laugh that could be heard corridors away, his capacity for plumbing the depths of the law with relentless focus and his utter inability to suffer fools. He once told an associate, now a successful partner at another firm, that he was better suited to working in a restaurant. In addition to eviscerating associates, his sharp mind could dissect complex legal issues, including in complicated sectors like telecoms and defence. Yet, alongside this legal acumen ran veins of restlessness and contrarianism that defined him as much as his professional skills.

Anand was almost a polyglot – speaking Hindi, English, Malayalam, Konkani and Marathi with varying degrees of fluency. This linguistic breadth mirrored his intellectual interests. He was as passionate about discussing Hindu mysticism and spirituality as he was debating politics or the finer points of foreign exchange control regulation. His support for legalising guns and prostitution in India raised a couple of eyebrows but reflected his willingness to stake out controversial positions when he believed in them, with persuasive supporting arguments.

'Prasad was always a bit different from the typical corporate lawyer,' noted one commenter on *Legally India* after news of his departure broke. This was a massive understatement that anyone who knew him would appreciate. These distinctive qualities that had made Anand a dynamic founder were, by the second half of 2015, also making him increasingly restless within the confines of conventional law-firm practice. His intellectual curiosity and contrarian thinking were butting up against what he was seeing as a growing sameness to his practice. This increasingly came up in conversations with the rest of us founders and me in particular, given that we were in the same office and chatted often.

His interests in politics and social issues – initially through a short-lived engagement with the Aam Aadmi Party (as a believer in free markets, he disagreed fundamentally with them on economic policy) – were deepening and the daily grind of law firm practice was delivering diminishing marginal returns to him personally despite his success at it. There was also a practical consideration – he felt he had earned enough money. Many successful lawyers realise this but are rarely able to act upon the realisation.

Managing the Exit

In early 2016, what had been occasional threats to leave solidified into a definite decision, following many internal discussions. Eventually, the firm sent out a carefully worded announcement to all colleagues:

We would like to inform you that Anand Prasad, one of the founding partners of Trilegal, has decided to leave the firm to set up his own independent counsel practice. As many of you know, Anand has always had a passion for political and social activism and this move will allow him to pursue these passions more actively.

As a first step, Anand will step down from the Management Committee effective March 31, 2016, with the intent to leave the firm on or before 31 March, 2017.

We are in the process of implementing a smooth transition of the firm's clients to other Partners and will ensure that all clients of the firm will continue to receive the same quality of service as they are accustomed to even after his departure. As part of the plan, Anand will gradually reduce active client management starting from 1 April, 2016. From then and until he leaves the firm, he will advise his clients jointly with other Trilegal Partners and lawyers with a view to effecting a smooth transition.

The announcement highlighted both Anand's contributions and his expansive approach:

Anand's larger than life personality has resonated through the firm from the very beginning. His contributions have been invaluable and he has helped grow and establish the firm to its current stature.

While we will doubtless miss his presence in the firm, this is an occasion to celebrate the years of his life that he has given to building the organiation and to support him as he embarks on this next, exciting phase of his career. We trust you will join us in wishing him the very best in the next stage of his professional life. And while he may no longer be a part of Trilegal, we hope to continue to work with him as an external counsel in the years to come.

Shortly after our internal announcement, *Legally India* reported: 'Trilegal founding partner Anand Prasad will be leaving the firm by the end of 2017. According to sources close to the firm, Prasad had been contemplating the move for some time and had discussed his plans with the partnership more than a year ago.'[72]

In an interview with *Bar & Bench*, Anand explained his thinking: 'After 16 years, I felt it was time for a change. I've always had interests beyond the law, including social reform and policy matters. The firm is in an excellent place, with strong leadership and a deep bench of talent. It's the right time for me to explore new avenues.'[73]

What followed was extraordinary in how ordinary it turned out to be – a carefully managed, year-long transition process designed to ensure minimal disruption to the firm, its clients and Anand's practice. Client relationships were systematically transferred, practice leadership was redistributed and the firm's operational structures were adjusted. This approach stood in stark contrast to the more dramatic splits and departures seen at other major Indian firms during the same period – notably the Amarchand Mangaldas split and the fierce lateral movement that it set into motion just a year earlier.

The Institutional Test

The significance of this transition extended far beyond a personnel change. One commenter on *Legally India* observed: 'This is a significant moment for Indian law firms – a founder leaving amicably shows real institutional strength. Most Indian firms wouldn't survive this.'

Indeed, for a firm founded just 16 years earlier, Anand's departure represented a critical test of Trilegal's institutional foundations. Would the edifice stand strong without one of its original pillars? Could the firm maintain its trajectory without the force of personality and legal talent that Anand had contributed?

These questions weren't lost on those watching from outside. Another reader comment captured the curiosity: 'Wonder what this means for Trilegal's management structure now? They had a three-person management committee, right?'

This was a practical question that required a practical answer. With Anand's departure, our three-person Management Committee would be down to two. Some people thought that as the remaining Delhi-based founder I should take his place, but I didn't want to, for the same reasons that led me to turn down the position in the first place. At the same time, I (and others) wasn't certain about how the balance would work. Delhi/NCR was a large part of the firm and would to some extent go unrepresented in management.

But the balance between Rahul and Karan was working well. Rahul was particularly keen that we maintain just two members on the committee, arguing that this would show that we didn't need one representative from each city in what had become a fully integrated firm. It was also a step in the direction of having a single managing partner at some point in the future.

On being asked if another partner would be brought into the committee, Rahul said:

> We'll figure that out, right now it is not necessary. You will hear more about it in the course of the next few months. Trilegal as a firm has always been very institutional. We've never wanted it to be about the founders; if you look at the name, you'll see that. In the future, we will set in place a professional management structure, which is independent of any individual personality.[74]

As we will see, we never added another partner and since Anand's departure, the committee has consisted of two members. This was another indicator of how far we had come from our original 'separate balance sheets in each city' structure.

Jonathan Brayne of A&O, no stranger to law firm leadership transitions after decades at one of the world's largest firms, sent us a short but thoughtful email that captured the moment: 'End of an era, guys. Very best of luck with the transition – but you're an institution now so I have no worries on that score.'

His confidence wasn't misplaced. By April 2017, when Anand finally left after the planned transition period, the process had been so smooth that *Legally India*'s headline was almost anticlimactic: 'Trilegal Co-Founder Anand Prasad Finally Leaves, As Announced Last Year.' The article noted: 'Sources within the firm confirm that the transition has been smooth, with his clients and practice areas redistributed among other partners.'[75]

What It Said about Us

The most telling aspect of Anand's departure was what didn't happen. No exodus of lawyers or clients. The firm didn't wobble or lose momentum. Revenue continued to grow, profitability wasn't affected and new partners – both homegrown and lateral – continued to join the partnership. In a market where law firms are often synonymous with their founding partners, I think it is fair to say that we had demonstrated a high level of institutional maturity.

Charandeep remembers how her initial feelings of concern were laid to rest. 'It was a very big question mark... is everything okay? Are we going to be alright? But then we came out beautifully and stronger.'

For Anand himself, the departure offered new horizons. Free from the constraints of law firm practice, he could pursue his interests in policy reform and social issues. For Trilegal, his exit and the quiet that followed transition was proving that, with the right approach, a law firm could indeed become greater than the sum of its founders.

29

Recognition and Renewal

On 9 April 2016, I stepped off a plane at JFK Airport in New York, bleary-eyed after the long flight from Delhi. I was in the US for meetings with potential clients and international law firms, and for my twenty-fifth reunion at SIPA – Columbia University's School of International and Public Affairs. As I switched on my phone and looked at my email, dozens of messages with the same subject line – 'Law Firm of the Year' – tumbled onto my screen.

They were all reacting to an email from Karan to the whole firm which had read:

Dear All,
   We always knew it but it's now official. According to Chambers we are India's best law firm!
   This recognition was based on independent research conducted by Chambers and included feedback from clients, peers and international law firms. The award is truly a recognition of all the hard work, effort and incredible team work that all our lawyers and staff have put in over the years.
   Take a bow everyone!

Trilegal had been named 'National Law Firm of the Year' at the Chambers Asia-Pacific Awards in Singapore.
   Waiting for my bags, I was overwhelmed by a surge of pride. We had always believed in what we were building, but recognition from Chambers, a respected industry commentator, felt really good.

A firm that had come into existence just 16 years earlier – a relative newcomer in a conservative profession dominated by traditional firms, some over a 100 years old, had been named India's top law firm for 2016. The long nights, the many little sacrifices, the constant push to prove ourselves – all of it felt a little bit more meaningful.

Celebration across the Firm

We arranged a town hall across the firm – simultaneous celebrations in each of our locations across India. Video links through Google Hangouts connected our offices as champagne corks popped in unison. Even across the slightly grainy video feed, faces beamed from screens, glasses were raised and a palpable sense of collective achievement vibrated in each room.

For many of our younger colleagues, this mattered – it validated the bet they had made on a maverick firm early in their careers. For the founders, it was a moment none of us could have imagined back in 2000. The years of being questioned about our model, the scepticism we had faced from the market – it made this recognition feel a little bit more validating.

The Founders' Moment

While congratulatory messages poured in from clients, competitors and friends at international firms, the exchanges among the founders carried a heartwarming blend of incredulity and shared achievement. We knew exactly where we had come from, and what this journey had meant to us.

Rahul captured the mood in an email to the rest of us:

> Gents,
> Just got back from the jungles of MP to this news. I think we've not done too badly even if we have to say so ourselves. Though now others are apparently saying so for us. We owe ourselves an extra special vintage of bubbly in London for this.

This referenced our upcoming trip to London for the farewell of David Morley, who was stepping down as senior partner of A&O. With Anand's recently announced plans to leave Trilegal, this would be one of the last occasions for the founders to celebrate together.

Rahul added a personal note: 'One other thing – my parents asked me to specially congratulate us all on this. They are probably happier than me.'

I responded: 'Our little firm hasn't done too badly eh…'

Karan's message highlighted what this meant personally and to our families: 'My Dad has forwarded the link only about 500 times to "near and dear". This is just awesome guys. Extra special celebration in London. What is especially nice is that all of us are still around together to savour this moment.'

External Recognition, Internal Evolution

The timing was meaningful, coming after a period of continuous change: Anand's departure announcement, the A&O relationship ending, moving to an all-equity partnership model and increasing interest from lateral partners.

But even as we celebrated, we were already deep into preparing for the next phase of our existence. Winning Law Firm of the Year raised the stakes. We were now an established player with over 40 partners and growing recognition. Success was bringing new challenges – how could we maintain our culture and values while continuing to grow and evolve?

Moreover, Anand's impending departure had precipitated a question we had only partially answered in Dubai: how should our governance structure evolve to deal with his departure?

Moving beyond Founders

We were already working with Brad Hildebrandt, an experienced law firm leadership advisor. His December 2015 session with the partnership addressed fundamental questions: how ready were we to move beyond founder-led leadership? Should leadership responsibilities be distributed more broadly? With Anand leaving, what should the Management Committee structure be?

Some preferred continuing with a three-member Management Committee, others felt comfortable reducing it to two, while a third group believed we were ready for a single managing partner structure. Brad's advice was measured: any change should be gradual. He recommended extending the Management Committee approach before considering a managing partner model.

The growing size of the firm meant we agreed to have a chief operating officer – we were finally ready to entrust significant day-to-day operations to someone who wasn't a lawyer and bring non-founders into management roles. But Brad felt it was too early for elections for leadership, emphasising that we were too small a firm for an election process. Elections – with manifestos, canvassing and potentially divisive campaigns – could create unnecessary friction in what was, after all, a commercial enterprise focused on delivering legal services. Cohesion and continued profitability was more important than electoral democracy.

The New Structure

By May 2016, a month after our Law Firm of the Year celebration, we had approved a new governance model with three key components:
- A chief operating officer would manage operations and support functions, acknowledging that professional leadership had become crucial.
- The Management Committee would go down to two members (Karan and Rahul, as discussed in brief in the previous chapter).
- A four-member Board would represent the partnership. Predominantly consultative, it would have a say in critical decisions like partnership agreement amendments, mergers or partner expulsions. Its composition was deliberately diverse: two founders (Sridhar and myself), a successful lateral (Sitesh Mukherjee) and a home-grown partner (Nishant Parikh). We wanted to signal that leadership opportunities existed beyond the founding group, and Sridhar and I were happy to have a formal role in management

outside the Management Committee. Moreover, it was beginning to be clear that Nishant was the outstanding leadership candidate from the next generation.

We also formalised practice groups for the first time – corporate, disputes and projects – headed by Nishant, Sitesh and myself, respectively. Practice differentiation was overdue, but there had been some resistance, particularly from Anand, who preferred a more fluid approach. But now, our scale allowed for clearer practice segmentation. Authority and responsibility were beginning to be distributed more widely, setting the scene for even wider participation in the future.

A Little Celebration

On 22 April, we gathered in London for David Morley's farewell – the last celebration that would include all the founders while still in the firm, as mentioned earlier. We enjoyed that 'extra special vintage of bubbly', celebrating both our award and our evolution into something well beyond what we had ever envisioned.

After more than 30 years in the profession, we are realistic about awards. The recognition is wonderful – it creates talking points with clients and motivates colleagues. But real kudos for a law firm comes through client praise, best demonstrated by them trusting you with more work. But it did feel good for our email signatures to carry the suffix 'National Law Firm of the Year' for the next 12 months.

Finding Our Purpose

The institutional changes we were making raised a deeper question we hadn't considered. In spring 2017, our new COO Sabiana Anandaraj sent an excited email to all partners: 'Congratulations all on the firm's new Vision and Mission statement – another step towards the journey to institutionalise!'

Sabiana had asked a simple question when she joined: 'What is the firm's vision and mission?' We had no clue; it wasn't something we had ever considered. But her corporate background brought structured thinking about institutional purpose.

After more than 15 years of existence the 'why' of our founding needed updating for our growing and increasingly diverse partnership. And, as we had learnt through previous reform efforts, the very process of articulating shared principles could serve to bring people together.

Designing an Authentic Process

Working with Brad Hildebrandt and then Aon Hewitt, we conducted 'Leadership Listening', where partners spoke openly about where we were, what we were proud of, what we wanted to change and what success looked like for us.

Common themes emerged – the first was an uncompromising focus on quality and excellence:

'Managing Crisis for Clients'
'Problem Solving'
'Not succumbing to undercutting and focusing on quality instead'
'Going after high value work and rejecting low margin work despite volumes'
One person was as clear as it could get: 'Best in the world at providing Indian legal services in each practice area'

The next set of ideas showed that we had succeeded in carving out a distinct identity for ourselves:

'Leaving a legacy'
'Building an Institution'
'Driving happiness and work satisfaction for every lawyer in the firm'
And simply: 'Being Different' – this was important and aligned well with our origin story.

We finally arrived at two statements that were short, crisp and meaningful to us:
- **Vision**: To be the best, most innovative law firm in India.
- **Mission**: To provide exceptional legal advice to clients and be the employer of choice, driven by our culture and industry-shaping work practices.

Living the Vision

For us these weren't marketing slogans but real aspirations. 'Best' encompassed delivering the highest quality legal services, being trusted advisors and an employer of choice. 'Most innovative' reflected our desire to continue to reimagine what a modern Indian firm could be. 'In India' emphasised our roots and Indian law expertise.

The mission balanced two equally important priorities: being exceptional lawyers and a great place to work. We established measurable goals: Top 3 rankings in every core practice area, Tier 1 status in major legal rankings, winning the *Financial Times* Innovation Award and being the preferred campus employer.

The mission and vision have guided many subsequent decisions – our growth and lateral partner additions from 2020 onwards reflected our commitment to being 'the best', while investment in bespoke technology demonstrated our innovation commitment. Even our decision to make our offices look and feel 'Modern Indian' is connected to the element of being rooted in India while being contemporary and forward-looking.

In 2019, RSG Consulting declared us 'Law Firm of the Decade'. We had learnt over the course of the decade that renewal and reinvention are not destinations but a never-ending effort. The award had been great, but our real challenge was to keep evolving while staying true to our principles. And that's always a work in progress.

30
The Guts of the Trilegal Lockstep: Our Levels-Based System

By 2017, we had evolved and fine-tuned what is now the guts of Trilegal's partnership system – a levels-based or 'gateway' structure that reimagined how lawyers would advance up our lockstep.

At its core, the system works like this: In order to hit the financial targets to advance through the lockstep, 100 per cent credit is given for work that a partner does themselves and 50 per cent credit is given for revenue from matters they refer to other partners. As partners advance through six distinct levels, they must progressively generate more of their targets through cross-referrals (from 8 per cent at entry level to 38 per cent at senior levels). To progress beyond Levels 3 and 4, a partner must promote lawyers from their practice to partner, in addition to meeting the financial targets.

The genius of the system is that as a partner becomes more senior, their focus shifts from 'what can I do for my practice' to 'what can I do for the firm and my colleagues', making individual advancement dependent on collaborative leadership and institution-building.

Note: The rest of this chapter details the mechanics, philosophy and implementation of this system. Readers more interested in the broader narrative of the firm's journey can skip ahead to the next chapter.

Building the Framework

A few years after our Dubai restructuring, the system we had implemented revealed a significant flaw. The criteria and roadmap for advancing through the lockstep were not clear. In particular, non-financial metrics had not been spelt out. This created two opposing risks.

As lawyers who understood the importance of due process, it was essential that fairness had to be done and *seen* to be done. There was discretion lurking in the administration of our lockstep which might not be exercised fairly. Our leadership (Rahul and Karan at the time) was trusted, but the success of any system should not depend on the identities of the people running it.

Ironically, at the other end of the spectrum, precisely to avoid allegations of unfairness, there was a risk that the Management Committee might default to financial metrics alone since non-financial criteria were vague. This could lead to a behaviour-distorting focus on revenue alone – exactly what we had always sought to avoid.

Further, our compensation system had no mechanism for rewarding exceptional year-on-year performance, re-exposing that old tension between fraternity and meritocracy. But our lockstep had worked well overall, fostering collegiality and building a culture that partners enjoyed. Any reform would need to preserve this.

External Guidance and Internal Deliberation

Brad Hildebrandt's consultation, which had helped restructure governance, also looked at compensation. Following months of partner discussions and additional advice from Aon Hewitt, we worked out the details of our levels-based compensation structure.

The approach maintained the financial target-based progression partners understood while overlaying clearly defined levels or 'gateways', each with specific financial and non-financial advancement parameters, as discussed previously.

Our 40-point lockstep was divided into six distinct levels, with automatic annual progression within levels but performance-based advancement between them. This created development runways – gaps between levels gave partners time to develop the business and capabilities needed for advancement.

The Philosophy behind the Framework

We built the system around interconnected principles reflecting how we thought partner responsibilities should evolve. Each Trilegal partner represents a unique financial unit with the capability and responsibility to manage transactions and clients autonomously. While advice should be sought from experienced partners and specialists from other practice areas when necessary, true partnership meant being largely self-sufficient within one's core practice area.

The main principles were straightforward: newer partners should focus on executing excellent work and building technical capabilities. As they mature, they should also build value by creating opportunities for others – first through cross-referrals, then developing new partners and ultimately building the firm's broader market presence.

The system began to acknowledge that senior partners' greatest contributions might not be measurable in traditional revenue metrics. Activities like managing the firm, mentoring juniors, building thought leadership or enhancing the firm's reputation through policy work would need recognition.

The Levels Structure

While financial targets increase by level, at Level 1, partners must achieve 92 per cent of financial parameters directly, with just 8 per cent from cross-referrals. By Level 5, partners may achieve nearly 40 per cent of their enhanced targets through cross-referrals (see Table 1). This created evolving incentives: as partners became more senior, their value shifted from just individual contribution to collaborative leadership. Advancement depended not just on personal success, but on the ability to work with and support colleagues across practice areas.

Table 1: The Level-Based System

Levels	Points	Total Revenue Target (₹)	Direct Revenue (₹)	Cross-Referral Revenue (₹)	Partner Development Requirements	Special Criteria
Level 1	5, 6.6, 8.3	6.0 crore	5.5 crore (92 per cent)	0.5 crore (8 per cent)	Entry via PSC Process	Automatic progression within level
Level 2	10, 13	8.75 crore	7.25 crore (83 per cent)	1.5 crore (17 per cent)	–	Merit-based entry from Level 1
Level 3	16, 19	10.0 crore	8.0 crore (80 per cent)	2.0 crore (20 per cent)	Must promote ≥1 partner	Practice building responsibility
Level 4	22, 25	13.0 crore	10.0 crore (77 per cent)	3.0 crore (23 per cent)	Must promote ≥2 partners	Enhanced leadership role
Level 5	28, 31	13.0 crore	8.0 crore (62 per cent)	5.0 crore (38 per cent)	Must promote ≥2 partners + support others' practice development	Collaborative practice building
Level 6	34, 37, 40	Flexible based on responsibilities	Variable based on role	Variable based on role	Management Committee-approved special responsibilities	Reasonable deviations permitted

Building Work for Others

Central to the structure was credit for cross-referral revenue. The idea of passing work to others was already embedded; having a lockstep meant sharing from the same pot. But with more partners, including laterals used to different systems, we needed to formalise this.

We limited referral credit to 50 per cent because greater credit should go to the partner secretly, and we wanted to avoid creating mere 'rainmakers' who weren't actually doing the work. To clarify, this wasn't actual money changing hands but notional credit towards lockstep advancement targets. This addressed a key issue in law firm economics: how to reward business development that doesn't directly benefit the business developer.

The Responsibility to Develop New Partners

Beginning at Level 3, partners were required to promote one junior colleague to partnership, and another at Level 4. At Level 5, expectations broadened to 'demonstrably supporting other partners' practice development'.

In a lockstep, firm growth fundamentally depends on partnership growth. We wanted this progression to create natural mentorship culture, where advancement required contribution to collective success. Partners needed to become stakeholders in the firm's broader health.

Flexibility at the Top

Level 6's flexible requirements acknowledged that senior partners' most valuable contributions might not be measurable in revenue terms.

I remember Shankh Sengupta, now head of our disputes practice, coming to my room some years ago and saying: 'I feel really sad when I see you hunched over documents – this is not what you should be doing for the firm at this stage of your career.' He made a strong point – senior partners should leverage their experience, contacts and market reach, not draft contracts that could be done equally well by partners with a third of their experience. I felt a sense of liberation: a well-established younger partner was exhorting me to create a second career within the firm, one that would benefit it intangibly.

Partners taking on firm-building responsibilities – building new practice areas, advising government on policy, expanding into new geographies or assuming management roles – might see a drop in individual revenue generation. But if they got it right, they could create significant value for the firm.

Fine-Tuning: The Bonus Pool

We introduced a small bonus pool representing 2–3 per cent of distributable profits, available to a maximum of four to five partners annually, providing a mechanism for recognising exceptional performance within the levels structure.

There had been resistance to this idea, including from me, driven by concerns about bad incentives and diluting our collaborative culture. We limited the pool to 5 per cent of profits and restricted how often partners could receive bonuses. This made bonuses more like 'thank you for extra effort' rather than year-on-year additional compensation.

Behavioural Changes We Expected

We anticipated several benefits:
- **Planning**: Partners would plan multi-year practice development towards the next level and not just focus on the current year's billings.
- **Collaborative Business Development**: Increasing cross-referral requirements gave partners financial incentives to appreciate and support colleagues' practices.
- **Investing in others' careers**: Partner-development requirements meant senior partners had tangible stakes in identifying and nurturing talent.

- **Balanced Development**: Combined financial and leadership requirements prevented advancement based solely on revenue generation.

Long-Term Institutional Implications

This had been the missing piece in our institution-building journey. The evolution from discretion-based progression to structured levels embedded our collaborative values directly into criteria for advancement. It would actually be easier for partners to succeed individually if they contributed to collective success through cross-referrals (there is only so much work that any one partner can do themselves).

The Management Committee's responsibilities increased significantly. Partner performance needed close monitoring to course-correct before gateway years – it is better to help partners reach targets than tell them they hadn't achieved them.

Despite increased objectivity, we maintained our 'black box' approach to individual compensation outcomes. Partners understood what they needed to do but received details relevant only to their own progression. Only the Management Committee knows everyone's numbers – even I for example, despite being a founder, have no access to them.

Balancing Culture and Performance

Throughout this evolution, maintaining our collaborative culture remained central. A learning for me was that cultural preservation didn't require avoiding all change, but ensuring that changes reinforced core values. The levels-based system arguably strengthened collaboration by making it an advancement criterion.

As we would discover, our levels-based framework would provide the basis for unprecedented growth over the next several years as well as the tools to manage it. What began as a solution to unclear advancement criteria turned out to be a driver of growth. We have made further tweaks to the system recently but the essence remains the same as in 2017.

Most Indian firms aren't explicit about compensation systems and advancement criteria for partners. But transparency without fairness would have been pointless, and fairness without clarity would have relied too much on leaders doing the right thing. The levels-based system gave us both.

But even the most carefully designed systems face unexpected tests. Ours was about to encounter a crisis that would challenge not just our compensation framework, but the very foundations of how we governed ourselves.

31
Crisis and Transition

As discussed in previous chapters, Trilegal's Management Committee had been in existence since 2012. Anand, Rahul and Karan were its original members. Anand stepped off the committee in March 2016 and left the firm in 2017. We had decided then to move away from the 'one city, one representative model' and the committee went down to two members. Rahul and Karan were the two members and by 2019, had been in management for seven years. The firm had grown significantly, and the levels system for lockstep progression required the committee to conduct several partnership reviews each year – its role had become more consequential.

By then, both Rahul and Karan wanted to get off the committee. Karan was moving to Bengaluru and did not want to go there as a committee member. Rahul was spending more time on policy-related work requiring extensive travel and Karan had begun to think it might be time to move to a single managing partner structure.

Informal discussions on leadership transition had begun well before Karan's Bengaluru move. This was also the year the partnership deed required us to re-evaluate our management structure. The senior group (Management Committee and Board) was slated to meet to discuss how to manage the leadership transition process but this meeting got delayed. In July 2019, Karan moved from Mumbai to Bengaluru.

Now, both members were in Bengaluru and both were reluctant to remain on the Management Committee. Up to this point, Sitesh had insisted that both Rahul and Karan stay on in management, arguing that founders still needed constitute the committee.

Formal Management Committee–Board discussions were finally scheduled for September 2019 to work out how to initiate the transition process. Regrettably, one partner, who had ongoing personal disagreements with the committee on an issue unconnected to firm management and governance, precipitated the process by writing to a group of senior partners, insisting that transition discussions be jump started. The email also contained certain thinly-veiled allegations against the committee and the founders. The result was a chaotic period of discussion, confabulation and intrigue, the likes of which the firm had never seen before.

The Crisis Unfolds

If anything so far has created the impression that we have always been an idyllically happy family at Trilegal, now is the time to address that notion. Yes, the founders had remained remarkably united on basic values, and the direction of the firm and relationships among partners had generally been harmonious. We had been free of the intrigue and politics that many law firms in India and abroad experience.

But, of course, there have been many disagreements over the years, including among the founders. Some of these have been quite deep. Our approach had always been to address differences among the senior leadership before going to the rest of the partnership. We remarked how this was what parenting guides recommended – parents should handle disagreements between themselves first and present a united front to the family.

In late 2019, we failed to do this, spectacularly. While the founders remained fundamentally aligned, that fateful email meant that it would no longer be possible to sort out the key transition-related issues among the senior partners and build consensus with the others. Perhaps we had become overconfident in our ability as founders to drive consensus and achieve the outcomes we believed in.

Consequently, following an extremely disruptive period in which many difficult discussions were had and unpleasant messages exchanged, on 7 November 2019, the Management Committee wrote to the partnership proposing the formation of a broad-based committee to develop a roadmap for governance transition.

The mail proposed convening to discuss: the current structure of governance and whether it needed modification; the process by which a new structure should be put in place; and the timing of the transition and what shape it should take.

As there had been loose talk suggesting that a small group had been making decisions on behalf of the wider partnership, we decided that any process to make changes to how the firm is to be managed would have to be overtly and self-consciously inclusive, transparent and representative.

The Governance Committee Process

The response to this proposal was encouraging. After a continued period of hard conversations, and no small amount of politicking, the partners who had volunteered to be part of the governance committee held their first meeting on 17 December 2019, followed by another on 8 January 2020.

There were three main questions:
- Did we need a new management structure or just a better process to select one?
- Should the new management comprise one, two or three people?
- What role should the Board play in the new structure, and how should it be composed?

The answers would touch on matters of trust, accountability and our long-term strategy towards building a lasting institution. By the January 2020 meeting, the direction was clearer: there would be a new management. Critically, and for the first time in the 20-year history of the firm, this would be selected through an election. The idea of a three-member Management Committee was rejected in favour of a two-person structure. Term limits for committee members and the method of selecting a Board were debated.

A third meeting, on 27 January, firmed up the framework. As the only founder who had never been on the committee and who was not planning to stand for election, I was asked to present the proposal.

We would elect a two-member committee for a three-year term, with each partner required to vote for two candidates. The election would be conducted digitally, by a third-party professional firm. The Board would be nominated – initially by the founders, in consultation with senior partners – with the intention of creating a more independent selection process in the future. Practice group heads would be rejigged and office heads introduced, creating a broader spine of leadership. The principle of 'one partner, one post' was adopted to ensure wider participation.

The proposal went to vote on 14 February 2020 and 48 partners voted and 46 approved. There was a clear mandate for reform. Elections were held shortly thereafter. Only two partners stood: Sridhar Gorthi and Nishant Parikh, and were elected unopposed.

Implementation

The new governance structure took effect on 1 April 2020, during the first wave of Covid-19. Sridhar and Nishant became Trilegal's first elected Management Committee. The Board comprised Rahul Matthan, Karan Singh, Charandeep Kaur, Kosturi Ghosh, Saurabh Bhasin, Delano Furtado and myself. Five practice groups were established with designated heads. Office heads were appointed in Delhi, Mumbai and Bengaluru. The changes were comprehensive but there was continuity, with several partners who had been in leadership positions continuing to remain involved.

There was an unexpected positive. Women, in the shape of Charandeep and Kosturi, were in the senior leadership of the firm for the first time.

What Had Gone Wrong?

In hindsight, none of us had acquitted ourselves particularly well through this period. While the firm had matured in many respects, we, the founders, were inexperienced in crisis management and defensive about the manner in which we handled disagreements.

As a consequence, the transition, which was on the cards in any case, took place in a tense, difficult and politicised environment, instead of in the orderly, consensus-building manner in which past changes to the firm's governance had taken place.

Rahul feels that our key strategic error was not having brought Nishant, the clear leadership candidate from the next generation, into the committee sooner. For Rahul, his hesitation to do so was based on a lack of knowledge of Nishant's capabilities and a sense that 'Nishant needed to mature'. Nishant, however, was convinced of his ability to step into a role in the committee right then.

Rahul reflected on the lesson, saying,

> When a change is required, whoever the successor is likely to be, we'll never feel they're completely ready for it. But as long as we feel that they are the right person, we just have to trust them, find a mentor for them on the job and get it done. I think the transition to Nishant was delayed by at least a year.

Sridhar feels that the underlying cause was that Karan's relocation to Bengaluru had left a leadership vacuum in both Delhi and Mumbai, creating a sense of disconnect with the leadership. And the founders hadn't been as consultative with each other as before – Sridhar and I had been more involved in firm-level decision-making in the past but had retreated to focus on personal and practice-related issues. As a result, the earlier cooperative 'secret sauce' among the founders had diluted and informal feedback wasn't finding its way to the committee.

No one doubted that the committee was acting in the best interests of the firm, but their approach to unpopular decisions was being seen as more top-down than desirable. Despite all this, Sridhar felt that but for the six-month delay, our historical goodwill would have contained the situation. But the six-month delay in transition planning turned out to be key.

For me personally, as someone with a deep dislike of confrontation, it was a very difficult period. Since I was perceived as someone who was relatively unbiased, I was dragged into many unpleasant conversations that I would rather have stayed out of. But the crisis brought us founders closer together and created a deeper sense of alignment, that has endured.

Karan agrees that mistakes were made:

> While we were fully committed to having open discussions on the transition process, we assumed that Rahul would continue in management and that we would be able to convince our partners of whatever solution we agreed amongst us. However, we hadn't asked partners what they felt. We thought we had all the problem statements and the solutions in our minds.

We had been true to our values and created a system in which each partner had equal say through their vote. However, despite best intentions, we hadn't given the fullest expression to this principle in practice. While some partners were trying to take advantage of the situation, perhaps others were just holding us accountable to our own ideals.

In hindsight, the six months from September 2019 to March 2020 were the most stressful and disruptive in the life of our firm. The 2020 elections were therefore more than a moment of significant governance reform. They were an assertion of growing maturity and the ability to deal with crisis. It had been messy and we had encountered serious disagreement, but we had channelled it into process, and emerged with something more stable and inclusive.

It is a terrible cliché that crisis often brings renewal. And we were in the process of going through a double crisis – first, management upheaval and, shortly after, the onset of a global pandemic.

We didn't know it then, but Sridhar and Nishant were taking over leadership at a time when the firm was on the threshold of the most spectacular period of growth that it had ever witnessed, one that carries through to the present day.

Part 6

Moving to Market Leadership

32
A Short Note on Numbers

What followed the governance crisis of 2019–20 was the most extraordinary period of growth in our history – growth so rapid and comprehensive that it transformed both our size and position in the Indian legal market.

Some readers might have found our story so far reasonably impressive – a successful start-up with new ideas and a lot of ambition. Interesting compensation and governance models, refined over the years. Others might ask, legitimately, 'Okay, that's all very well but what has this actually delivered? A few industry awards and some lawyers with decent reputations – but how do we really know whether any of this has worked in substance?

Here's the answer: our past had laid the foundation for a transformation that took place in 2020–25 that took everyone by surprise, even us. Revenue almost quadrupled, the size of the partnership trebled, and the firm may just have become India's largest, by both revenue and number of lawyers.[76]

In our first 20 years, we had built a moderately sized firm with a good market reputation – more with clients than with our legal industry peers – that at times exceeded its size. We did well on indicators like client satisfaction but market perception lagged. No longer. Our recent growth has been so dramatic that I struggle to wrap my head around the scale. With it, our standing has shifted – we are in every conversation about India's top firms.

And numbers don't lie. Here are key statistics shared at our partner meeting in May 2025 – the first performance data, to my knowledge, ever officially released by an Indian law firm.

Revenue

2001: Just under ₹2 crore
2025: Approaching ₹1,600 crore

At some point in 2024, we crossed the magic ₹1,000 crore mark for the first time.

This represents a compounded annual growth rate of 16 per cent over 25 years. However, what's remarkable is the recent acceleration:

2020: About ₹400 crore
2025: Approaching ₹1,600 crore

Revenue per lawyer has grown fivefold over the firm's lifetime, reflecting productivity gains through better systems, technology adoption and higher-value work.

People

2000: 6 founders and 2 associates
2025: 145 equity partners plus over 1,000 lawyers

Sometime in 2024, we crossed 1,000 lawyers. When the firm opened for business, we had fewer than 10. Again, it is recent growth that is striking – in mid-2020, the firm had approximately 350 lawyers.

Rahul captured the moment in a LinkedIn post: 'Trilegal, the law firm that a few of us set up nearly 25 years ago, crossed 1000 lawyers. No matter how successful we thought we would be in 2000 when we signed the partnership deed, I don't think any of us expected that, 25 years later, the firm would be this big.'[77]

Add non-lawyer staff and the firm currently supports the livelihoods of over 1,500 people and their families. The growth of our partnership shows similar acceleration:

> **2010**: 11 partners
> **2012**: 25 partners
> **2020**: 52 partners
> **2025**: 145 partners

We added five partners net in our first decade. We doubled that by 2012, then doubled that again by 2020. And we have almost trebled the partnership since then.

Demographics

The composition of the partnership has changed significantly. The founders happened to all be men and for many years we were rightfully accused of being a 'boys' club'. We promoted our first woman partner, Charandeep Kaur, in 2009, with Kosturi Ghosh following in 2010, but progress was slow initially.

Today, 34 per cent of our partners are women – likely the highest proportion among major Indian law firms. Kosturi recalled: 'She [Charandeep] and I were the only women in the partnership for a long time... it was a bit difficult at first – not because anyone made us feel out of place, but being women we were just different. It's good to see that we are now beyond the 30 per cent mark – it's a very different partnership today.'

Recent partner promotions reflect this shift, with women dominating:

> **April 2024**: 7 out of 11 new partners were women
> **October 2024**: 3 out of 5 new partners were women
> **April 2025**: 5 out of 8 new partners were women

Age demographics are striking too. We started by calling ourselves a young and dynamic firm. This was true; I was the oldest partner at 32. And, in some ways, we remain a young firm. Thanks to the recent promotions, 58 per cent of partners are under 40 and 81 per cent are millennials.

Our 2024 Board refresh reflected this diversity: three women, three founders, three lateral partners, with representation across practices and our three regions (Delhi NCR, Mumbai and Bengaluru). The physical expansion has kept pace. From the tiny offices of our foundation year, we now operate from six locations across three cities, occupying over 250,000 sq. ft of quality office space.

Practices

Our practice portfolio has expanded both in breadth and depth. The most striking growth since 2020 has been in newer or previously smaller areas:

White Collar and Investigations: 31.2x
Capital Markets: 23.5x
Real Estate: 22.4x
Financial Regulatory: 20x+

More established practices also saw substantial growth:

Corporate Tax: 8.5x
Disputes: 6x+
Funds: Nearly 5x
Banking: 3x+
Energy and Infrastructure: 3x+

We have also added entirely new practice areas: intellectual property, climate change, aviation disputes, private clients, trust and estate planning, and international trade.

Today's practice distribution reflects both breadth and depth:

General Corporate: 56 partners
Disputes: 23 partners
Banking: 11 partners

A Short Note on Numbers

Energy and Infrastructure: 11 partners
Capital Markets, Employment, Real Estate, Tax, TMT: 5–8 partners each

Clients

2001–12: 1,336 clients
2013–25: 8,698 clients

This reflects a mix of domestic and international clients across multiple sectors and includes long-term relationships and new clients. Billable hours have grown correspondingly:

2010–11: 326,590 hours
2024–25: 1,962,220 hours

This reflects not just volume increases but also the complexity and value of matters handled.
Industry-specific growth over the past five years has been notable:

Life Sciences: Nearly 8x over five years
TMT: Close to 4x
Energy and Infrastructure: Close to 4x
Manufacturing: 3.5x
Private Equity: 3x+

Standing

We believe that we are now one of only three full-service Indian law firms to exceed 1,000 lawyers, alongside CAM and Khaitan & Co Many of our practices are ranked in the top tier by market observers such as Legal 500, Chambers, ILFR (International Financial Law Review) and Asian Legal Business.

When we hit the 1,000-lawyer milestone in 2024, I reflected on what this meant in a LinkedIn post: 'The little law firm I was part of setting up with Anand Prasad, Karan Singh, Prem Ayyappa, Rahul Matthan, and Sridhar Gorthi in the year 2000 now has 1,000 lawyers. Hard to believe, given our rather humble beginnings – the professional and personal journey has been beyond our wildest dreams.'[78]

The response was overwhelming. Dozens of alumni, clients, well-wishers shared and even competitors sent congratulations. Former colleagues affectionately recalled memories of their formative years with us.

What This Tells Us

We have gone from start-up law firm to being (possibly) India's largest law firm. The growth spans every dimension – people, practices, clients and capabilities.

External factors have helped; our story is rooted in India's growth and the economic expansion of post-liberalisation years. But at the same time, we appear to have outpaced our closest competitors more recently – an independent survey suggests that the largest six law firms grew headcount by 83 per cent on average over the past five years – we have trebled in the same period.[79]

What strikes me is not just the scale, but what it represents in human terms. Each number represents careers built, clients served and relationships forged. The following chapters dig into the reasons for this growth – how the foundations laid over two decades enabled this unprecedented expansion.

33
The Power of Compounding

When Albert Einstein allegedly called compound interest 'the eighth wonder of the world', he was describing a mathematical principle that applies far beyond how your money in the bank multiplies year on year.

Our lockstep model has, particularly in the past 10 years, created its own version of compounding – one in which individual success drives growth through a process of creating new partners and consequent revenue expansion, which in turn contributes to firm building. Comparing the number of internal candidates who made it to partner in the five years before and after 2020 tells its own story. But partner promotions are only the tip of the spear of a broader effect that covers all aspects of firm growth.

The Lockstep Imperative

We have seen how the levels-based lockstep requirements introduced in 2017 incentivise partner promotion. At Levels 3 and 4, partners need to promote team members to progress through to the next level.

Economists would call this the 'positive externalities' of our system. When a more experienced partner mentors a candidate towards partnership, the mentor advances through the lockstep, the candidate becomes a partner and the firm gains another equity owner invested in its success. Each new partner eventually faces the same requirements, creating a cascade effect.

The Business Foundation

A partner sponsoring a team member for partnership must have a business case to do so. This requires demonstrating that they have enough additional work and client relationships to pass on to the candidate, and that they are not cannibalising their own practices in order to get through to the next level. Clearly, the overall profitability of the firm should not fall as a result of a new partner entering the partnership, however talented and well-liked they might be.

Partnership candidates are encouraged to build relationships with other partners and practices in the firm in the run up to making partner – this increases their chances of referrals after they get through. Since existing partners know that new partners are key to firm growth, they are invested in their success.

2020: The Mathematics of Growth Takes Over

The data reveals 2020 as a clear inflection point – the levels-based system introduced in 2017 was taking effect. While the firm had been growing steadily in the preceding five years, the rate of internal partner elevations took off in 2020. Through the 2020s, partners promoted in the 2015–19 period and our successfully integrated laterals were reaching lockstep levels that required them to promote candidates.

Partner promotion data over the past 10 years shows the acceleration of this organic growth. In the five years leading up to 2020, the firm promoted 19 partners – an average of just under four annually. In the five years up to March 2025, that number increased to 49 partners – almost 10 per year on average. This represents a 158 per cent increase, reflecting the compounding effect taking hold.

The growing new partner cohort sizes reflect this. The largest cohorts in the 2015–19 period saw four partners promoted. In contrast, the 2020–24 period saw cohorts of 6, 7 and 11 partners, with April 2024 representing the largest single promotion in the firm's history. The April 2025 cohort of 8 partners brings the total number of partner promotions since April 2020 to 57 – five more partners than the entire firm had in April 2020.

I often remark that my favourite days at work are 1 April and 1 October – the two days in the year on which we announce partner promotions. For me, this validates our system.

New Partners Means Firm Growth

When clients see expanded capacity and expertise within the firm, as represented by a growing number of partners, they feel more confident, tend to give more work and refer group companies or other clients.

As newly promoted partners develop their practices, their work volumes increase and they need more associates to handle their expanding workload. These associates develop skills and experience, and some will become partner candidates themselves in future years. As partners deepen their specialisation and build more focused teams, existing clients are more likely to give additional work and refer other clients. The client base compounds as individual relationships deepen and the overall portfolio expands. Growing partner numbers, expanding associate ranks and increasing client engagement create multiplicative rather than additive revenue effects.

Network Effects

Each new partner brings relationships and expertise that benefit others while expanding the firm's overall capability. A partner focused on private equity work might have the opportunity to introduce a capital markets partner to the client as they move towards an IPO. Corporate partners' joint ventures can fail or their clients can go bust, requiring disputes or insolvency specialists.

With almost 150 partners today, the scope for internal referrals is exponentially greater than when the firm had 40 partners. Fifty per cent attribution for cross-referrals towards meeting levels-based targets aligns firm growth objectives with financial incentives.

The expanding partnership creates capacity for larger, more complex engagements. Clients increasingly look for firms that can handle multiple aspects of sophisticated transactions. However, this virtuous cycle depends entirely on maintaining quality. The more partners we promote from within, the more rigorous our selection process must be.

Quality Control and PSC Discipline

Making up an increasing number of partners from within means you have to be that much more careful about the process. Promoting people who aren't up to the mark – particularly because partners may feel the pressure to promote candidates just to progress through the levels system – is a recipe for mediocrity, drops in profitability and worse.

As a result, our selection process has become tougher. Sponsoring partners prepare detailed nomination reports on candidates' capabilities, monitored for a year or more before they come up for partnership. Details of hours billed, transactions worked on and clients serviced are included, as are testimonials from clients and colleagues. The business case for partnership is much more important than it used to be, and is established between the sponsoring partner and the Management Committee as a threshold condition for a candidate to be considered.

A senior partner is appointed as lead assessor, conducting due diligence by speaking to partners they have worked with, younger lawyers they have supervised and clients. A report is prepared with details of issues to be explored during the actual PSC interview, which has largely followed the format we developed during the A&O years. The client simulation exercise has been dropped, in favour of a more rigorous technical assessment and a deeper analysis of the softer skills that go up to making a good partner – including personality, client and market awareness, and a sound understanding of how the firm itself operates.

Following an often intense PSC interview, a recommendation is made to the partnership, which then votes on the proposal through a secret ballot. As a testament to the rigour of the process – while sometimes candidates do not pass the interview (in some cases they can come back for another attempt six to twelve months later) – no candidate ever recommended by the PSC has ever failed to make partner.

The system is sustainable only if standards are maintained.

Cultural Transmission

When the system works, each partner candidate understands the values of the partnership and the value of being a partner. Requiring partners to develop partner candidates creates opportunities for technical and cultural mentorship. This means that the firm's culture stands a good chance of being transmitted to the next generation. Partners promoted as recently as 2019 are creating partners from their own practices in 2025.

At a recent event to celebrate our twenty-fifth anniversary, I puffed my chest out when I overheard a newly promoted partner explaining to a client: 'The system creates a cycle where success requires helping younger lawyers in our teams eventually become partners. As a result, every partner has a stake in building the next generation.'

The contrast between the five years before and after 2020 – 19 partners versus 57 partners – shows the power of good incentives. When individual advancement requires promoting other partners, and this in turn demands business justification, the outcome is compound growth. Internal promotion provides sustainable, compound growth rooted in culture and values, but there are also other ways in which a firm can grow its partnership. Our foundation had created the platform for us to take bolder risks and pursue more ambitious growth strategies.

34

Leadership, Scale, Risk and Growth

By 2020, we had reached a scale that changed the menu of strategic options available to us – we found ourselves in a fine-dining restaurant instead of a family eating joint. But the compounding story left me feeling that reality was more layered – this wasn't just destiny by lockstep playing out in some pre-ordained fashion.

While thinking about this, I recalled a conversation that Rahul and I had about our recent growth, which revealed two somehow competing explanations for our transformation.

The Importance of Leadership Transition

Rahul, like me, is a great believer in the power of compounding, but he feels strongly that there was another, essential ingredient to our growth – a big shift in leadership style.

As a technology lawyer, Rahul evokes what happens with successful tech start-ups:

> Karan and I constituted the Management Committee when we were an entrepreneurial firm, and we had an entrepreneur's approach to management. And there are very few entrepreneurs who have been able to scale. You can count them on your fingertips. Jeff Bezos, Mark Zuckerberg – beyond them, very few. You need to get someone else in... In Google, Sergey Brin and Larry Page were there, but they had to bring Eric Schmidt in. And Eric Schmidt does the scaling. Sheryl Sandberg does the scaling at Facebook.

This echoes Larry Greiner's classic 'crisis' of leadership, a version of which we had navigated back in 2012, when partner feedback in Dubai revealed the need to evolve from founder control to more institutional governance. There was no crisis this time around but nearly a decade later, we needed to pivot again. Just as Google brought in Eric Schmidt to move from entrepreneurial chaos to scalable structure, and Microsoft found renewal under Satya Nadella, successful firms often require new leadership styles for different growth phases. For us, this evolution came out of the crisis of 2019 and the elections that followed. 'We needed Sridhar and Nishant. We needed a different approach to scale,' says Rahul.

When Sridhar and Nishant became members of the Management Committee, they were keenly aware that they were following a period of great success, but they also felt the need to assert their own style. 'Rahul and Karan, with Anand before them, had been very successful, in many ways,' Sridhar acknowledged. 'But we needed to prove ourselves... We asked ourselves: "Okay, what's our way of doing this?"'

The need to carve out their own management path, while being mindful of their responsibility to steward the firm through its next phase, made them more willing to take what Sridhar called 'proper, calculated, strategic risks' for growth. This meant a departure from the more cautious style that had suited us in the past. Earlier, when we had less, the negative consequences of a risky decision could have affected the firm more severely. Now, they had the platform to be bolder.

Nishant was sharply focused on growth – he frames this as 'building the right capability stack and becoming the most meaningful law firm for our clients'. For him, the driving force was specialisation – he felt that we needed to expand our service offering. He said, 'We would do one or two matters for several clients but they would go to other firms for other work because we didn't have the practices.' Beyond breadth, depth was equally important: For instance, the market did not think of us as a serious disputes firm. 'We didn't have the numbers our competitors did,' said Nishant. The idea was to become embedded into our client's business, to work with them not only on events such as acquisitions or disputes but also to stay engaged with them in everyday operations. This is what makes advisors 'sticky' with clients.

His belief was that law firms had limited themselves to traditional practice areas and needed to take a cue from accounting and consulting firms who offered a wider set of services to their clients. This wasn't going to happen on its own. Nishant describes how he has spent thousands of hours over the past five years understanding market needs, trying to spot trends and identifying practices that needed more depth. Practically, as we will see later, this meant bringing in practices like climate, international trade, private wealth, compliance (particularly in financial services with regulators becoming more vigilant and aggressive) and corporate governance.

Nishant's approach to growing the firm has been tremendously successful. Earlier, we saw how he was identified early for leadership. But anointed ones don't always succeed. Nishant has. As a second-generation leader, he thinks about the firm like a founder and has developed the ability to see the larger picture in his decision-making – qualities that have been instrumental in our growth over the past five years.

Market Context: Why Timing Mattered

As Sridhar said, 'Almost by definition, lateral movement is a function of how we are perceived.' Our reputation was evolving from that of a promising medium-sized firm to one approaching the elite group that constituted the so-called 'tier-one'. Lateral partners from established firms could now feel that they were moving to something better rather than taking a step down.

Our success in bringing in quality laterals in 2015–19 laid the ground. 'They became very good brand ambassadors for the firm,' Sridhar noted. 'It was not just us saying "Look, look, we are meritocratic and transparent...", people from outside came in and said, "Dude, what they are saying – it's true."' This countered market narratives that if you left the elite circle of traditional firms, your career was 'finished'. Moreover, this wasn't just about professional success. As Nishant said, 'These guys became very successful here in Trilegal – but they were also much happier. Professionals really want that today.'

Word of lateral partners rebuilding better versions of their practices with us built a momentum of its own. This improved market perception, combined with our compounded scale, had enabled a change in our approach to strategic decision-making. As an excited Nishant says, 'I think we have the best set of partners ever assembled in India!'

Strategic Execution under New Leadership

As laterals succeeded, we became more comfortable with the idea of bringing in more experienced partners. Scale meant that the risk of any one prominent individual not fitting in had dissipated. It helped that what senior laterals wanted was changing. Sridhar cited the example of Sai Krishna, who joined from AZB: 'Sai came from a firm with a very different culture from ours ... but wanted to leave that for exactly the reasons we appreciated – growth, autonomy, equitable sharing, transparency, free flow of information.'

Nishant also admitted to being greedy: 'In my mind, I could see some great practitioners in other firms. And I always thought it would be great if we could have them with us.'

Increased risk appetite didn't mean lowering standards. To the contrary, it meant greater rigour. We applied strict filters: a lateral candidate had to bring a blue-chip practice that would add meaningfully to our capabilities, the highest possible reputation for competence and integrity, validated by clients, and their motivations had to align with our values.

As laterals testify (see next chapter), the process was demanding and the Management Committee imposed self-discipline. 'We first have to convince the Board, and then the partnership. That keeps us honest and maintains our credibility,' Sridhar explained. This means that for 9 out of 10 people who approach us, we politely do not take the conversation forward. This meant that Nishant and Sridhar spent hours getting to know potential laterals, explaining the uniqueness of our structure and creating the right expectations for them once they joined.

There was a competitive imperative too. In 2020, our revenues were around ₹400 crore, which we surmised was somewhat lower than our nearest competitors. 'We said to ourselves that if we don't catch up, it's a very insecure place to be... If we don't move up, we slip down,' Sridhar noted. Nishant was even more passionate: 'Growth is life.' Adding partners was not just about adding revenue but also about increasing the nodes of collaboration among partners.

Ironically, this happened during Covid-19 – after an initial slump, we saw a huge uptick in work. We needed more partners to do the increased work. Our capital markets practice shows how scale enabled strategic thinking. Bhakta Patnaik was the sole partner in a practice area experiencing a cyclic slump. 'He came to us and said: "There's a weakness – capital markets is a one-partner practice. Clients are asking what will happen if I fall sick?"' Sridhar recalls. Without an immediate financial case, we promoted Brajendu Bhaskar from within and brought in Richa Choudhary from AZB. The timing was fortuitous; within three months, the capital markets exploded.

The practice has since handled some headline-making deals. The Unnati Foundation listing was the first-ever NGO to be listed on India's Social Stock Exchange. The NTPC Green Energy IPO paved the way for sustainable products listings. They also advised on Harsha Engineers (oversubscribed 74.7 times), Premier Energies (which debuted at a 120 per cent premium) and Ecos Mobility, alongside HCL Technologies's pioneering overseas tender offer. Finally, the practice handled the Adani FPO that was fully subscribed but ultimately withdrawn after the Hindenburg allegations, a watershed moment that led to enhanced market disclosure requirements. 'From a revenue of under ₹10 crore, it is now a market-leading practice and crossed ₹100 crore of revenue last year,' Sridhar explains. Scale creates option value – the ability to make investments that might not pay off immediately but position you for opportunities as they come along. This included Vijay Parthasarathi and Vinay Sirohia joining from CAM in 2024.

With the pandemic as a catalyst, Nishant and Sridhar also drove a shift in the firm's business mindset, bringing greater commerciality to our practice. The chaos caused by the world coming to a standstill required the new Management Committee, finding their feet in management, to go back to first principles and evaluate how the business of the firm ran at practice and individual partner levels.

Navigating the uncertainty of the initial phase of Covid-19 was hard and at first required conservatism; the Management Committee adopted zero-based budgeting and was careful about distributing bonuses. But when results exceeded expectations, bonuses were enhanced and paid out immediately and salary increments given. This was noticed by lateral partner candidates. Sridhar recalls, 'Many laterals said that the way we conducted ourselves in the pandemic told them more about our values than anything we could have said.'

Scale and Compounding

Sridhar differs from Rahul on his emphasis on leadership transition being the key factor. He feels that the foundation was strong, and that our systems and culture were perhaps designed to promote compound growth regardless of who was leading.

What connects all these transformations – the ability to specialise, willingness to take risks, capacity to attract laterals and our enhanced market positioning – was scale. Karan is passionate about this: 'Scale is the horizontal feature that enables everything else.'

However, scale also brings challenges. As Geoffrey West identifies in his excellent book *Scale*, organisations face inherent growth tensions as they grow.[80] The same scaling that enables new capabilities can create complexity and distance from original values. Unlike cities, which become more innovative as they scale, companies (or law firms) typically become more efficient and bureaucratic but less innovative. This creates a challenge that many firms face and we will continue to – capturing the benefits of scale while maintaining the entrepreneurial spirit and cultural values that enabled it in the first place.

Older partners sometimes observe that the culture of the firm is changing, romanticising the past with comments like 'we are not the firm we used to be'. But Karan argues that things are better on balance; Trilegal partners have greater stability, wealth and status today than ever before.

The majority of partners agree that the firm's culture is positive and enabling, and behaviour that doesn't conform with our values is the exception. In my view, each partner has a responsibility to re-create the culture they yearn for; after a point, this can't be handed down.

Both Were Necessary

Through this analysis, two explanations for our rapid recent growth emerge. Rahul believes that leadership transition was essential; entrepreneurial founders needed to give way to leaders who could scale. Sridhar feels that it might have happened anyway. I think he is being modest about what Nishant and he have achieved in the past five years. You can of course never know what might have happened with different leaders, but the change in leadership style has been key to our growth in this period.

To me, the foundation built in our first two decades was the necessary but not sufficient condition for our transformation. Without the lockstep, the culture of collaboration, the democratic governance and the scale we had achieved by 2020, it would have been difficult to execute the aggressive growth strategies that Nishant and Sridhar adopted.

But having the right platform doesn't automatically generate the vision or courage to use it strategically.

What made the difference was leadership being willing to see the possibilities that scale created and bold enough to pursue them. The willingness to move beyond the cautious incrementalism that had served us well in earlier phases catalysed our latent potential into explosive growth. The foundation enabled the transformation, but it required new leadership to make it happen.

35
Becoming a Lateral Magnet

Our lockstep incentives had all but ensured that we would promote partners internally. But while we were growing our partnership from within, another form of compounding was taking place.

The Validators

We have seen how the lateral partners that joined the firm during the 2015–20 period had brought breadth and depth to many of our practices. What we hadn't anticipated was the impact this would have beyond their individual practices. Each successful integration iteratively validated that Trilegal was becoming a credible – and even attractive – destination for a certain type of high-quality, independent-minded law firm partner.

What might earlier have been considered a risky career move – joining a relatively young firm without the pedigree of the traditional market leaders – was now becoming a strategic professional choice. As I spoke to many partners who had joined us laterally, one name kept coming up: Ganesh Rao, who had joined as a lateral himself in 2018.

His own path to Trilegal began during a sabbatical. Says Ganesh, 'Everyone assumed I was leaving AZB, and people started reaching out – one of them was Nishant Parikh. I told him I wasn't planning to move, and even if I were, not during my sabbatical.' When he returned to work, he came across Trilegal in a deal between the Aditya Birla Group and Varde Partners. He says, 'I saw Yogesh Singh and

Sridhar Gorthi work together, and the positive dynamic between founder and non-founder partners was refreshing.'

This led to a series of meetings to join Trilegal and, soon after, Ganesh and his close friend and partner Aditya Jha (who has also played a key role as a validator) came on board. Ganesh felt that in his previous firm, his investment fund practice didn't have the freedom to grow – it was considered just a bolt-on to the corporate practice. As he says, 'Trilegal was the opposite, they offered a platform and support. That was a real pull.'

However, there was some uncertainty. Ganesh recalls, 'I opened my Trilegal laptop and had zero emails. Aditya and I still joke that we came with a full lunchbox and an empty inbox. But people like Sridhar, Nishant and Karan said, "Let's get on a plane and introduce you to people." That made a huge difference.' Going with senior partners to meet clients made him feel like a part of Trilegal, not just an add-on. And it worked. 'I wanted a firm where partners help each other, and I got it. You don't need to hoard relationships. People are aligned, both culturally and economically,' Ganesh reminisces.

Ganesh hadn't anticipated becoming an evangelist for other laterals, but he had the perfect credentials for it. He had been in two traditional firms with the same team, for 12 years, building a credible practice and being part of the inner circle. This career trajectory made him relatable to others whose practices were doing well but who felt that something was lacking in their professional lives.

Pre-2020, he spoke with Arjun Ghose and Harsh Maggon, who joined the firm. Post 2020, conversations with him were important for Shruti Rajan, Vishrov Mukerjee, Pranav Atit and Anuj Berry. Vishrov noted, 'I really only spoke to Ganesh, who was a college pal. Once I had a thumbs up from him, it was easy.' Pranav's experience was similar. He remembered that Ganesh said to him, 'Why are you wasting your time? A few years from now you'll want to come anyway – might as well do it now.' Shruti, who joined us in 2020, had a deeper connection – she was Ganesh's classmate from The West Bengal National University of Juridical Sciences in Kolkata, and they had worked together at the undivided Amarchand Mangaldas.

Anuj Berry also spoke to people he knew, including college friends like Ganesh and Shruti, and Bhakta, whose younger brother was a friend. He recalls, 'Bhakta said to me: "If you have an entrepreneurial spirit, this is the place for you. Don't expect that people will throw files at you here and you just execute. You have to hunt for your own work. If you have that ability, it'll be great."'

What Drew Them In

These partners shared something beyond professional ambition. As Shruti put it, 'There are two paths available to an Indian law firm lawyer – ride on someone else's credentials or bet on yourself.' Shruti and others felt that Trilegal's environment would support ambitious lawyers who wanted to back themselves.

Rahul Arora joined in late 2019. He found a culture that made collaboration intuitive. 'Last year, I worked with 39 other partners,' Rahul said. 'Show me a partner in another firm who can say that.' But what stood out most for me was him saying this: 'The first feeling you get is – I am in a place which is mine. You feel a sense of ownership.'

Shruti found that collaboration 'just happened' across practice areas: 'If I was pitching to a client, I would reach out horizontally to someone from employment or corporate – a peer – without thinking twice. That was not what I had seen elsewhere, where "collaboration" was only top-down.'

Nitesh Jain got the freedom to open a new litigation-focused office in the Fort area in Mumbai when he joined in 2021. He recalls, 'Nishant said, "Do what you want to build a practice ... identify and run that office." That's what attracted me – the confidence and freedom that was given.'

Vishrov, who joined in 2023, expressed it like this: 'The firm allowed me to be entrepreneurial without being alone.' I had goosebumps when I heard him say this – it was exactly how I had felt soon after we set up in 2000.

The trust that came with partnership also mattered. Richa Chaudhary, who joined in 2021, said: 'I was given a free hand, which made me feel like a real partner. I don't want to be called partner to be a glorified senior associate, but here I'm considered responsible enough to take the right decisions to build my practice.'

Pallabi Ghosal, who joined with Sai Krishna in 2022, liked the transparency: 'The level of financial data shared with partners is quite amazing. I don't think even the senior-most equity partners in traditional firms have any idea of how you can look at firm performance. When you're trusted with all this information, you feel like a real partner, not just one in name.'

Common themes emerged: transparency in explaining our partnership model during interviews, collaborative culture as the default rather than the exception, institutional support without micromanagement and partners quickly thinking long-term. As Rahul said, 'Once Trilegal, always Trilegal. The firm spoils you. It gives you autonomy, support and a culture that is hard to walk away from.' Nitesh agreed and said, 'I don't think I can go back to any other system now.'

Rigorous Integration

If a PSC is demanding in what it asks of home-grown partners, then similar standards must apply to laterals as well. Many laterals were surprised by the evaluation process. Unlike traditional firms, where even potential associate hires might meet only one or two senior partners, here lateral partners found themselves speaking with five or six partners, each weighing in with complementary questions.

Pranav was struck by this: 'It felt like real partnership-level due diligence, not one person making a unilateral call.' Anuj was initially puzzled – 'I thought, why am I doing this beauty parade, meeting so many partners' – but he found it gave insight into the firm's collaborative culture and helped his decision-making.

The process went beyond technical competence to probe cultural fit and long-term thinking. Pranav recounted what was supposed to be a casual, 10-minute conversation with Rahul that became an hour-long exercise: 'Rahul grilled me – not on law obviously, but on long-term thinking and vision.' While initially disconcerted, Pranav later realised why Rahul did that. He said, 'Rahul was probing because he cared about cultural fit. Now that I'm here, I want the same process to be followed for everyone!' Anuj was reassured by Karan when he was worried about cultural dilution. Karan told him, 'We have strong gatekeeping, not everyone makes it through.'

The thoroughness at Trilegal created confidence. Pranav concluded: 'The process had teeth. For every person who makes it through, I realised that many more don't.' Nitesh reflected similarly: 'You're speaking to partners, and you're actually asking them questions, they're encouraging you to ask more. That showed me what this partnership concept is really about.' Vishrov told me that our laterals jokingly call themselves 'the expats', reflecting their shared experience in joining the firm. They've found there's a common journey – a process by which an 'expat' becomes 'home grown' by working with many other partners and sponsoring their own candidates through the selection process.

The Senior Partners Arrive

By 2022–23, these individual success stories had created the foundation for something bigger – senior partners and their teams began to see the firm as the choice for the next stage of their careers.

Two key moves demonstrate this: Sai Krishna's team moving from AZB in 2022, bringing three partners plus associates; and Amit Khansaheb's team from SAM in 2023, arriving with eight partners and 40 lawyers. Sai and Amit were well established in their previous firms, but worried about their younger partners, wanting them to have greater control over their own careers.

For Sai, the move represented three decades of shared history, having roomed with Sridhar at NLS. An earlier move hadn't worked out when a key member of his team required partnership to move and we couldn't guarantee that. But in 2022, in a deal in which he was representing ASK Wealth Managers and Trilegal was acting for Blackstone, he came across Nishant and things moved fast. What stood out to Sai was the absence of conditions. When he offered to defer his own equity points until performance milestones were hit, prioritising junior partners, Sridhar and Nishant rejected this on principle: 'We're confident you'll hit your numbers.' And the results validated this. The team's performance exceeded expectations, working with existing Trilegal partners (Kunaal Shah in Mumbai, Rahul Arora in Delhi and Mridul Kumbalath in Bengaluru).

Back in 2000, Amit Khansaheb's father was an early client. 'I heard about Trilegal in the year it started because my Dad, when he was with Degussa Huls, was one of the first few clients,' Amit recalls. He describes himself as 'an open advocate' of Trilegal before joining, laughed at by former colleagues who said our model would be unworkable at scale.

The opportunity to join us arose in 2023 through personal connections, involving Anand and Nikhil Sachdeva from Amit's team (Amit claims he had wanted to join for 15 years before he did). The entire team was evaluated and he too liked the transparency of the process. But what he craved was the fraternity he experienced after he joined: 'For the first time in my life I felt that everything I do benefits everyone. If I bring a hundred rupees to the firm, everyone gets a piece of it.'

Individual laterals from 2015 onwards had served as market validators, showing that our model could work for people joining from other firms. The team moves of 2022–23 showed this had reached critical mass. While our internal growth created partners systematically and organically, our lateral partners allowed us to scale overnight. Quality lawyers weren't just willing to join us – they were bringing their teams, clients and accumulated expertise to us.

36

Specialisation: Building Practices from Within

Our scaling since 2020 resulted from multiple factors working together – compounding partner promotions, new leadership and lateral hires. Add specialisation to that; we had the ability to develop genuine specialists in key practice areas.

Specialist lawyers bring enhanced value. They can anticipate implementation challenges, predict regulatory changes and contribute to policy initiatives that can transform the relationship with a client from service provider to trusted adviser. Specialisation creates advantages that compound with other strengths. For example, we get significant renewable energy acquisition work not just because of our M&A skills, but because of our sectoral depth.

We are certainly not the only firm with specialists. However, what distinguished us was that our lockstep enabled early risk-taking in emerging practice areas before they became mainstream and obviously lucrative. Partners could invest time and resources without immediate economic pressure, developing knowledge ahead of market demand. The foundations were laid early, long before our recent growth. As the following examples illustrate, we had been making calculated bets on emerging practice areas throughout our first two decades.

Banking and Finance: Building on Regulatory Innovation

Our banking practice emerged from the intersection of client relationships and regulatory change. Karan was recommended to Citibank. As a firm with no banking pedigree, we offered to review their mandate letters for free, giving us a foot in the door.

Simultaneously, Karan's team, including Sawant and Ameya, was studying the then new SARFAESI Act of 2002. This Act enabled banks to get bad loans off their books by allowing them to sell stressed assets to specialised reconstruction companies without going to court – a major breakthrough in India's banking sector.[81]

Seeing that this created opportunities for asset reconstruction and securitisation work (packaging loans into tradeable securities), Karan bet on our building banking expertise, and when we showcased what we had learnt to Citibank, they were impressed. 'The first matter we got from Citibank was a first-of-its-kind securitisation. We did not know the product and were starting with a version of it that had never been done,' said Ameya. He remembers it as an exciting, intellectually stimulating phase – three people sitting late into the night in our tiny library, learning together and building excitement and camaraderie as they did so. This left a strong impression: 'It was exciting – here were the three of us, gung-ho about building something new. As a young lawyer, I was getting everything I liked: research, writing, drafting.' He recalls a similar encounter with Asia Pacific Loan Market Association (APLMA)[82] documents: 'None of us had read an APLMA document before. For three days, we read it cover to cover, discussed it and then built the confidence to do a new type of transaction.'

There has been lots of banking work since – project and acquisition financing, debt placements, regulatory work and much more. But a nice reminder of that early work came in 2021, when we advised Piramal Capital & Housing Finance on its ₹34,000+ crore bid and competition clearance in the Dewan Housing Finance Corporation Limited insolvency resolution. This was done under the 2016 Insolvency and Bankruptcy Code, and also involved competition law issues, but it doesn't take much imagination to trace these roots back to the SARFAESI Act work two decades earlier.

Energy and Infrastructure: Building Knowledge and Taking the Long View

My projects background provided the base, but building a comprehensive energy and infrastructure practice required luck, patience and selective risk-taking. Early matters like Power Grid, Petronet LNG and Bangalore Water with Vivendi and Suez helped build our projects CV. However, very early on we adopted an approach that would define the practice: investing in knowledge whilst the market was still developing.

It started with renewables. Initially, India's wind power projects were built mainly for tax breaks – investors could write off 80 per cent of costs in the first year. If you saw wind turbines in Maharashtra or Karnataka in the mid-2000s, they were probably owned by cricketers and Bollywood stars, for tax benefits, not project revenue. Contracts were a couple of pages long and largely meaningless.

In 2006, when British Petroleum (now BP) decided to invest in this emerging area with Suzlon as the construction contractor and equipment supplier, they weren't going to accept any celebrity-facing bare-bones contracts. With a referral from Sandeep Katwala at Linklaters in London (who had also sent us Vodafone), I found myself drafting India's first proper, bankable wind farm contracts from scratch, contacting lawyer friends in London for precedents and advice.

Halfway through this work, Sridhar introduced me to Mahesh Makhija from China Light & Power (now Apraava Energy), who needed help on a similar transaction with Enercon India as their contracting counterparty. Our BP experience won us the mandate. Nearly 20 years later, Apraava has 3,000 MW (megawatt) of renewable energy assets – almost all developed with Trilegal's legal assistance – and Mahesh Makhija has been a friend ever since.

Apraava's second project was with Suzlon. When negotiations began, Suzlon handed us a set of draft contracts, cheekily calling them their 'standard form'. I didn't know whether to feel flattered or to ask for a commission when we saw that they were the same contracts we had drafted for BP and negotiated with them!

The sector clearly had potential. Rather than waiting for new clients and business models to arrive in India, we decided to build expertise ahead of demand. We attended renewable energy conferences in Europe, learning about the trajectory of regulatory developments and how these projects fit into European climate commitments and evolving deal structures. I initially went by myself and later with Neeraj Menon – now head of the energy and infrastructure practice at Trilegal and one of India's top lawyers in this space. We built relationships with developers who we thought would eventually invest in India. And when they did, we knew how to relate their experience in Europe to the law, regulation and contract models they would find in India.[83]

Today, this practice is the largest specialist infrastructure and energy practice in India, risk-managing for clients in a practice area that depends heavily on local and central government authorities and the interpretation of regulation.

With Neeraj, Saurabh Bhasin, Nayantara Nag and Amar Narula as the senior lawyers, this practice also attracts significant M&A work to the firm. Next-generation partners like Gautam Chabra, Niharika Puri, Swathy Pisharody, Riyaz Bhagat, Megha Kaladharan and Astha Shrivastava add depth in diverse areas such as smart city infrastructure, housing and hospitals, water and waste systems, river system regeneration, large industrial developments and nuclear power. It is a matter of some pride that the majority of partners in the projects practice started their careers with the firm and have grown with the practice. The practice is complemented by the electricity, roads and airports sector-focused regulatory disputes practices run by Deep Rao, Jafar Alam, Janmali Manikala, Milanka Chaudhury and Vishrov Mukherjee.

We have used this knowledge-led muscle we developed in building the renewable energy practice to other sunrise infrastructure sectors, including battery storage, electric vehicles and green hydrogen. In each, we built knowledge ahead of the curve, sometimes partnering with industry associations and government on policy initiatives, giving us a 'ground floor up' view of the development of these industries.

Actis's renewable energy platforms in India illustrate how the market itself has grown in scale over the past decade – and our practice with it. In 2014, it set up Ostro Energy, aiming for 1 GW (gigawatt) of wind and solar capacity, which was sold to ReNew Power four years later. That was followed in 2017 by Sprng Energy, which reached close to 3 GW of assets, with a pipeline more than double that size before being acquired by Shell in 2022. The most recent venture is BluPine Energy, launched in 2022 with $800 million of committed capital and a 4 GW target across solar, wind and energy storage. We advised Actis on all these platforms, seeing each grow larger and more complex as India's renewable energy sector itself scaled up.

Technology: Geeky Interest and the Policy Interface

Our technology practice was perhaps the prime example of leading with intellectual curiosity rather than client demand. In the late 1990s, just a few years out of law school, Rahul Matthan wrote *The Law Relating to Computers and the Internet* – India's first technology law book (published in 2000). There was virtually no jurisprudence in this area then.[84] The timing was fortuitous. For the few technology-related cases that reached Indian courts, it was often the only available reference. An early software dispute decided by the Supreme Court cited the book, giving it credibility.

The post-Y2K outsourcing boom brought us HealthScribe, which pioneered the 'follow the sun' outsourcing model.[85] HealthScribe was cited in Thomas Friedman's *The World Is Flat* as one of the companies that kicked off India's outsourcing revolution.[86] This was in parallel with our work on technology and innovation policy through the Strand Life Sciences and Simputer engagements and the maps advisory work.

The HealthScribe entrepreneurs established FirstSource, initially a subsidiary of ICICI and also a client, expanding beyond medical transcription to broader outsourcing. Building on this, we handled World Network Services (now WNS), Citibank's captive outsourcing operation. Captive outsourcing became a big part of our practice, and years later we helped Telenor with their outsourcing initiatives across Asia. This was the foundation for our extensive work with global capability centres today.

Telecoms clients gave the next big impetus to our tech practice. Data protection work emerged from representing Vodafone and Telenor, who operated under strict European privacy regimes. As a result, we were among the first Indian law firms to understand the significance of data protection. This became crucial when Aadhaar was being developed – Rahul was pulled in by Nandan Nilekani to advise on India's digital identity programme. This has led to a deeper role for Rahul and his team in the development of law and policy in the tech space over the past decade and a half. This deep understanding of data protection led to us working extensively with all the major tech platforms. Today, Nikhil Narendran manages our Amazon and Google relationships, Apple work is in Jyotsna Jayaram's hands and Rahul focuses on Meta policy matters.

The practice, which now also includes Jaideep Reddy, Kirti Balasubramanian and Jishnu Sanyal as partners, advises technology clients and new age businesses on product development, industry-defining litigation, data protection and cutting-edge areas like cryptocurrency, digital public infrastructure and AI.

So, geeky individual passion, supported by institutional patience, has created lasting competitive advantage. By maintaining a commitment to understanding technology deeply – from the early days of the internet to today's AI and data governance challenges – we've built what we believe to be India's leading tech law practice.

Employment Law: From Side Hustle to Core Practice

Our employment law practice shows how one person's initiative, plus institutional support, can transform what I used to call a 'cottage industry' into a major practice. Employment law work used to be an offshoot of our corporate practice. When foreign companies established Indian operations, they needed contracts to hire country heads and local representatives. After joining the Employment Law Alliance around 2002[87], our employment work grew, but no one was able to give full-time attention to the practice.

The catalyst came when Ajay Raghavan came up for partner in 2009. His partnership proposal was a passionate pitch to build a dedicated employment practice. As Ajay said:

> I didn't instinctively love corporate law – I was more drawn to areas of practice with real people in them. The turning point came with a large telecoms client who said employment law advice in India was hopeless – too much quoting of the letter of the law, too little practical guidance. I researched the international market and found that not only did large firms have dedicated employment law practices but in jurisdictions like the US boutique firms did just employment. I saw a huge opportunity.

He recalls, 'There was initial pushback when I pitched employment law – I honestly didn't think you guys would say yes. We agreed I'd continue corporate work and build employment on the side. It was daunting, but I hit my numbers in year three – and after that, the practice just took off.'

Soon, Ajay was able to ditch his corporate work and focus exclusively on employment law until leaving the firm in 2020 for entrepreneurial and philanthropic opportunities. Where Ajay left off, Atul Gupta and Swarnima, whom Ajay mentored and trained, took over the practice and have grown it further. His legacy: a market-leading practice with six partners and a clutch of premium clients, handling everything from sensitive sexual harassment matters to sophisticated executive compensation structures – far beyond our simple employment contract beginnings.

Japan: Persistence and Relationships

The roots of our Japan-related work lie in the two years that I spent in Tokyo in the late 1990s with Ashurst. The connections I built brought us occasional work from Japan. By 2009, our Japan practice was respectable but not much more. As Charandeep was coming up for partnership, we were working on a deal for Yamaha Motors, and I noticed that she got along well with our Japanese clients. When I suggested that she build a Japan-focused practice once she became partner, we were aware this would require cultural sensitivity beyond legal expertise.

Building our Japan practice over the past two decades shows the value of long-term effort in a unique market. As Charandeep reflected: 'Initially we didn't know how it would go. But we persisted, with multiple visits a year, and today we have one of the largest Japan practices – and one led by a woman, which is something quite unique.'

In a country thought of as insular, we decided, counterintuitively, to lean into our Indianness. Charandeep would wear a sari during Japan trips; our tradition-respecting Japanese clients appreciated our respect for our own traditions. 'In Japan, I often hear: "You are a mini-brand in yourself, Charandeep san, because of what your firm enabled you to build." That would never have been possible without the support and trust I had here,' Charandeep says.

These stories reveal patterns that became crucial for our rapid growth after 2020. Timing mattered – our best initiatives combined knowledge building with key moments when that knowledge became valuable. Patience was crucial – whether in supporting Ajay's employment law initiative or investing years in Japanese relationship-building. Individual initiative, backed by institutional support, created competitive advantages that compounded over time.

We created a foundation that enabled the more aggressive growth strategies that Nishant and Sridhar would follow: initiative enabled specialisation, which attracted better work and better lawyers, leading to growth that enabled even more granular specialisation and further scale. This platform allowed us to take the calculated risks that would define our next phase of development.

37

Specialisation: Strategic Practice Development

The foundation we had built largely through organic growth and individual initiative created the platform for more ambitious practice development strategies. Particularly between 2020 and 2025, we moved beyond waiting for practices to emerge naturally toward strategic intervention – identifying gaps, recruiting specific talent and building comprehensive capabilities that could compete with anyone in the market. We had done this before, with litigation in particular, but this approach came into its own after 2020.

This shift required new leadership willing to take calculated risks and the scale to absorb them. It also reflected a maturing market where clients increasingly expected full-service capabilities and deep specialisation simultaneously.

Private Equity and Private Credit: Building from the GFC

The origins of our private equity and private credit practices demonstrate how market disruption can create unexpected opportunities. In the early 2000s, Karan and Sridhar had handled occasional venture capital and private equity work through niche mandates from houses like Morgan Stanley, CLSA and Barings, but we weren't yet on the radar for major deals.

The 2006–08 period saw private equity money flooding into India. Large US private equity and hedge funds established dedicated India pools. Deals were structured with exits planned via IPOs or strategic sales or by having recourse to the promoter by selling the stake back. When the global financial crisis hit, this boom turned to bust almost overnight. Portfolios crumbled, exits stalled and valuations collapsed. Fund managers were spending much of their time dealing with stressed investments.

By 2011–12, funds were grappling with underperforming investments and seeking advisers free of conflicts of interest to help navigate their way out. This created an opening for us. We hadn't been involved in structuring many of the original deals, and many funds wanted to use a different set of lawyers to get themselves out of the mess they found themselves in.

Nishant took the lead on this. We pooled our private equity, litigation, restructuring and financing capabilities. We discovered first-hand how the regulators, courts and arbitration tribunals looked at deal structures, exit rights and governance set-ups. Each investment had its own unique solution. It took deep efforts over years and a mix of aggressive and subtle strategies to help clients like D.E. Shaw & Co, Farallon, 3i, Citadel and Goldman Sachs exit their positions. We got a good taste of what works, and more importantly, what 'not to do' for foreign clients investing in India.

The foreign currency convertible bond (FCCB) disputes of that era became particularly valuable – combining finance, litigation and restructuring work. Through this crisis-related work, Nishant built relationships with fund managers who later joined or founded some of the largest global private equity fund platforms in India. Those connections became the foundation for our entry into the bulge-bracket space. By the mid-2010s, firms like Carlyle and Blackstone, Macquarie, Goldman Sachs, Apollo and CDC had become regular clients.

More recently, the Indian market has matured into separate pools of private equity buyout firms, VC and minority investors and private credit – each class of investor has developed its own playbook that has made India a booming market for private capital. The pattern mirrors other practice developments: market adversity created institutional opportunity. By committing to the post-GFC clean-up work, we built expertise, credibility and networks that have since underpinned one of our most important practices. Today, private equity capital drives significant firm growth, but its strategic foundations were laid during the market dislocations of 2008–12 – and in a young partner's willingness to take calculated risks in a period of great uncertainty.

Litigation: Building from Scratch

Building our disputes practice required a different approach. Anand's early experience as a litigator helped, but creating a serious disputes capability needed more than that. Shankh Sengupta, our current disputes head, insists that what we built is unique: 'Litigation is a practice steeped in tradition, often passed down through generations. We are an aberration. We've built our disputes group – which is about 10 years younger than the firm – from scratch and today we have over 25 partners.'

Initial disputes work came from overseas clients who lacked established litigation relationships in India, and expected their court-related papers to reflect the rigour and attention to detail they were used to in transactional documents. Many traditional litigation firms, focused primarily on advocacy, weren't geared up to do this. Our investment of time and effort to produce detailed, well-researched and nicely formatted briefs mattered to foreign clients. This led to representations of TIW opposite Shyam Telecom, and the Salvation Army and the American Society for the Prevention of Cruelty to Animals against the Wadias.

However, we still needed standalone disputes credibility. Existing clients were going to other firms for their most important disputes, regardless of how happy they might have been with our performance on transactions. This risked losing client relationships, just as lacking capital markets capability had done earlier. We couldn't build this internally. Disputes lawyers think differently and need day-to-day courtroom experience – predicting how judges might react, which arguments are likely to play out in court, and the interaction between procedure and advocacy. This would require a lateral strategy. Bringing Sitesh Mukherjee into the firm in 2009 marked our transition from decent litigation support to genuine disputes depth. His electricity sector regulation expertise complemented our power sector clients. Shankh Sengupta joined as a senior associate in 2011, became partner a few years later (in 2014) and now heads the practice.

A defining moment came during the FCCB crisis. As discussed, between 2011 and 2013, Trilegal was involved in the majority of the FCCB-related disputes in India, as many of our private equity clients held these instruments. Shankh recalls our success in protecting these clients' interests, which helped establish the firm's credibility in commercial courts and among leading senior advocates. This gave us the heft to represent existing clients like Telenor in a major corporate battle with its joint venture partner Unitech (as discussed earlier) as well as companies like Agusta Westland, implicated in a high-profile case for corruption in a matter relating to the purchase of helicopters by the Indian government.

When Sitesh left the firm in 2020 to become an independent counsel, his farewell email pointed out the growth of the practice: 'It has been a wonderful journey at Trilegal. I started the disputes practice at the firm with three lawyers, and now we are a team of 50.'

But the real transformation came after 2020, with Nishant driving a dramatic expansion. He believes that the dispute resolution practice 'should be the jewel in the crown for any full-service firm. It makes clients come to you when the stakes are high. And when we deliver results, the relationship strengthens and benefits the entire firm. There is nothing better than being with a client in the trenches.'

As a result, our disputes practice has seen a significant scale-up – from five partners and 30 lawyers in 2020 to 27 partners and 200 lawyers today, covering broad corporate commercial disputes and niche areas like financial and securities crimes, real estate, environment, insolvency, the energy and infrastructure sector, tax and intellectual property.

Partners such as Shankh, Anuj Berry and Ashish Bhan now lead a strong white collar defence practice. This is often supported by the investigations practice, led by Kunal Gupta, which offers forensic investigation capabilities supported by AI-based technologies and run by a multi-disciplinary team of lawyers, accountants and software engineers. Specialists in this practice now represent clients before criminal investigation agencies and courts and tribunals that adjudicate economic crimes.

Two recent matters illustrate how the disputes practice has evolved. We secured competition approval for the ill-fated Zee–Sony merger in 2022, but the deal faced multiple challenges. A wave of litigation followed: shareholder challenges to merger terms, competing broadcasters seeking to block the combination and multiple proceedings before the National Company Law Appellate Tribunal (NCLAT). Nitesh Jain, who led much of this work, recalls the complexity of steering parallel cases while trying to keep a billion-dollar deal alive. The matter ultimately collapsed in 2024, but it demonstrated the importance of a top disputes team inside a full-service firm.

Similarly, our work with BYJU's began on the transactional side, advising Blackstone on its billion-dollar acquisition of Aakash Educational Services. In later years, the focus shifted to disputes: investor petitions, governance conflicts and proceedings before the NCLAT. Both these cases reflect how the disputes practice has grown to handle sensitive, high-profile matters at the intersection of corporate governance and investor rights – often following from the same client relationships that began on the deal side. Reflecting the cross-practice nature of this engagement was the fact that three senior practitioners were involved: Yogesh Singh on the corporate side, Shankh and many others on the disputes front, and Sampath Kumar on compliance. Sampath recently rejoined the firm after some years away with a major accounting firm and is in the thick of the firm's enhanced offering to clients on corporate governance services.

From almost nothing in 2009, we are now well established as a top litigation practice. As Shankh notes: 'We are now a preferred destination for young lawyers starting their litigation careers, with even judges and senior counsel recommending candidates to us.'

Real Estate: Plug and Play

In mid-2019, Rahul Arora arrived for his interview with me at 360° in the Oberoi Hotel in Delhi armed with a file full of numbers and bold plans to grow his infrastructure projects-focused real estate practice. I was impressed with his enthusiasm and ambition, and following a few more interviews, he was voted into the partnership. Little did he know that the practice in which he was the first full-time partner would, in five short years, become India's leading corporate-focused real estate practice. Up to that point, only Kunaal Shah in Mumbai did real estate, but he was also doing other work.

Rahul's practice exploded, surpassing our (and his) wildest expectations. Our infrastructure practice provided him with a stack of clients, who were happy to get real estate advice under the same roof. Encouraged, we took on another real estate specialist, Mridul Kumbalath, in Bengaluru in 2021. This gave us strong real estate capabilities in Delhi and Bengaluru, but we lacked the depth to represent the sophisticated private equity and corporate clients who were increasingly dominating India's real estate market.

The solution: Sai Krishna joining us from AZB. The team of partners he brought with him – Pallabi Ghoshal, Shivani Kabra and Vivek Bajaj - included specialists in the M&A, financing and funds aspects of real estate. As Sai explained: 'We wanted to give clients a complete package, a one-stop shop that married the existing core real estate capabilities at Trilegal with corporate real estate experience.' A fortuitous lack of conflicts of interest meant that virtually all of the new team's client work could transfer.

'For us, the corporate plus real estate integration sets us apart. It's yin and yang,' Sai observed. This was well timed for how the market had evolved. Our larger real estate clients aren't traditional property developers but institutional investors. 'Between Blackstone, GIC (Government of Singapore Investment Corporation), Brookfield –

they own the biggest commercial office portfolios in India,' Sai explained. Collaboration fuelled this – Rahul Arora worked with 39 different partners across the firm last year. 'That's the beauty of it,' said Sai. 'Real estate might not be glamorous, but it touches almost everything – projects, tax, disputes – so it naturally pulls more partners in.'

Rebooting the Finance Practice

After Sawant Singh left the firm in 2008, and while Karan did some financing work, Ameya Khandge was our only dedicated financing partner for a while. With Aniruddha Sen and Kannan Rahul joining the partnership in the mid-2010s, we added more depth. Aniruddha focused on private credit and restructuring, and Kannan brought in excellent bank, private credit and sponsor relationships. The trio managed to grow a premium practice in a competitive and fee-sensitive market.

In recent times, private credit has offered great solutions to corporates and has become a large asset class in India. Deals in this space are complex and bespoke, requiring good quality lawyers to help structure and document them. We have doubled down on private credit and sponsor relationships, and added Joseph Jimmy, Prasan Dhar and Pallavi Banerjee to the partnership. We also brought in Aditya Bhargava, who has a nice practice focused on developing innovative debt resource raising solutions for banks and non-banking financial companies (NBFCs).

Nishant and Sridhar adopted a new vision for how our specialist practices should develop. Rather than remaining 'support practices' dependent on flow of work from the corporate and disputes teams, they believed that each practice should be standalone and independent.

'If you think like a support practice, you will not go out and promote your expertise,' Nishant explained. 'And if you're not promoting yourself and pitching for cutting edge work, you will remain dependent.'

This philosophy transformed how we approached practice development between 2020 and 2025. Instead of viewing employment law, tax, competition or regulatory practices as adjuncts to larger deal teams, we built them into market-leading offerings that could win mandates independently. Reflecting this approach, Himanshu Sinha and Samsuddha Mukherjee have grown the tax practice significantly in the past five years, Aparna Mehra and Gauri Chhabra joined from SAM to boost our competition practice (which already had Gautam Chawla and Rudresh Singh) and Shruti Rajan came from CAM to add depth to our financial regulatory practice.

The Virtuous Circle in Action

The strategic developments after 2020 reveal patterns different from our earlier organic growth, but equally powerful. Strategic thinking enabled targeted capability building, which attracted sophisticated work and top talent, leading to growth that created even more strategic options.

Our corporate practice, the largest practice in the firm, became what Nishant called a 'deals factory' – a machine for generating transactions that drove visibility and client relationships. This wasn't just about quantity; the market had evolved to demand size, scale and depth in ways that fundamentally changed how deals got done.

Many acquisitions today create intensely competitive bidder interest, and clients demand a level of engagement that only large, experienced teams can provide. 'Bidders win deals partly by demonstrating certainty of execution to sellers and offering to get deals signed in double quick time,' Nishant says. Large transactions routinely require lawyers from multiple practice areas – the number of lawyers staffed on a deal can run up to a few dozen.

Our clients also demand sectoral expertise. 'Focusing on sectors as diverse as financial services, technology, infrastructure and energy, healthcare, and industrials helps us offer the right mix of lawyers for every deal,' Nishant explained. With more than 60 partners in the corporate practice today, we can field teams with the combination of deal-making skills and sector knowledge that sophisticated transactions demand.

The firm has many excellent deal makers today, a mix of home-grown and lateral partners. Amit Khansaheb, Ashwyn Misra, Arjun Ghose, Delano Furtado, Gautam Singh, Harsh Maggon, Kunal Chandra, Vaibhav Kothari, Vishruta Kaul are just some of the senior lawyers that make us competitive for the most complex transactions.

We created a new virtuous circle: vision enabled acquisition, which attracted better work and better lawyers. This led to integration benefits, which enabled even more ambitious strategic moves. Since 2020, we have built market-leading positions not just through scale, but through thoughtful combination of internal development and external acquisition.

Network effects emerge – our real estate, litigation, private equity and employment law practices benefit enormously from cross-referrals from other practices. Different approaches suit different strategic opportunities – sometimes organic development, sometimes lateral acquisition, sometimes hybrid models that combine both. Underpinning everything was the lockstep. The economic logic was simple: Since everything goes into a common pot, there was clear justification for specialisation. Cross-referral attribution reduces friction in referring work to colleagues. The lockstep removed the barriers, allowing partners to do what came naturally.

This combination of organic foundation and strategic acceleration has, I believe, created a firm with both the entrepreneurial culture of our early years and the comprehensive capabilities that sophisticated clients demand. The challenge now is maintaining this balance as we continue to grow.

38

Support Functions: Getting Out of the Way

There is a pathology that lawyers worldwide share. Much of what we do is adversarial – litigation and negotiations – which means we express our views forcefully and are prone to viewing discussions as zero-sum games. And since clients invest millions relying on our advice, we must appear authoritative when delivering it. Put these two things together, and it means that we think we know everything, claiming mastery in whatever we are talking about.

This often extends beyond law into areas in which we have no special knowledge. Law firm partners who wouldn't dream of questioning a surgeon's medical advice will second-guess practice development strategies, technology implementations or HR policies. Professional conditioning that makes lawyers effective advocates for clients also makes it hard for us to accept non-lawyer expertise.

Worldwide, quality support functions enhance lawyers' ability to serve clients and firm leadership. In the past five years, we have finally had success in our support functions becoming mainstream and more integrated into our core legal work. We had to start by hiring support professionals whose skills were so strong that even sceptical lawyers would acknowledge their value. They also needed to have the tenacity to win approval from opinionated Type-A lawyers. Growing scale and reputation helped us convince top professionals to join, many of whom had never considered law firms. We are finally evolving from the amateur, *jugaadu* approach to support functions that characterised our early years.

Learning to Manage People

We always wanted a work environment that drew us into the office each day and created a positive experience for our colleagues. This meant an office that was more structured and fairer, and less hierarchical and formalistic than what the market offered.

Balancing that aspiration with the reality of running a law firm wasn't easy. We had no training on how to manage people and had contrasting views about what incentivised them beyond financial rewards. This made our HR practices rudimentary, and how an individual experienced life in the firm depended disproportionately on how partners and other senior lawyers treated them.

Being Obsessed with Performance Can Affect People Practices

In our early and middle years, we accepted and even rewarded partners who delivered excellent work but did so through being harsh with juniors or dismissive of peer – behaviour that undermines our values. Our *raison d'être*, after all, was to deliver high-quality legal services and some partners believed that this could be done only by driving lawyers hard, sometimes very hard.

When the firm was smaller, a financially successful partner's contribution to the bottom line was more significant, making us hesitant to take action against poor behaviour. Today, no individual partner can move the needle on our balance sheet, which makes enforcing values easier. With 145 partners, bad behaviour from a few is easily contrasted with good behaviour from many, especially when Gen Z is (justifiably) unwilling to accept treatment that even millennials might have tolerated.

Adopting Better Approaches

Our A&O alliance in 2008 was a milestone for our HR. Genevieve Tennant, their head of HR, generously shared policies, manuals and frameworks. Smita Gaur, a consultant who served as our de facto head of HR for years, spent time in London with A&O, adapting best practices for us. Allen & Overy's approach aligned with our commitment to equality and fairness – we have always maintained complete pay parity across practice areas, cities and genders.

Today, HR teams are embedded in practice teams. They discuss resourcing and productivity with partners while checking continuously with lawyers, essentially asking: 'Do you have what you need to be successful?' This creates an early warning system, identifying ahead of time that someone is unhappy and might quit, allowing swift intervention.

We've overhauled fresher recruitment, moving from 'big batch' campus hiring to pre-placement offers (PPOs) following internships. Over 80 per cent of our 70 graduate hires in 2024 came through PPOs – genuine assessment over several weeks beats snapshot interviews. The results are encouraging: first-year attrition among fresh graduates dropped from 40 per cent to 12 per cent (the market average is around 33 per cent). Instead of annual engagement surveys, we do 30-day and 90-day check-ins – regular conversations that give us a better understanding of how our young lawyers are faring.

Business Development: No More Fake Email Addresses

It's a truism that the most effective business development that a law firm can do is by its partners and other lawyers doing good work, and then speaking knowledgeably about it to clients. This principle hasn't changed for us. But much else has.

'Innovative' efforts like creating fake email addresses are no longer called for. Today's business development involves managing our international law firm relationships and LinkedIn presence thoughtfully and producing sophisticated materials to help partners with client development.

Business development for lawyers must be knowledge-based to be credible; given legal restrictions on advertising and the sophistication of clients, we can't just tell potential clients how great we are. The only sustainable way to attract work is by demonstrating subject matter expertise – writing in public forums, policy work and doing a good job when on the other side of a deal. Also, it pays to remember the human side; showing knowledge about shared interests in geopolitics, cricket or music to clients can create strong bonds as well as reflect intelligence.

Knowledge Management: From One Person's Initiative to Client-Facing Products

Our KM is still run by Aimi Hodiwala-Rale, but her team now includes eight lawyers and two support staff, operating across two divisions: learning and development, and client support.

Learning and development evolved with the launch of the Trilegal Academy for Excellence (TAE) in 2017, offering over 100 hours of annual programming structured around legal writing, professional skills, legal knowledge, and accounting and finance. We've just launched an AI-powered learning management system – TAE eCentral – that tracks and improves learning across the firm.

Client support involves taking our internal knowledge and developing it into knowledge products for clients and the world in general – which has become what Aimi describes as 'a mini publishing enterprise'.

We became the first Indian law firm with a YouTube channel through our Unlocked video series. When Covid-19 made professional production impossible, we pivoted to video chats on business and legal topics with clients in a more casual, DIY style. Our Private M&A Deal Trends Report uses our own data and experience to create insights for the M&A community.

Professional Leadership across Functions

As mentioned earlier, making our support functions more relevant to our work required bringing in credentialled professionals whose capabilities would command respect. Appointing Sabiana Anandaraj as our first COO in 2016 was a turning point. As Karan said when she left: 'Sabiana joined us when we were starting a journey of institution building. That meant changing our attitude towards creating systems and processes.'

Parul Gupta joined as head of HR in 2023, bringing almost a decade of senior HR experience from Microsoft. As Sridhar observed: 'When we were a small firm, no really talented HR person wanted to work for us. As we are growing larger, we are attracting top people.'

Finance: A Story of Indiscipline

And that brings us to finance.

Law firm economics isn't rocket science. It depends on a sequence of closely interlinked processes: diligent time recording, careful management of work-in-progress (inventory), prompt invoicing and the challenge of collections. This is what translates intellectual effort into revenue.

But law firms, unlike many other businesses, can't predict the intake of new clients or how much business they might get from an existing one, particularly since retainer business contributes a low proportion of revenue for most large Indian firms. Services are provided first and payment received later, often much later. This means a high component of fixed cost and a low component of 'predictable cash flow', one of Karan's favourite phrases on law firm finance.

This puts extraordinary stress on making timely collections. Unlike businesses that have access to bank debt, working capital facilities or customer advance payments, law firms must rely almost entirely on disciplined collection of outstanding invoices to maintain cash flow.

Our partners aren't great at this. When it comes to servicing clients, we are world class but when it comes to financial responsibility, something seems amiss. We have long struggled with the most fundamental business disciplines of all – time recording, timely billing and, most importantly, collections. This dysfunction is confounding when considered against our fantastic recent performance. As Karan notes, 'This is what has been counterintuitive in this phase of scaling. Imagine how much better our recent growth would have looked with financial discipline.'

Indiscipline is admittedly concentrated among a minority of partners, often some of our busiest and most successful ones. I think several factors contribute: success and financial comfort may breed complacency. Our partners' relative independence and professional autonomy, coupled with our consensus-building culture – which has led to light touch management – may have undermined financial responsibility. There are also psychological factors; partners can feel insecure about sending large bills, worried about client relationships. Ironically, when bills arrive months after work is completed, clients may forget the scope and quality of work done, forcing us into the awkward position of offering discounts to keep the peace.

We've begun implementing targeted measures: partners with significant unbilled work face restrictions on team expansion and building development expenses. Financial discipline has become a metric for bonus eligibility and partnership selection, since an associate with poor time recording habits tends to become a partner who doesn't send bills on time. Our new CFO is planning to enhance technology use in the finance department, creating hope for systemic improvement. But this nut remains to be fully cracked.

Technology: A Different Evolution

The next chapter looks at the unique path of our technology evolution. While Avnish Kshatriya recently joined to head the function, lawyers are deeply involved in imagining how we use technology at Trilegal.

The Challenge of Scale

As we grew from 52 partners in 2020 to 145 today, and from tens of lawyers to over 1,000, each support function has had to negotiate this dramatic increase in scale. Simultaneously, our clients have become more sophisticated in their expectations from us – demanding, for example, better knowledge products and information security on the one hand and the deeper use of AI on the other. So, as these functions evolve into genuine practice enablers, improving them is a continuous process. But at least that old lawyer pathology of dismissing support expertise is ebbing, as our support functions themselves have upped their game.

39
The Lawyer-Led Innovation of Our Technology Backbone

Rahul Matthan personally registered the domain 'trilegal.com' through Network Solutions soon after we decided to call ourselves Trilegal in early 2000. In 2025, Microsoft recognised the firm as an 'AI first mover' in India and South Asia. Between these moments lies a story of technological evolution and lawyer-led innovation.

What began as a homespun 'cheap and best' approach, driven by the fact that initially we didn't have enough money for big investments in equipment and software, has transformed into a sophisticated legal technology infrastructure. Our IT system 'processes over one million transactions a year and maintains 99.98 per cent uptime for critical systems' (I am told this is a good thing). En route, we had to ensure that growing sophistication supported rather than hindered how our lawyers work, while reflecting and building on our collaborative culture.

First, We Need Email

From the very beginning, our approach to technology was driven by lawyers who understood both the law and the technology, rather than techies trying to understand how lawyers function. We had some interesting options for our email system in those early days, before Office 365 and Google Workspace made corporate communications plug and play. Rahul, thanks to his interest in computers and

The Lawyer-Led Innovation of Our Technology Backbone

technology, drove our tech strategy. He roped in Anurag Johri, a friend who provided IT solutions for start-ups, as our IT consultant. Anurag established an email server running on Linux – chosen not for the ideological reason of it being open source but simply because it was cheaper. Using anything else would have meant paying licence fees, which we saw as an unnecessary cost.

When Nikhil Narendran joined as an associate some years later, he was struck by our unconventional approach. He said,

> When I joined, the person handling IT was Johnny [Johnny Pinto]. He did everything, from configuring laptops to troubleshooting systems. We used a lot of open source and free tools. For instance, our email client was Thunderbird – something I loved as a techie, but it shocked me because every other law firm I knew used Microsoft.

The system worked, just about, until growth and changing needs demanded something more robust. The story of Anurag calling Rahul shouting 'Who's Panna?!' in exasperation, when a lawyer with that name crashed our email by emailing several dozen retreat photos to all@trilegal.com is part of firm lore.

Another test came with a memorable incident in the early noughties. Heavy downloads were spotted by our fledgling IT department, slowing emails and Internet access on our fragile dial-up connection. The Head of IT was asked to investigate. He called Rahul back, short of breath, and said, 'Sir, the files are all porn!' The firm obviously had a no-porn-at-work policy and serious action was deemed necessary. The IT Head was beside himself. He said, 'Sir, it's one of the female lawyers!' None of us had thought that reprimanding a young woman for downloading porn would be part of our job description.

Clueless about what to do, a partner call was arranged. One of us suggested that the downloaded files be examined more closely, either because he had more of his wits about him or perhaps because of a deeper interest in the subject matter. The list of files was summoned and reviewed. All the files had the same name, with a code of cryptic letters and numbers next to them – 'Grey's Anatomy S1E1', 'Grey's Anatomy S1E2' and so on.

Imagine our relief at realising that this was a 'mere' copyright violation and that we wouldn't have to confront the 'female lawyer' for something far worse. She was summoned and told to lay off activity that could harm the firm's IT system and its reputation. But the cognitive processes that led our IT head to see the word 'anatomy' and jump to the conclusion 'OMG, porn!' remain a mystery.

Beyond the comedy, this incident highlighted the realities of managing technology in a small but growing professional services firm in the early 2000s. Bandwidth was precious and individual usage could impact the entire organisation. But this was still early days and being relatively low tech had its advantages. As Kosturi Ghosh observed: 'What was really great then was no smartphones, which meant no constant email. Once you left office, you were off the email grid.'

From Survival to Strategy

Upgrading our email systems meant moving to Microsoft. But this was more than an email system change – it also surfaced a commitment to software compliance. This, similar to our decision to be squeaky clean on taxes when we set up, wasn't necessarily the norm in small businesses. This was also informed by Rahul's professional experience. He was representing the design software makers Autodesk on copyright violations, conducting raids on architects' and designers' using unlicenced software. Determined that we would never face the same situation, we maintained more software licences than we had employees, making sure that no one could point fingers at us.

Our lawyer-first approach often meant that we were ahead of the curve on technology adoption. We were probably the first Indian law firm to roll out a BlackBerry to every lawyer, first to shift to laptops for all and, by 2011–12, before 'cloud' was even a thing, we had moved to Microsoft servers and adopted Office 365.

Early adoption sometimes came with risks that provided learning experiences. A big lesson arrived dramatically during a cable cut that cut off access to Office 365. Our system was brand new, and we had only one route to Microsoft's servers. For two days, we were completely locked out of our email – there was no backup system. Lesson learnt. A fundamental principle that would guide all IT infrastructure decisions was adopted: Redundancy is paramount. We immediately implemented Mimecast, which we still use. It copies every email we receive on Office 365 before it reaches us, so if Office 365 fails we can access Mimecast and function normally.

The decision to move to Microsoft servers wasn't driven by tech fashion trends but by organisational necessity. Our decentralised structure required systems that could work seamlessly across locations. As Nikhil explains: 'There are of course no "headquarters" for Trilegal. We started in three cities together. That same decentralised, collaborative mindset is in our IT too – our document management system, our data lake for documents, is built to be decentralised and interoperable with other firm-wide software.'

Early cloud adoption proved prescient when Covid-19 arrived – we had been ready for remote working long before 'working from home' was a thing. 'That early investment paid off,' said Nikhil. What seemed like a luxury and perhaps risky technology bet in 2011 had become essential infrastructure by 2020.

Custom Solutions for Unique Needs

When Sabiana joined as COO, and we could afford to become a little more sophisticated, we evaluated existing enterprise resource planning (ERP) solutions for the essential activities of time recording and billing. We couldn't afford the state-of-the-art Thomson Reuters system we would have liked, so we custom-built our billing software instead. This was another example of the consistent choice we made – to build tailored solutions rather than accept off-the-shelf options. This was driven not by abstract technology preferences but by understanding what we needed and refusing to compromise. It became a nice metaphor for our overall approach as a law firm: if existing models don't work for us, we will create ones that do.

Consequently, apart from our Microsoft backbone, which has become basic infrastructure for most law firms, we've built or customised almost everything ourselves. This includes the ERP, client relationship management (CRM) systems and document management systems (DMS). Our time-recording and billing system evolved through multiple generations – starting homespun, moving to OSource (a domestic start-up when we began to work with them) and eventually migrating to Microsoft Dynamics (now Dynamics 365). Each transition prioritised the user's experience, building systems where the front-end looked as close as possible to what our lawyers were used to. 'What we're using now is two generations away from OSource, but still looks and feels quite like the original system,' explained Rahul.

Our IT systems architecture reflects the workflow of our firm. When a new client file opens, it starts in the CRM system, tracking business development history. The engagement letter is created from CRM information. Once the engagement is confirmed, the matter shifts to the ERP for time recording and (eventually) billing. Mapping lawyers to a matter involves our human resources management system (HRMS). So, when a matter is opened in the ERP, it pulls the matter number from CRM and staffing from the HRMS. The time recorded in the ERP then flows back to the HRMS for lawyer appraisals. Enough acronyms for you? The logic of this system was conceptualised and built from scratch by us, rather than buying expensive solutions like Elite (the benchmark Thomson Reuters system for law firm enterprise management).

Document Management: Solving the Unsolvable

This custom approach proved particularly valuable in document management – historically one of the most challenging aspects of law firm technology. Commercial solutions had failed spectacularly. We tried MatterSphere from Thomson Reuters, but it didn't work for us, lacking mobile solutions when our litigators were already using iPads extensively in court.

So, we built a solution from scratch: a custom, AI-powered DMS built on Microsoft's SharePoint system. This places us in rare company; we're the first among India's largest law firms and among a handful globally to achieve this, something recognised by Microsoft in a published case study.[88]

Innovation as Institutional DNA

Three years ago, we formalised our decades-long 'mixing and matching, developing and trying out' approach by creating the Digital Innovations Group (DIG). As Nikhil emphasises: 'Our innovation team includes lawyers, information security folks and legal technologists, all working together daily. That means our tools remain co-designed by the people who actually deliver legal work.'

The DIG is a symbiosis between IT professionals and lawyers, including people like Dipti Sharma (an engineer who became a lawyer and now leads our legal tech function) working with Dhruv Nagarkatti (our chief transformation officer, who joined us from PwC). Nikhil himself is an engineering college dropout. This combination means that innovation supports lawyering.

Our AI approach exemplifies this philosophy. Rather than buying generic solutions, we worked with partners like Lucio AI to build tailored AI tools for various activities, including invoice review and compliance audits (more about AI in Chapter 40). 'Lawyers don't want to reinvent their workflows and therefore need to be in the room when legal technology is being built,' says Nikhil. The importance of this initiative meant that in addition to Nikhil, Karan is also part of the leadership team on AI adoption.

Technology Enabling Culture

Our current IT operations has grown dramatically to support the firm's growth. Email infrastructure alone encompasses approximately

32 TB (terabyte), growing at 6 TB annually. File storage exceeds 32 TB, comprising more than 43 million files, stored primarily on a multi-cloud environment hosted on more than 40 servers. Our IT infrastructure tracks over 3,000 devices in real time – a dramatic evolution from when large email attachments could bring us to a grinding halt.

This infrastructure enables the data sharing that makes our lockstep work effectively. Our almost 150 partners get end-to-end visibility of their practices through dashboards providing near real-time data about hours, active files, amounts not yet billed to clients and outstanding invoices, accessible on both laptops and mobile devices. This transparency, which also enables accountability, would have been unimaginable in our early days (and is still rare in other Indian firms).

Cross-referral tracking that supports our levels-based system requires integration among CRM, billing and performance management. Technology makes it easier for us to reward collaboration systematically rather than relying on informal recognition. Our security philosophy balances protection with autonomy. As Rahul notes: 'We have a fairly open approach to IT. Anyone can bring whatever device, whether Mac or anything else, and we will configure it for our system.'

Supporting Individual Initiative

Years ago, when Nikhil was thinking of leaving to build legal technology solutions elsewhere, Rahul told him: 'When you're at Trilegal, why go outside? Build it in the firm.' Perhaps Rahul was seeing a bit of himself in Nikhil here. Nikhil believes that this captures something essential about our approach – enabling people to mould individual interests to the firm's needs rather than restricting them to traditional roles.

After Nikhil's impressive presentation to the partnership on our digital innovation projects in Dubai in 2023, Sridhar and Nishant told him: 'Even if you take a hit in your book [revenues] because you're spending time on this, don't worry – just do it.' As Nikhil reflected, 'When I came in, I didn't fit into the Trilegal Bangalore culture at all. But the firm overlooked my shortcomings and helped me build on my strengths.'

What Technology Means for Us Today

Technology expenses account for over 11 per cent of the firm's overall expenses (excluding salaries) – high even by global standards – reflecting our belief that technology is helping us to be better lawyers. Over the last three years, our IT budget has grown by over 40 per cent year on year, reflecting a deep shift in how we view technology – from grudging expense to competitive advantage.

The habits formed by early financial constraints, forcing non-standard solutions like Thunderbird, created a DNA that serves us well today. The inability to afford commercial software led us to build tailored systems, and the need to coordinate across cities drove early cloud adoption.

It is clear to me that our willingness to build custom solutions rather than accept off-the-shelf limitations reflects the same independent thinking that shaped our choice of partnership structure. Just as we rejected traditional law firm hierarchy, for democratic governance and wide profit-sharing, our technology evolution rejected conventional wisdom about purchasing enterprise software in favour of building systems aligned with our specific needs and style.

40

Impact, and Lessons for Institution Building

It is difficult to write about your own impact without sounding self-serving. But here are some thoughts on how we may have affected the Indian law firm space. We don't claim sole credit; other factors will doubtless have been at work as well.

Legal journalist Reena SenGupta says that Trilegal made 'institutional values plausible in the Indian legal market' and changed 'the expectations of an entire generation of lawyers – in terms of fairness, transparency and voice'. Other market observers identified the two biggest factors shaping the Indian law firm market over the past 20 years – the Amarchand Mangaldas split and the emergence of Trilegal. (I'd add to this the reforms that Khaitan & Co made a decade or so ago.)

Impact on the Legal Market

Opening Up the Equity Conversation

Our partnership model was fundamentally different from anything that had come before. As discussed throughout the book, we started with salaried and equity partners, capped founder equity and introduced an all-equity lockstep. A legal guide noted, 'Trilegal stands out in the Indian legal landscape for its all-equity lockstep model, which emphasises transparency, democracy and meritocracy.'[89] I think it is fair to say that our model has prompted others, traditional firms and newer ones, to rethink their structures, creating a discernible shift across the profession towards broader equity distribution.[90]

A legal market recruiter identified two landmark innovations by Indian law firms. First, Amarchand Mangaldas democratised associate hiring through merit-based campus recruitment, moving away from the old solicitor route[91]. Second, Trilegal did something similar for partners, creating a meritocratic equity structure that other firms took a decade to start catching up with.

Governance

We always operated on the principle of 'one partner, one vote'. We transitioned away from founder control and held our first democratic management elections in 2020. Since a partner can be removed with a 75 per cent vote, it has been possible, for over a decade, for the Trilegal partnership to get rid of the founders.

As a result of Jyoti Sagar's unprecedented stepping back in 2013, to our knowledge JSA is the only other large firm with a similar governance approach. Wider participation of partners in management outside controlling families has become much more common in large firms.[92]

Influence on Newer Firms

Allen & Overy's David Morley commented that 'it was not just the governance framework that impressed us – it was the fact that the founders capped their own equity to create a future-facing institution'.

Reena SenGupta described Trilegal as 'a role model' for younger founders. In her research for Resight India[93] she found that 'Trilegal's story had encouraged many to start their own firms'. Our model – non-family, institutional, meritocratic – has become aspirational. Some breakaway firms are 'trying to build differently, often echoing Trilegal's early path'. Our success has 'legitimised the idea that new entrants can challenge legacy structures, without dynastic backing'.

Some firms like Argus Partners and DSK Legal have apparently adopted structures similar to ours, at times with advice from people who know our system.

Why Change Remains Limited

Despite our examples, only some firms have adopted this model. Several factors explain why. Firms that could have acted didn't move early enough, and change later becomes reactive and unsustainable. Many founders maintain a 'sole proprietor mentality', focusing on extraction versus building something that lasts. Changing a legacy system may require a clean break.

With six equal founders, we had to share from the beginning. A client noted that we 'applied a corporate governance framework to the firm in terms of building institutions, whereas there's usually a promoter mindset to how many other firms are run'.

Yogesh Singh, who heads our corporate practice, feels that many comparable firms 'have tried to do what Trilegal is doing without taking one final step'. Other founders are unable to 'share without ego because they feel that as they are bringing in the business, they need to be rewarded disproportionately'.

Our Approach to Wider Impact

We didn't intend to change how law firms operate, but have tried to do our bit towards broader professional and social objectives.

Policy Work

Rahul's work on technology policy, from early engagement with Nandan Nilekani on Aadhaar to his decade-old *Mint* column, has been exceptional and exemplifies our approach to policy work – persistence and focus on impact.. This has led to involvement in behind-the-scenes pro-bono advice on digital public infrastructure, advice on UPI[94], ONDC (Open Network for Digital Commerce) and the DEPA (Data Empowerment and Protection Architecture) framework, data protection, privacy[95] and AI regulation – contributing ideas quietly rather than just seeking access to policymakers. Other practices, like energy and infrastructure, have worked with state, central and foreign governments on policy reform.

This work is supported by the firm. Senior partners are increasingly expected to use their experience for original and public intellectual contribution. This is becoming the culture – younger partners have picked up this baton, with regular involvement in industry associations and government appointed committees.

In 2022, Karan and I co-founded Trustbridge[96], a policy research and impact non-profit foundation that aims to improve the rule of law for better economic outcomes. We contribute time, ideas and connections, in addition to funds – active participation in trying to make change, not just financial support to a cause we like.

Enabling Genuine Pathways for Women Partners

We have 34 per cent women partners today, possibly the highest percentage at major Indian law firms. We are not interested in paying lip service to diversity; women partners contribute in unique ways to and improve people practices, partnership dynamics and client retention. Having many excellent women partners isn't just the right thing to do, it is also good business.

The lockstep and PSC require us to promote on merit alone. This means intervening early to ensure that competent women lawyers have the confidence and skills to reach the PSC and have a genuine shot at partnership. Our growing ranks of women partners are role models for those on the path.

Mentorship, evaluation and parental leave systems reduce attrition and normalise ambition. Our maternity policy and lockstep flexibility (partners can choose to temporarily freeze their points for personal reasons) help women lawyers have families. When Richa Chaudhary became pregnant soon after she joined, she was surprised by the support. She recalls, 'The support that I got made it possible not just for me to sustain my practice through that period, but to grow.'

The Agami Partnership: Legal Innovation and Access to Justice

Our long-term partnership with Agami[97] represents a commitment to supporting legal innovation and access to justice, with initiatives like the Data for Justice Challenge, which created a hub for sharing and building information to improve justice delivery.

Agami also works on developing online dispute resolution (ODR) mechanisms in partnership with NITI Aayog and other institutions, boosting technology-enabled dispute resolution in India.

Social Initiatives and Community Impact

The Ocean Cleanup project approached us for legal work on systems to collect plastic where rivers enter oceans. The initiative has become so popular that associates are waitlisted to work on it.

Our Karam Foundation partnership supports female law students from underprivileged backgrounds with personal mentoring time from partners, going beyond the internships they requested.

Our long-term work with Catalysts for Social Action (CSA) in Maharashtra means engagement with systems reform in childcare. Rakesh Tiwari, a trustee at CSA, described our role as 'quietly pivotal'; lawyers help with compliance, process design and long-term sustainability.

Many partners see corporate social responsibility (CSR) as an extension of the firm's values. 'You can't claim to believe in fairness inside the firm and ignore inequality outside it,' said Karan. Yogesh Singh describes the firm as offering a 'whole life' approach to supporting lawyers who want to contribute beyond their legal work.

10 Lessons for Institution Building

Based on our internal experience and the market changes we think we've influenced, here is what we have learnt about building lasting institutions.

Founders Create Culture, but Must Step Back Eventually

Initially, the firm's identity and the founders' personalities were deeply intertwined – we worked through common values, effort and mutual trust. Each of us had unique strengths that created a powerful counterbalance in our foundational years. We were opinionated and ambitious, disagreeing sometimes on practical applications of our values. But we trusted each other's intentions. We compromised for harmony and survival, creating a culture of consensus. As Edgar Schein said, 'The only thing of real importance that leaders do is to create and manage culture.' In accommodating each other, we were writing the firm's cultural code.

However, we also learnt that we would have to let go. Institutions that last must move beyond their founders. The 2012 Dubai retreat marked a shift from founder-led to something broader. The 2020 elections took this one step further. A critical mass of partners had to feel shared ownership for us to develop the alignment we aspired to. And once things open up, you can't go back.

Find a Mentor

The founders lacked mentorship; no one showed these inexperienced lawyers how to build practices or handle the complexity of running a law firm full of flawed, ambitious humans with messy emotions. Moreover, the uniqueness of our model meant we had no one to copy. Our solution was to lean on each other and learn from our many mistakes.

Part of what held us back from seeking advice was the perceived need to project high confidence. We couldn't be seen to not know what we were talking about, internally or to clients. That alpha approach got things done, but sometimes created an echo chamber. Not having mentorship made us more aware of the need for it.

Culture without Structure Can Only Get You So Far

For several years, we relied heavily on belief, instinct, energy and informality. While we were a small firm, that worked well. As we grew, we felt the limits of culture without structure. We expected people to behave institutionally but hadn't built the institution.

To scale our values, we had to embed them in processes: lockstep compensation, structured evaluations, democratic governance and transparent advancement criteria. What's more, we kept writing it down – our partnership deed is often ammended, rarely consulted and contains the source code of our culture, open for all partners to see.

Find Ways to Tap into Internal Initiative

Many of our practice areas and systems were built from within. Aimi built KM from scratch. Ajay built employment law when others weren't thinking about it. Rahul, and then Nikhil, built our tech stack to reflect our working practices.

If the opportunity exists, people with initiative will grab it. Laterals like Ganesh Rao and Aditya Jha in funds, Rahul Arora in real estate, Nitesh Jain building the Mumbai litigation practice and many others saw the opportunity and ran with it. The flexibility to experiment and the willingness to let thoughtful initiative take its course has become part of the firm's DNA.

Establish Trust First, Collaboration Will Follow

We chose high trust over constraints; we shared client relationships across offices even before unified financials. The lockstep and referral credits made this economically rational, but the foundation was trust.

Most people respond better to faith than suspicion. As Richa Chaudhary noted: 'At Trilegal, every single action shows that faith and the culture that "I trust you". That makes a huge difference.'

Another lateral partner was surprised that he could plan his own business development trips without permission. We were surprised that he was surprised.

Lasting respect comes from working with others and consistent contribution to the collective, and not from intellectual heft, big books of business or fancy titles.

You Have to Balance Collegiality and Merit Continuously

An enduring challenge has been balancing collective culture with recognition of exceptional performance. We wanted credit sharing and collective thinking, but effort and outcomes must also have consequences. The lockstep reduces economic competition between partners, while advancement criteria and bonus pools recognise performance. But this balance requires constant work – what works today may not work in a few years' time.

Flexibility Enables Resilience

We've made numerous pivots: altering our lockstep structure, moving to all-equity, bringing laterals into a firm that had largely grown organically, getting into and out of the A&O relationship, bringing in elections for leadership and absorbing shocks like the Phoenix departures. Each situation required different types of resilience and a capacity to adapt. We've learnt to let go, recalibrate and get going again. Flexibility made scaling easier.

Transparency Works, Especially If You Play the Long Game

We were always open about how we were structured. We had written partnership deeds (when many operated on handshakes), shared advancement criteria, elected management – none of this was standard.

A legal recruiter noted our 'willingness to explain not just mechanics but philosophy' as highly unusual in the Indian market.

We spent time explaining not just 'how' the system worked, but 'why'. Transparency feeds back into trust.

Persistence Doesn't Just Pay, It Compounds

Reena SenGupta identified persistence as crucial to our success. Many firms 'burn out due to founder fatigue' – the exhausting, emotionally charged work of managing a services business built on people. We prevented this by institutionalising early.

Building something unprecedented requires long-term commitment. Persistence in principles, combined with flexibility in execution, creates the foundation for institutional growth. The compounding effect of consistent value-based choices over 25 years created something much larger than the sum of its parts.

The Central Lesson: A Sharing Model Can Deliver Great Success

In an age of cynicism about business ethics and institutions, including law firms in India, the experience of our choices offers a different pathway. A model based on well-designed, merit-based sharing can build an institution. Moreover, people like how it feels to be in a collaborative environment.

We've made mistakes and course-corrected repeatedly, but stayed true to a basic conviction: the firm must be bigger than any one of us. The market response – from lateral partners choosing to join us, to younger firms modelling elements of our approach, to traditional firms implementing reforms – suggests these alternatives resonate with many in our profession.

Our lockstep model has attracted interest from quarters outside the legal profession. V.P. Rajesh, my financial advisor, and Ambrish Arora, the architect who designed several Trilegal offices, have both consulted me on adapting our equity-sharing approach for their own firms. Both were drawn to the incentive structure it creates, aligning individual success with collective growth while reducing internal competition.

41
25 Years of Change and What Next?

Over the past 25 years, enormous changes have taken place in the Indian law firm landscape. These span how law firms operate, how the profession is perceived and how the broader business environment has evolved. We have had a front-row seat to witness not just our own evolution, but the broader transformation of the Indian law firm ecosystem.

Changes We Have Witnessed

The Rise of Institutional Firms

The most basic shift has been the emergence of non-family and non-founder dominated firms; this trend is well established and irreversible.

This is striking when considered against India's broader business landscape. Roughly 75 per cent of India's top 2,000 listed companies remain promoter-held, illustrating how difficult it is to build non-family institutions. Yet, in law, newer firms constitute the vast majority of the top 100, though traditional firms still dominate the top tier.

The market has moved decisively towards wider equity distribution and greater involvement of non-founders in management. This is one of the fundamental drivers of newer firms' rising importance.

Professionalisation of Practice and Management

Where deadlines were once missed by weeks and client service varied wildly, law firms have significantly improved how they deliver legal advice. Pressure from increasingly sophisticated clients and better structured competitors has transformed performance.

The exponential growth in deal volume has created demand for institutional capacity to handle multiple large and complex mandates simultaneously. Transactions have also become more sophisticated, requiring deeper specialisation and cross-practice collaboration that larger, better-organised firms now provide.

This extends beyond legal practice to support functions. One observer noted, 'If the leader of a firm uses the word "admin" – they have a problem – the craft of management is under-appreciated in law firms.' Successful firms have grasped the difference between administration and strategic management, investing in professional business development, HR, KM and technology.

Specialisation Becomes the Norm

Firms used to follow generalist models where partners handled diverse practice areas and start-up law firms (including us) had to do whatever work came through the door. But firms that developed real specialisation could distinguish themselves in what was still a relatively small legal market.

Developing expertise in emerging areas like technology law and renewable energy attracted clients to smaller firms when traditional firms weren't yet large enough to exert gravitational pull through scale. Over time, established firms reacted and developed similar offerings.

Today, a dominant, brilliant, charismatic senior partner can no longer credibly claim domain expertise in multiple practice areas. Specialisation is the norm, with all top firms maintaining dedicated teams for corporate law, disputes, banking, competition law, capital markets, employment law, intellectual property and numerous other areas.

Professional Respectability

When I went to Delhi University (St. Stephen's College) in 1985, three types of people studied law: those from families of lawyers following their forefathers' footsteps, those studying for the civil services exam who wanted hostel accommodation that being in the law faculty qualified them for and those with inclinations towards university politics or hooliganism (sometimes the same thing).

Three relationship-driven professions – accounting, banking and law – historically favoured the Lutyens Delhi or South Bombay English-speaking upper classes where influence resided. As India's economy expanded, the middle classes started getting into these professions, which changed the culture and the work ethic.

Outside elite legal families, law's social respectability was questionable. This has changed dramatically, and law firms are largely responsible for that. With entry-level salaries at ₹15–20 lakh in top firms and senior associates earning ₹45–60 lakh, the profession's economic appeal has transformed its social standing. Lawyers used to perform poorly in the arranged marriage stakes. Today, people can lead a matrimonial ad by saying that the groom is a lawyer in a tier-one firm.

The Top Indian Lawyers Are World Class

The profession's technical competence has transformed. In 1991, Indian lawyers didn't know how to handle global deals. Today, cross-border transactions into India that were once led by foreign lawyers overseas are typically managed by Indian lawyers in Indian firms. The best Indian lawyers are world class.

Indian law firms sometimes act as global lead counsel even when transactions span multiple jurisdictions. This includes international M&A, capital markets transactions with overseas listings, global project financings governed by English and US law, and international arbitration proceedings.

Top international firms have recruited Indian graduates directly for decades, and not just for India-related work. Scores of Indian lawyers, having earned their spurs in top Indian firms, are partners and practice leaders at international firms, making this career path routine rather than exceptional. However, due to undercutting competition, this rise in quality has not translated into proportionately higher fee levels – something will have to give here.

Evolution from Risk Management to Business Enablement

Economic growth and increasing complexity in transaction structuring, the law itself and stricter oversight by enforcement agencies have elevated legal advice's importance in business decision-making. Companies have begun to speak of law firm fees as investments rather than costs. One CFO explained that rising legal expenses are an investment in business and operational sustainability and that compliant companies tend to experience faster and more sustainable growth.[98] Many companies prefer ongoing legal advice from a 'trusted advisor' rather than transaction by transaction consultation, creating opportunities for deeper relationships.

Corporate lawyers, who started off by being contract drafters and providers of legal memoranda, moved on to becoming risk managers and now are transforming into business enablers. In the tech sector, lawyers are called when products are being designed to provide guidance on regulatory compatibility. For new business models, lawyers are involved early so that time and effort is not wasted on legally unsustainable structures. Increasingly, lawyers get calls on M&A deals before bankers – this was rare even five years ago.

The Rise of Institutional Capital

One of the most significant transformations in India's corporate finance ecosystem has been the explosive growth of various fund types. The Indian Venture and Alternate Capital Association represents over 430 funds, with combined India assets under management of over US $350 billion.[99]

Private equity (PE) and venture capital (VC) have become important growth engines. Investments in PE–VC reached $43 billion in 2024, with VC funding alone at $13.7 billion.[100] Sovereign wealth and pension funds bring patient, long-term capital. They prioritise infrastructure, strategic sectors and stable returns over aggressive growth, as do specialist infrastructure and real estate funds. Hedge funds, while smaller in absolute terms, represent sophisticated alternative strategies.

For law firms, this has created new practice areas and dramatically elevated the professional sophistication required across traditional ones – transforming not just how deals were structured, but quality standards across the board.

Growing Legal Capabilities within Companies

In-house legal departments generally used to be backwaters, housing lawyers whose work mainly involved coordinating with external counsel. Now, in-house legal capabilities have transformed. Companies that once relied exclusively on external counsel now have sophisticated internal legal teams. For companies with larger in-house departments, law firms are brought in for specialised advice, regulatory work, litigation and large matters requiring extra capacity.

Going in-house has become an excellent option for competent lawyers seeking quality legal work. Sophisticated companies now pay substantial salaries for in-house legal heads, and want them working alongside commercial teams in making business decisions. The perception that work-life balance is better in-house has made these roles attractive to associates and younger partners seeking alternatives to traditional law firm tracks.

A Transformed Disputes Landscape

Today, law firms are much more deeply involved in disputes – in preparing complex briefs for senior counsel but especially by arguing more matters themselves. As sector expertise becomes more relevant, specialist litigators in law firms are more relevant, especially in regulated sectors.

Alternative dispute resolution has grown tremendously, particularly arbitration and disputes in specialised forums like NCLAT; the Competition Commission of India; and sectoral regulators in electricity, oil and gas, telecoms, real estate and securities markets.

There are many more top-quality senior advocates beyond the traditional 10–20 'super seniors'. Some say this dilutes the position; others say it democratises litigation. From a law firm perspective, we have access to more excellent senior advocates, which benefits our clients.

Legal Education Needs to Improve

Legal education has expanded enormously, with the 'five-year law school' model pioneered by NLS in 1988, offering direct entry from high school. For the first 15–20 years, these schools attracted top students, almost comparable to IIT-level engineering talent.

But the explosion of law schools created challenges. There was one national law university when Rahul or Sridhar went to NLS – today there are 27, plus countless other schools following the five-year model. As demand has grown and law schools have mushroomed, quality control has been problematic. More students meant shifting towards mass entrance examinations – the Common Law Admissions Test – with only objective questions and nothing that tests critical reasoning.

There are fundamental issues with the five-year system beyond entry exams. Unlike engineering or medicine, the practice of law is difficult for a 17-year-old to understand. People don't really know what they're getting into, and we observe people not finishing, finishing and not practising law or practising for a couple of years and then leaving the profession. Tellingly, NLS, which started the five-year programme, has introduced a three-year programme, perhaps signalling a shift in thinking.

The 'Socialist' Campus Hiring System Must Go

Campus recruitment operates through what I call a 'socialist' approach, designed to ensure everyone in the graduating cohort gets a job, rather than enabling the best candidate to get the best job. It does not facilitate the best matches between firms and candidates.

In most major law schools, the recruitment coordination committee (RCC) – a student-run body – exercises complete control. Students cannot communicate directly with firms; all interactions flow through the RCC. It decides which firms to invite, allocates interview slots based on salary packages and ranks students by CGPA.

The RCCs implement 'no-hold' policies – students receiving offers above a certain financial threshold are automatically withdrawn from further recruitment. They can apply for only 2–3 positions, and securing one offer ends participation entirely. Students must accept or decline offers within 24–48 hours, with no negotiation allowed. This absence of market principles prevents multiple offers or optimising choice – ironic, given that these graduates will go on to serve clients in India's highly market-driven business environment.

The major law schools need to sort out campus recruitment. If they don't, the top firms will move to hiring almost exclusively through internships and PPOs, a trend that is already well established.

Trends That Will Shape the Future (in Reverse Order of Probability)

Here are trends that will reshape law firms in the coming decade, from what I feel are the most certain disruptions to the most speculative possibilities.

Legal Technology and AI: The Great Disruption

My career has seen the arrival of computers; the rise and fall of fax machines; the advent of the Internet, email and Google searches; and the use of enterprise software in law firms. Each innovation enhanced efficiency.

Artificial intelligence will do much more than all that. It will bring about a fundamental shift in law firm operating and business models. Early applications focus on document review, legal research and routine drafting, but implications extend far beyond efficiency gains. Without knowing quite where it all is going, leading firms are already investing significant time, effort and money on AI adoption.

The integration of AI with KM will be transformative. Functions that focused on precedent storage and document retrieval will evolve into AI-powered systems that analyse patterns across transactions; provide instant guidance on complex, even novel legal questions; and perhaps even anticipate regulatory changes.

Down the line, the convergence of AI, data analytics and KM will create new capabilities. Law firms will develop proprietary tools that predict case outcomes, identify optimal transaction structures and provide real-time compliance guidance. This will transform the economics of legal service delivery, allowing firms to provide higher-quality advice more efficiently. The economy and the market for legal services is growing, so I don't immediately anticipate job losses in absolute terms for a while, but the pace of creation of new jobs will slow.

Artificial intelligence could have a democratising effect by making knowledge more accessible, but I think it is more likely that it will create a new caste system: firms that successfully integrate these capabilities into delivering legal services will gain competitive advantages. Humans in law firms will continue to matter but will lose relative importance if they don't use AI.

Existing Trends Will Deepen

Four major trends from the past 25 years will accelerate and deepen.
- **Deeper Governance Evolution**: The trend towards governance reform in law firms will accelerate. Founder-centric models will give way to fully professional management structures with elections and succession planning. Performance management will become more sophisticated, with data- and AI-driven evaluation.

Homespun approaches to management will be replaced by professional business leadership.
- **Continued Specialisation and Sector Focus**: Specialisation will deepen, with firms developing granular expertise in response to regulatory complexity and client sophistication. New practice areas will emerge around climate change, ESG compliance, data governance, and emerging digital and new energy technologies. Sector-specific expertise will be critical as clients demand their lawyers understand their industries and businesses deeply.
- **Enhanced Focus on Talent Retention and Well-Being**: The growing recognition of mental health and work-life balance issues, especially post-pandemic, has already driven changes in how firms approach talent management. Current attrition rates, reportedly as high as 33 per cent, are unsustainable. Successful firms will invest in career development, diversity initiatives and genuine work-life balance rather than mere lip service.
- **Business Model Evolution and Pricing Innovation**: Traditional billable hour models already face pressure. Clients prefer predictable pricing and will demand greater AI integration to cut costs. They will choose firms that demonstrate value through innovation rather than time on the clock. Alternative fee arrangements – success fees (currently not permitted but should be reconsidered), value billing based on transaction value and salience, and litigation financing structures – will become more acceptable.

Foreign Law Firm Entry: Not So Easy

The regulatory framework now permits foreign firms to practise foreign law and international arbitration, while prohibiting the practice of Indian law. However, several factors suggest foreign firms may not establish large presences in India.

Regulatory uncertainty is a constraint. The Bar Council of India's rules on foreign firm operations are unclear and continue to evolve, creating resource planning problems for international firms. Local bar associations and the Society of Indian Law Firms have consistently opposed foreign firm entry, viewing it as a threat to domestic practitioners' livelihoods.

Economic realities present the biggest challenge. International firms face a mismatch between their global cost structures and Indian market rates. Partners accustomed to billing over $1,000 per hour will struggle with clients who expect to pay half that or less. This will make it difficult to attract and retain expat talent from global offices.

Further, well-established Indian lawyers, even those with English or US law qualifications, may remain cautious about joining international firms, preferring the autonomy and familiarity of successful Indian practices.

These constraints suggest foreign firms will remain relatively small in India, focusing on niche areas like international arbitration and cross-border regulatory work.

Here's my take on a model that can change this dynamic. International firms can't make substantial profits in India because rates are far lower than in their home jurisdictions. But they could establish larger presences in relatively-low-cost India to service international work in emerging markets. Why should international work in Vietnam be serviced from Singapore, or Kenya transactions from Dubai?

It will require effort: Indian lawyers may need some training in foreign law, clients would need convincing that India-based teams can handle their international matters and there may be regulatory issues in certain jurisdictions. But if India is the home of global capability centres for the world's largest corporations, then why not for the world's largest law firms?

Indian Firms Will Go International

Ritvik Lukose from the recruiter Vahura says, 'What Rajah & Tann has done outside of Singapore – I'd really love to see Indian firms follow that model and build out overseas.'

This will happen. Indian law firms will do more international work for two reasons. First, Indian capital is becoming more international.

Second, Indian firms have an expanding range of skills which are relevant internationally, particularly in emerging economies. Some Indian firms will set up offices in key jurisdictions to service such work.

Potential markets include the Middle East, Africa, Central Asia and Southeast Asia. In particular, favourable regulatory environments in the Middle East are promising for establishing offices for regional work and as a hub for Africa and Central Asia.

In the next 25 years, the pace of change will accelerate. The firms that thrive will be those that can capture the benefits of scale and technology, while maintaining the human relationships and professional judgement that remain at the core of legal practice.

Like our firm, the profession has come a long way from the time when six young lads set up Trilegal in 2000. Today's legal market offers opportunities for innovation, entrepreneurship and impact that would have been unimaginable back then. The challenge for the next generation of law firm leaders is to manage these possibilities while preserving the values and culture that today's young workforce aspires to.

Appendix: A Note on the Regulation of Law Firms

The Bar Council of India (BCI) occupies a central position in regulating the legal profession in India. Established under the Advocates Act, 1961, it serves as the apex regulatory body responsible for overseeing the conduct, education and discipline of advocates across the country. While its mandate is broad, its authority is at times unclear and its regulatory approach has evolved in response to changes in the legal landscape.

Regulatory and Administrative Functions

The BCI's core function is to maintain standards of professional conduct and etiquette among advocates. It operates both as a statutory body and as a self-regulating institution, and is charged with balancing the interests of the legal community with broader public responsibilities. Its primary functions include:

- **Setting professional standards**: The BCI prescribes the Code of Conduct for lawyers, which is binding on all advocates enrolled in India. This code includes rules against advertising, prohibits contingency fees and imposes confidentiality obligations.
- **Granting recognition to law degrees**: The BCI plays a role in accrediting law schools and universities and determining whether their programmes meet the required standards for producing competent legal professionals.
- **Disciplinary oversight**: The BCI has the power to investigate and take action against advocates guilty of professional misconduct.

It operates as the final appellate authority in disciplinary matters initiated by State Bar Councils (SBCs).
- **Regulating the entry of foreign lawyers**: In recent years, the BCI has actively shaped policies regarding the participation of foreign law firms and practitioners in the Indian legal market.

Disciplinary Mechanisms and Professional Misconduct

The BCI is vested with disciplinary authority over lawyers, although much of this function is decentralised to the SBCs. The Advocates Act empowers SBCs to receive complaints against advocates and take disciplinary action where necessary. If an advocate is found guilty of misconduct, the BCI has the power to:
- Warn, reprimand or suspend the advocate from practice.
- Remove the advocate's name from the roll, effectively disqualifying them from legal practice.

Regulation of Legal Education

A crucial, but at times overlooked, function of the BCI is its role in regulating legal education. The council is responsible for setting minimum standards for law degree programmes, approving syllabi and accrediting law schools. Key aspects of its involvement include:
- **Accreditation of law schools**: Law schools in India require BCI approval to confer degrees recognised for legal practice.
- **Curriculum guidelines**: The BCI prescribes syllabi for three-year LLB and five-year integrated LLB programmes, aimed at ensuring uniformity in legal education.
- **Bar examination**: Since 2010, the All India Bar Examination (AIBE) has been a mandatory qualification for advocates before they can practise in Indian courts. This was introduced to filter out underqualified graduates and improve professional competence.

The BCI and Law Firms

The regulatory framework governing law firms in India is not as clear as it could be. Unlike other jurisdictions such as the US or the UK, which have dedicated regulatory bodies for law firms, India does not. Instead, the regulation of law firms operates within the broad contours of the Advocates Act, 1961, a statute primarily designed to regulate individual lawyers.

As a consequence, while is clear that all lawyers who work in law firms fall within the regulatory purview of the BCI, the BCI has little or no regulatory power over a law firm as such. The BCI's disciplinary jurisdiction, for instance, applies only to individual advocates, not to law firms as entities. This creates a peculiar enforcement gap: while an individual lawyer can be sanctioned for professional misconduct, the firm itself can escape regulatory scrutiny.

This means that law firms operate largely through self-regulation, interpreting the terms of the Advocates Act in a manner that would make sense for groupings of lawyers in a firm. Law firms in India are structuring as partnerships under the Indian Partnership Act, 1932, or as Limited Liability Partnerships (LLPs) under the Limited Liability Partnership Act, 2008.*

The BCI's stance on the regulation of lawyers and, therefore, by extension, law firms, law firm regulation is a product of its institutional philosophy, which is still rooted in the ethical foundations of the middle of the last century. It views the legal profession not as a commercial enterprise but as a noble vocation guided by principles of integrity, independence and client service. This has meant severe restrictions on advertising, contingency fees and external investment – rules that have remained largely unchanged even as law firms have grown in size, complexity and sophistication.

---

* They cannot incorporate as companies or raise external capital due to BCI restrictions prohibiting non-lawyer ownership in legal practice.

Appendix: A Note on the Regulation of Law Firms 311

The Regulation of Foreign Law Firms in India

The BCI, its members and most Indian law firms have traditionally resisted liberalisation. The fear has been that that much larger, well-capitalised international firms would crush domestic practices. In *Bar Council of India v. A.K. Balaji* (2018), the Supreme Court upheld restrictions on foreign firms practising in India, reinforcing the BCI's authority to regulate the profession.

However, in a marked shift in 2023, the BCI introduced new rules permitting foreign law firms to establish a presence in India under strict conditions – they may advise on home jurisdiction and international law but are barred from appearing in Indian courts and hiring Indian qualified lawyers. They would also come within the regulatory purview of the BCI. This regulatory change, while significant, remains both controversial and unclear, with subsequent amendments and many issues in the new rules open to interpretation.

It remains to be seen how things will evolve.

Notes

1. Simon Sinek, *Start with Why: How Great Leaders Inspire Everyone to Take Action*, Portfolio, 2009.
2. Jim Collins, *Good to Great: Why Some Companies Make the Leap... and Others Don't*, Harper Business, 2001.
3. Peter F. Drucker, *The Effective Executive: The Definitive Guide to Getting the Right Things Done*, Harper Business, 1967.
4. Jim Collins and Jerry I. Porras, *Built to Last: Successful Habits of Visionary Companies*, Harper Business, 1994.
5. Malcolm Gladwell, *Outliers: The Story of Success*, Little, Brown and Company, 2008.
6. Emmie Martin, 'Here's Why Warren Buffett Says That He and Charlie Munger Are Successful', *CNBC*, 5 May 2018, https://tinyurl.com/bdhr9h4u.
7. Phil Knight, *Shoe Dog: A Memoir by the Creator of Nike*, Scribner, 2016.
8. Richard Feloni and Sarah Wyman, 'I Asked Everyone from a Billionaire Tech Founder to a Former Navy Seal Commander What It Means to Be Successful, and Money Was Only an Afterthought', *Business Insider*, 28 August 2018, https://tinyurl.com/mrb9wvhw.
9. 'Jeff Bezos - About Luck', *YouTube*, 27 May 2024, https://tinyurl.com/nv8w7erw.
10. Marc Galanter, 'Lawyers in the Mist: The Legal Profession in Popular Culture', *Dickinson Law Review*, Vol. 122, No. 1, 2017, https://tinyurl.com/2p9uvdna.
11. The standout example is *Court* (2014).
12. *Indian Judicial Data Grid*, https://njdg.ecourts.gov.in/njdg_v3/.
13. Peter Attia, *Outlive: The Science and Art of Longevity*, Vermilion, 2023; This idea was foreshadowed by Louis M. Brown, who developed the concept of 'preventive law' in the 1950s, aiming to prevent legal problems before they arise, much like preventive medicine. (L.M. Brown, *Preventive Law*, Prentice Hall, 1950.)
14. Depending on the nature of the business of the target company, these documents could be more or less complex – contracts relating to a small manufacturing business will tend to be less detailed and complex than contracts relating to a complex financial services business or a power plant. For example, contracts relating to a coal-fired power plant could include fuel transportation and supply agreements, construction and engineering contracts, an operation and maintenance agreement for the power plant, a power purchase agreement to sell the power, financing agreement with banks and financial institutions, insurance agreements, etc.
15. 'Heineken Acquires Additional 14.99% Stake in UBL', *MoneyControl News*, 23 June 2021, https://tinyurl.com/ksv859tb.
16. 'India: Datasets', *International Monetary Fund*, https://tinyurl.com/ynchs7dw; 'India GDP Per Capita', *Trading Economics*, https://tinyurl.com/bderh6mh.
17. Vishal Gupta, 'Only 20 Lakhs Advocates Are Registered in India– Law Ministry', *Latest Laws*, 13 August 2023, https://tinyurl.com/39n4ytmr.
18. 'Rankings: ALB Asia Top 50 Largest Law Firms 2024', *Asian Legal Business*, 22 November 2024, https://tinyurl.com/2n5ch7fx.
19. *Resight India 100: Star Firms & Market Analysis*, RSGI, May 2025, https://tinyurl.

com/yhuj4wz9.
20. Sourajit Bhattacharya, 'As of December 1, 2024, India Has Approximately 7,421 Law Firms', *LinkedIn*, April 2025, https://tinyurl.com/33jebtf7.
21. Dabiru Sridhar Patnaik, 'The Science of Law', *Centre for Post Graduate Legal Studies*, 6 January 2017, https://tinyurl.com/yamu9hm2.
22. Estimates vary from 67–95 per cent. Dia Rekhi, 'End to Family Drama: How India's Smaller Family Businesses Are Investing in Succession Planning & Family Constitutions', *The Economic Times*, 21 May 2025, https://tinyurl.com/3kxwemtf; 'Listed Company Promoters: Trust Trusts for Planning Succession', *Financial Express*, 20 September 2016, https://tinyurl.com/4n9u7dtc; Avinash Goyal et al., 'Five Differentiators of Outperforming Family-Owned Businesses in India', McKinsey & Company, 2 August 2024, https://tinyurl.com/2s3arpjd.
23. M. Rama Jois, *Legal and Constitutional History of India: Ancient Legal Judicial and Constitutional System*, LexisNexis, 2004.
24. Pleaders represented clients in lower courts. They often had practical legal knowledge but might not have had formal legal education. Vakils were a step above pleaders – they had formal legal training and could practise in higher courts, like the district courts and even the high courts, though they ranked below British trained barristers.
25. 'Crawford Bayley & Company', *Law.Asia*, https://tinyurl.com/3u49r67y.
26. *Little & Co.*, https://tinyurl.com/ysxxrnfr.
27. For a detailed history of the firm, see: Aditi Roy Ghatak, *Amicus Curiae: Khaitan & Co is 100*, Rupa Publications, 2018.
28. This included the Birla, Bajaj, Godrej, Mafatlal, Kirloskar, Modi, Shriram, Thapar and Wadia groups of companies.
29. Satish John and Maulik Vyas, 'Khaitan & Co: Lawyers for India Inc, for 100 Years', *The Economic Times*, 25 March 2012, https://tinyurl.com/bdh39tcb.
30. 'Founders' is not a formal designation in Trilegal. The founders are partners and enjoy the same rights and privileges as any other partners in the firm.
31. An advocate on record (AOR) is a designation unique to the Supreme Court of India. Only advocates who have passed the AOR examination conducted by the Supreme Court are entitled to file matters and appear before the Supreme Court. They are essentially the gatekeepers to the highest court in India.
32. A 'right of first refusal' gives a party the first opportunity to buy something (shares, property) before it is offered to others.
33. A 'Texas shoot-out clause' is a dispute resolution mechanism where one shareholder sets a price at which they're willing to either buy the other's shares or sell their own shares to the other, forcing a clean break between shareholders in dispute.
34. Phil Moyse was a well-known name in London's money markets and is credited with professionalising MAI's operations and helping it compete in what was becoming a highly electronic, high-frequency and globalised brokerage market.
35. This legendary red wine from the Rhone valley in the south-east of France became a favourite of the Trilegal founders, and is still called into service at special occasions.
36. Prem was not the second member of the firm though. Before he joined, Johnny Pinto joined as an office boy. Twenty-five years on, Johnny is still with Trilegal and now is the head of billing for the Bengaluru office.
37. Jayanth K. Krishnan and Patrick W. Thomas, 'Being Your Own Boss: The Career Trajectories and Motivations of India's Newest Corporate Lawyers', *The Indian*

Legal Profession in the Age of Globalization: The Rise of the Corporate Legal Sector and Its Impact on Lawyers and Society, David B. Wilkins, Vikramaditya S. Khanna and David M. Trubek (eds), Cambridge University Press, 2017.

38. P. Bourdieu, *Distinction: A Social Critique of the Judgement of Taste*, Richard Nice (trans.), Harvard University Press, 1984; Galanter and T. Palay, *Tournament of Lawyers: The Transformation of the Big Law Firm*, University of Chicago Press, 1991.
39. Alexis de Tocqueville, *The Old Regime and the Revolution*, Stuart Gilbert (trans.), Anchor Books, 1955.
40. R. Rubin, *The Creative Act: A Way of Being*, Penguin Press, 2023.
41. N. Wasserman, *The Founder's Dilemmas: Anticipating and Avoiding the Pitfalls That Can Sink a Startup*, Princeton University Press, 2012.
42. H.E. Aldrich, *Organizations Evolving*, Sage Publications, 1999.
43. M.S. Cardon et al. 'The Nature and Experience of Entrepreneurial Passion', *Academy of Management Review*, Vol. 34, No. 3, 2009, pp. 511–532, https://tinyurl.com/d4w4tzdr; B. Clarysse and N. Moray, 'A Process Study of Entrepreneurial Team Formation: The Case of a Research-Based Spin-Off', *Journal of Business Venturing*, Vol. 19, No. 1, 2004, pp. 55–79, https://tinyurl.com/mrh3sthj.
44. B. Clarysse and N. Moray, 'A Process Study of Entrepreneurial Team Formation: The Case of a Research-Based Spin-Off', *Journal of Business Venturing*, Vol. 19, No. 1, 2004, pp. 55–79, https://tinyurl.com/mrh3sthj.
45. Wei Hu, Yan Xu, Fuqiang Zhao and Yun Chen, 'Entrepreneurial Success – The Role of Psychological Capital and Entrepreneurial Policy Support', *Frontiers in Psychology*, Vol. 13, 2002, https://doi.org/10.3389/fpsyg.2022.792066; Alexander Newman, Martin Obschonka, Julia Moeller and Gemma Garima Chandan, 'Entrepreneurial Passion: A Review, Synthesis, and Agenda for Future Research', *Applied Psychology*, Vol. 70, No. 2, 2021, pp. 816–60.
46. M.S. Granovetter, 'The Strength of Weak Ties', *American Journal of Sociology*, Vol. 78, No. 6, May 1973, pp. 1360–1380.
47. B. Horowitz, *The Hard Thing about Hard Things: Building a Business When There Are No Easy Answers*, Harper Business, 2014.
48. N. Wasserman, *The Founder's Dilemmas: Anticipating and Avoiding the Pitfalls That Can Sink a Startup*, Princeton University Press, 2012.
49. J.L. Pierce, T. Kostova and K.T. Dirks, 'Toward a Theory of Psychological Ownership in Organizations', *Academy of Management Review*, Vol. 26, No. 2, 2001, pp. 298–310.
50. Simon Sinek, *Start with Why: How Great Leaders Inspire Everyone to Take Action*, Portfolio, 2009.
51. N. Wasserman, *The Founder's Dilemmas: Anticipating and Avoiding the Pitfalls That Can Sink a Startup*, Princeton University Press, 2012.
52. H. Schultz and Joanne Gordon, *Onward: How Starbucks Fought for Its Life without Losing Its Soul*, Rodale Books, 2011.
53. Richard Susskind, *Tomorrow's Lawyers*, Oxford University Press, 2017.
54. E.H. Schein, *Organizational Culture and Leadership*, Jossey-Bass, 2010.
55. Richard Susskind and Daniel Susskind, *The Future of the Professions: How Technology Will Transform the Work of Human Experts*, Oxford University Press, 2015.
56. The Enron scandal (2001) involved one of the US's largest corporations using fraudulent accounting practices to hide billions in debt and inflate profits. Once

valued at $70 billion, Enron collapsed within months of the deception being exposed, wiping out shareholders and employees' retirement savings. This also led to the dissolution of Arthur Andersen and prompted major regulatory reforms including the Sarbanes-Oxley Act. Enron became synonymous with corporate fraud and demonstrated how quickly even seemingly successful companies could collapse when built on financial manipulation.

57. J.G. March, 'Exploration and Exploitation in Organizational Learning', *Organization Science*, Vol. 2, No. 1, 1991.
58. H. Mintzberg, 'The Structuring of Organizations: A Synthesis of the Research', *University of Illinois at Urbana-Champaign's Academy for Entrepreneurial Leadership Historical Research Reference in Entrepreneurship*, 1979.
59. R.H. Coarse, 'The Nature of the Firm', *Economica*, Vol. 4, No. 16, 1937, pp. 386–405.
60. C.F. Sabel, 'Learning by Monitoring: The Institutions of Economic Development', *Handbook of Economic Sociology*, N. Smelser and R. Swedberg (eds), Princeton Sage, 1994.
61. Bruce Sterling, 'The Year in Ideas: A TO Z.; Simputer', *The New York Times*, 9 December 2001, https://tinyurl.com/mwn6c3e7.
62. Rahul Matthan, 'Geographical Data – Do We Have a Fundamental Right to Access It?', *Current Science*, Vol. 79, No. 4, 2000, pp. 499–503, https://tinyurl.com/ms2byw9x.
63. Rahul Matthan, 'Radical Map Reforms', *Ex Machina*, 16 March 2021, https://tinyurl.com/nks4wpw4.
64. 'Vodafone Wins Bid for Hutchison Essar', *Forbes*, 11 February 2007, https://tinyurl.com/4zjfzc7u.
65. See appendix, 'A Note on the Regulation of Law Firms in India'.
66. *Wisden Cricketers' Almanack*, founded in 1864 by cricketer John Wisden, is the world's most authoritative and longest-running annual cricket reference book, known as the 'Bible of Cricket'. It features records, statistics and commentary on all aspects of the game.
67. Nirupam Bajpai, 'Global Financial Crisis, Its Impact on India and the Policy Response', Working Paper No. 5, Columbia Global Centers | South Asia, Columbia University, July 2011, https://tinyurl.com/yvtf6uz3; Rajiv Kumar and Pankaj Vashisht, 'The Global Economic Crisis: Impact on India and Policy Responses', *Asian Development Bank Institute*, November 2009, https://tinyurl.com/53r2mc3y.
68. Maulik Vyas, 'Trilegal Ends Its Five Years Alliance with US-Based Law Firm Allen & Overy', *The Economic Times*, 27 September 2012, https://tinyurl.com/puh7hu65.
69. Charles Handy, *The Empty Raincoat*, Hutchinson, 1994.
70. Abey Francis, 'Greiner's Model of Organizational Growth – Phases of Organizational Growth and Crisis', *MBA Knowledge Base*, https://tinyurl.com/yuteve7w.
71. 'Amarchand Mangaldas Split Is Now Official', *Business Standard*, 7 May 2015, https://tinyurl.com/434eamka.
72. Kian Ganz, 'Anand Prasad Exit Interview: Trilegal Co-founder about "Happiness Quotient" Politics, Becoming Counsel, Handover', *Legally India*, 26 February 2016, https://tinyurl.com/2wajrbx4.
73. Pallavi Saluja, '[Exclusive]: I Have Been Socially Inclined for a Very Long Time, Says Trilegal's Anand Prasad', *Bar and Bench*, 26 February 2016, https://www.barandbench.com/news/exclusive-politically-socially-inclined-long-time-trilegal-anand-prasad.

74. Pallavi Saluja, 'Breaking: Trilegal Co-Founder Anand Prasad Leaves for Counsel Practice, Politics', *Bar and Bench*, 26 February 2016, https://tinyurl.com/y2dhh2jc.
75. Kian Ganz, 'Anand Prasad Exit Interview: Trilegal Co-founder about "Happiness Quotient" Politics, Becoming Counsel, Handover', *Legally India*, 26 February 2016, https://tinyurl.com/2wajrbx4.
76. Indian law firms don't release much data; this is an impressionistic view.
77. Rahul Matthan, 'Yesterday Was a Milestone', *LinkedIn*, 2024, https://tinyurl.com/yevx7yrx.
78. Akshay Jaitly, 'The Little Law Firm I Was Part of…', *LinkedIn*, 2024, https://tinyurl.com/3czfbe4k.
79. *Resight India 100: Star Firms & Market Analysis*, RSGI, May 2025, https://tinyurl.com/yhuj4wz9.
80. Geoffrey West, *Scale*, Weidenfeld & Nicolson, Oxford, England, 2018.
81. The asset reconstruction business in India enabled by the SARFAESI Act has grown into a multi-trillion-rupee sector, with over ₹7 trillion in stressed assets handled annually in recent years and more than ₹1 trillion in assets acquired by asset reconstruction companies since 2016.
82. Standardised legal templates developed by the APLMA for use in syndicated loan transactions in the Asia-Pacific region
83. For the calendar year 2024, investments in the renewable energy sector exceeded US $32 billion (approximately ₹2.75 lakh crore).
84. Rahul Matthan, *The Law Relating to Computers and the Internet*, Butterworths India, 2000.
85. The 'follow the sun' outsourcing model is a global workflow strategy used by organisations – especially in IT services, software development and customer support – to provide round-the-clock service or development by leveraging teams in multiple time zones.
86. T.L. Friedman, *The World Is Flat: A Brief History of the Twenty-First Century*, Farrar, Straus and Giroux, 2005.
87. *Employment Law Alliance*, https://tinyurl.com/59zkaujz.
88. 'Decoding the Fine Print', *AI First Movers, Microsoft*, https://tinyurl.com/5n8tpmur.
89. 'Trilegal', *ICLG*, https://tinyurl.com/597wn5vr.
90. Priyanka Gawande, 'Rising Stars Secure Equity Stakes at Top Law Firms', *mint*, 30 June 2025, https://tinyurl.com/ypurbxzh.
91. The Bombay solicitor's route is a unique legal career pathway, administered by the Bombay Incorporated Law Society. Candidates must complete a law degree and then serve a three-year clerkship under the supervision of a registered solicitor with at least five years of experience. Then, they must pass the rigorous solicitors' examination. The division between solicitors and advocates no longer exists in Indian law but some Mumbai firms prefer for their partners to be registered solicitors.
92. 'Framing a Future', *India Business Law Journal*, 2019, https://tinyurl.com/mryamx53.
93. *Resight India 100: Star Firms & Market Analysis*, RSGI, May 2025, https://tinyurl.com/yhuj4wz9.
94. As seen in: Rahul Matthan, *The Third Way: India's Revolutionary Approach to Data Governance*, Juggernaut Books, 2023.

95. As seen in: Rahul Matthan, *Privacy 3.0: Unlocking Our Data-Driven Future*, Harper Collins, 2018.
96. *TrustBridge*, https://tinyurl.com/yhm93feh.
97. *Agami*, https://tinyurl.com/4kbn7tun.
98. Alekh Shah, 'India Inc CFOs See Legal Spending as a Strategic Investment, Targeting below 4% of Costs, With Growth Aligned to Revenue', *CFO News*, 10 September 2024, https://etcfo.com/s/ffj94dg.
99. 'About Us', *IVC Association*, https://tinyurl.com/38pnzxt6.
100. 'India PE-VC Market Rebounds in 2024 to $43 Bn; VC, Growth Investment Spur Momentum', *The Economic Times*, 7 May 2025, https://tinyurl.com/59ert5rz.

Acknowledgements

This book exists thanks to a writing exercise in March 2022, when I discovered a microblogging platform called Nicheless and decided to write 300 words daily for a month to build my writing muscle. After a few pieces on the rich North Indian vocabulary for the word 'slap' and my childhood in Kashmir, I drifted into anecdotes about Trilegal's early days. When a couple of posts about our first invoice and how we named the firm passed 6,000 views, some people suggested there might be a book lurking behind these tales. My economist friend Ajay Shah was characteristically direct: Stop sharing snippets and write something serious about building institutions.

Writing about your own firm, especially while still in it, presents unique hazards. You risk either hagiography or banality, neither of which is of any interest to readers. And client confidentiality must be respected. I've tried my best to be an honest steward of the Trilegal story – holding it at this moment in time on behalf of the partners, lawyers and staff who built what was always a collective enterprise.

The book draws on conversations with many of the nearly 150 current Trilegal partners and some who have left. A deep source of satisfaction through this journey has been discovering how successive generations of partners made our early vision their own and elevated it beyond anything the founders imagined (and hopefully will continue to do so for years to come). The cliché that 'it takes a village' has rarely been more apt.

Geoffrey Picton-Turbervill, the late Ian Scott and Philip Hurst gave me my first job as a lawyer when there were precious few Indians from India being hired by London law firms. Along with other Ashurst colleagues – Charez Golvala, Clive Tucker, Henry Knowles, Huw Thomas, Ian Johnson, Ian McNeil, Jeremy Sheldon, John McClenehan, Judy Sharrock, Myles Mantle, Paul de Cordova, Paul Griffin – they provided lessons and guidance I still follow today.

Deepak Adlakha and Muneesh Sharma offered counsel and

Acknowledgements

friendship during my Dua Associates stint, and helped me figure out what practising law in India was all about.

Our firm would not have existed but for clients who believed in us before logic suggested they should. Heartfelt thanks to all our clients but particularly those who trusted us when we had no scale, no brand and very little beyond enthusiasm: Amitabh Pande, Chris Watson, K.V. Rajshekhar, Lashit Sanghvi, Mahesh Makhija, Pankaj Wadhwa, Prabhakar Dev, Rajesh Kapadia, Sandeep Katwala, Shaun Parmar, S.K. Bhatt, Varun Batra, Victoria Rigby Delmon, Vinay Ganga and many others. That early faith kept us going through our most uncertain years and I am proud to say that many of those relationships endure. Thanks too, to our many, many friends and colleagues in law firms around the world.

Steve Hirschfeld trusted a small Indian start-up to join the Employment Law Alliance, opening doors to international collaboration and credibility well beyond our size and reputation.

David Morley, Jonathan Brayne and Wim Dejonghe generously reflected on 'the A&O days' – that improbable alliance between a Magic Circle firm and six young lawyers who thought they were reinventing the Indian law firm. Thanks to them and many, many more A&O partners for the trust and camaraderie.

Rajen Gandhi provided advice, insight, friendship and has been part of the journey from the very beginning.

Moray Maclaren, Reena SenGupta and Ritvik Lukose provided crucial external perspectives on how our choices resonated in the wider market, helping me understand what our experiment meant beyond our own experience.

Several colleagues and friends helped me see the firm, profession and this book from angles other than my limited founder's view: Aditi Jaitly Jadeja, Ajay Shah, Ambrish Arora, Bhavin Patel, Manish Sabharwal, Manu Nair, Nayantara Patel, Nish Bhutani, Prashanto Sen, Rajesh Jha, Rashi Gadekar, Renuka Sane, Ritin Rai, Susan Thomas, Tanvi Nagpal, Vijay Singh Chauhan, Vikas Ahuja and V.P. Rajesh tested ideas, sharpened perspectives or just listened to me work through my thoughts.

Saket Shukla and Sawant Singh offered candid, good-humoured and generous perspectives about their time at Trilegal.

Nishant Parikh brought his characteristic sharp eye and steady patience to explain the firm's spectacular growth in the 2020s, helping me understand the strategy that he and Sridhar put in place with a granularity that has enriched the narrative.

Deep gratitude goes to all the Trilegal partners and colleagues who sat through interviews with me – you will meet them in the book. (My apologies to those whose insights did not make the editorial cut.) These weren't just fact-gathering sessions; they gave me fresh insights into an institution I thought I knew inside out. Many stories were novel, refreshing and often very funny. I wish I could have written chapters on our retreats, parties and many (mis)adventures, but as my publisher firmly reminded me, that would have produced a book for insiders rather than something with a wider purpose.

Special thanks belong to my projects practice colleagues, particularly Amar Narula, Astha Shrivastava, Gautam Chabra, Megha Kaladharan, Nayantara Nag, Neeraj Menon, Niharika Puri, Riyaz Bhagat, Saurabh Bhasin and Swathy Pisharody, for tolerating Monday meetings, bad jokes and rants about the world while helping build what I believe to be the country's leading energy and infrastructure practice.

Ashish Bhan, Deep Rao, Charandeep Kaur, Gautam Chawla, Gautam Singh, Jafar Alam, Ketan Gaur, Kunal Chandra, Kunaal Shah, Mohit Rastogi, Sampath Kumar, Sanjam Arora, Sneha Vardhan, Tine Abraham and many other partners who have dropped by for chats over the years have helped me whittle away my embedded founder's view and see the firm and the profession around us through fresh eyes. Your perspectives reminded me that institutions belong to their present, not their past. Thanks to Manpreet Kaur for her years of patience and support.

Thanks to everyone at my publisher, including Nishtha Kapil, Smita Mathur and particularly Chiki Sarkar, who, to my abiding surprise, said yes immediately when I pitched the book to her. Her advice to a first-time author – to ensure that the book was written with integrity, provided insight and wasn't full of self-praise – was invaluable. I hope I have managed to do some of that.

Scores of unnamed colleagues, including many Trilegal alumni, across the legal profession have shared perspectives – recently and over the years – about the peculiarities of the Indian legal market and the distinctiveness and impact of the Trilegal experiment. These insights helped place our story in its broader industry context.

My parents, Ashok Jaitly and Jaya Jaitly, gave me the freedom to follow my own path and instilled values that somehow found their way into the firm – sometimes consciously, sometimes by accident.

Isabelle, who I believe would have made a much better lawyer than me, provided honest, sharp insights that improved this book. Your patience and sacrifice supported an often uncertain journey, and your belief in what I was part of building sustained me through crisis and triumph.

Anoushka, Amaya, Auxanne and Ilyssa were the best stress relief imaginable (though Monday mornings sometimes came as sweet relief!). Coming back to the chaos that is our home reminded me that life was larger, funnier and richer than whatever drama or success had unfolded at the office. This book might explain a bit more about what Daddy was doing when he was 'in the office'.

And finally, my fellow founders – Anand Prasad, Karan Singh, Prem Ayyappa, Rahul Matthan and Sridhar Gorthi – what I owe you all, in a variety of different ways, is impossible to put into words. Thank you for the trust, friendship and common belief that has sustained us through the vast majority of our professional and adult lives. We have grown (up) together and created something that enabled each of us to become better versions of ourselves while building careers and a firm that none of us could have imagined from that first meeting on Sridhar's floor in Bandra. Each of you taught me something that appears in these pages and much more that does not. This book, like the Trilegal story from day one, is as much yours as it is mine.